The Great Movie Musical Trivia Book

by

Jeff Kurtti

Introduction by
Shirley Jones

APPLAUSE BOOKS • NEW YORK

The Great Movie Musical Trivia Book

by Jeff Kurtti

Library of Congress Catalog-in-Publication Data

Kurtti, Jeff
    The great movie musical trivia book / by Jeff Kurtti ;
introduction by Shirley Jones.
      p.   cm.
    Includes bibliographical references and index.
    ISBN : 1-55783-222-6
    1. Musical films --United States--Miscellanea. I. Title.
PN1995.9.M86K87   1996
791.43'6--dc20   96-1837
                                      CIP

British Library Catalogue in Publication Data

A catalogue record for this book is available from the British Library

APPLAUSE BOOKS

211 W. 71st St.
NEW YORK, NY 10023
PHONE 212-595-4735
FAX 212-721-2856

406 VALE ROAD
TONBRIDGE KENT TN9 1XR
PHONE 0732 357755
FAX 0732 770219

FIRST APPLAUSE PRINTING, 1996

Contents

Part One: MGM Musicals

Part Two: Broadway to Hollywood

Part Three: Flights Of Fancy

Part Four: Americana

Part Five: Animated Musicals

This book is dedicated to the loving memory of my friends

Rob Roy MacVeigh

and

Michael Chervenock

and to

Robert Tieman

with my eternal gratitude
for his invaluable friendship and editorial assistance

Introduction by Shirley Jones

Shirley Jones today.

Depending on which way you look at it, the movie musical was either my panacea (having whisked me to instant stardom at the age of 19 via my very first feature film) or my torpedo (sputtering through its last phase of popularity at the peak of my career). Either way, I straddled that transitional era in Hollywood…and I suppose I should be grateful for having survived it.

The beginning was right out of an old Hollywood "B" script. It was my first New York audition, a short time after leaving home in Smithton, Pennsylvania…my very first tryout, for a chorus spot in *South Pacific*. After all the eliminations, from the hundreds who showed up, it was down to about six. A voice from the darkened seats out there asked if I would be kind enough to do my song one more time, "for my

partner, Mr. Hammerstein," who was on his way to the theater from his office. And there were returned the immortal words that would live in New York Shirley Jones Infamy: *"Certainly…and what is your name, sir?"*

When that day ended, I had become the first (and last) actress ever to be put under personal management contract to the Rodgers & Hammerstein office. And not a bad day that was.

From there it was the road company of *Me and Juliet,* and less than a year later—I was still 19—I was given the lead in the much-awaited film version of R&H's *Oklahoma!* Directly after that, I was asked to screen test (along with every viable musical star on the planet) for the super-coveted role of Julie Jordan in R&H's *Carousel.* And I did. More miraculously, I got the part, re-teaming with my *Oklahoma!* "Curly," Gordon MacRae, a terrific and down-home guy with just about the

As Laurey in *Oklahoma!* (1955).

As Marian the Librarian in *The Music Man* (1962).

most glorious natural voice I'd ever heard. A few years later, I was offered the role of Marian the Librarian in the Hollywood version of the Broadway smash *The Music Man*, opposite the original, one-and-only Harold Hill, Bob Preston.

It still astonishes me when I realize how young I was for all that to happen so quickly. And I suppose it's fair to say that the momentum from that phenomenal burst of class-A exposure is still at work. It even led me to the opportunity to play Lulu Baines in the 1961 classic *Elmer Gantry*, with Burt Lancaster and Jean Simmons, which sent me home with a gold statuette they call "Oscar."

And of course, there was "The Partridge Family," my television "mini-musical" that still circles the tube, picking up new generations of fans with every pass.

And when you add all that to the home video explosion, with all those early musicals in release and re-release, I often feel as if I'm in some sort of "Twilight Zone" time warp.

Today, I spend most of my time traveling the country doing my symphony concert, with all those timeless American musical masterpieces—and I take great note of people who are inclined to memorialize that time and those works in one sort of compilation or another.

Such was my fascination with *The Great Movie Musical Trivia Book* when the manuscript was sent to me. If you're a fan of the celluloid musical, get ready—you are about to have one terrific time. It has just the right measure of humor and intelligence to make it the perfect "bathtub book," if you will. It is sharp, thoroughly researched, and filled with the kind of information that will challenge your best recollections.

I hope you enjoy *The Great Movie Musical Trivia Book*. For me, I'm having a bit of a time believing that I actually lived part of it!

Shirley Jones
Beverly Hills, California
April 1995

As Julie Jordan in *Carousel* (1956).

Author's Note

My head is jammed with trivia. Ever since I can remember, facts and figures, anecdotes and legends have clung to some kind of mind-Velcro I've got. It is a great resource at times, a great bet-winner and party-starter. It can also annoy you, vex you, and drive you slightly crazy. Anthropologist Stephen M. Fjellman summed it up: "...I can't remember where a lot of my ideas come from. I'm a really lousy scholar. What I heard yesterday on 'Entertainment Tonight' goes into today's piece. Tomorrow I'll forget where I heard it. I'll probably tell some class it's from Heidegger."

You would think Trivial Pursuits® would be like heaven for me. But I find that more often than not, trivia—and that includes trivia books—barely whets my appetite for real information, or at least something more than a pat answer to a pat question. Most of what people consider trivia is really just minutiae, to which you might easily attach the phrase "but who cares?"

I always want to know more. My favorite kind of "trivia" books are *The Straight Dope* and its sequels by the great Cecil Adams, Tom Burnam's *Dictionary of Misinformation* and its sequel, and Jan Harold Brunvand's Urban Folklore series. They not only answer the question, but also provide more depth, background, revealing anecdote, context, and a little personal commentary.

More than a simple answer to a question, in this book you'll get background—a little tangential information, a dash of biography, a pinch of historical context, some myth and speculation—and my own opinion to boot. It's part trivia, part history, part "making-of," part "behind-the-scenes," part film commentary, and (I hope) fun,

informative, and interesting.

Someone out there may be asking, "But where's *The Sound of Music*? Where are Fred and Ginger? Where's *my* favorite movie musical?" Since a trivia book about movie musicals in general would have to be pretty shallow to cover even part of the ground, I decided to write a mind-bending book about ten of my personal favorite movie musicals. The great part of it is that I have already begun work on a mind-bending sequel about even more great movie musicals—including *The Sound of Music*!

The ten quizzes are each separated into three levels. The first level deals with characters, events, and locales within the story of the film. The second level tends toward the actors, directors, and creative forces behind the scenes of the picture. Level three is more difficult, more "backstage," and derives from extensive personal research and interviews.

Credits and cast lists for each film are included at the end of each chapter. In some cases, individuals who contributed to a given production but are not credited on the actual film or contemporary publicity materials are included as well.

It is my hope that this book will become to you what those I have mentioned have been to me: a friend on the shelf that can be read and re-read, used for reference or to settle (or start) an argument. At the very least, all this might enable you to start driving *your* friends and colleagues a little crazy.

Jeff Kurtti
Los Angeles, California
September 1995

Chapter One
The Wizard of Oz

1060

The Wizard of Oz *is probably the first live-action movie musical any modern child can remember seeing. The film represents a convergence of great talents employed by Hollywood's finest movie factory, in the zenith year of 1939, all in service to a rather bizarre "American Fairy Tale" first published in 1900.* The Wizard of Oz *has achieved the status of a classic, due in part to its melodious score, colorful production, and the casting of a young talent named Judy Garland in the leading role. This status is equally accountable to annual television airings and the simple, homespun philosophy that, as picturesque and exciting as other places may be, "there's no place like home." The film's dedication sums it up nicely: "For nearly forty years, this story has given faithful service to the Young in Heart; and Time has been powerless to put its kindly philosophy out of fashion. To those of you who have been faithful to it in return...and to the Young in Heart...we dedicate this picture."*

■

Level One: The Easy Stuff
Story & Characters

Previous page:
"Lions and
tigers and bears,
oh my!" The
principal cast of
The Wizard of Oz
in a classic
publicity pose.

Q: Mean old Miss Gulch is referred to by her first name just once. What is it? What is the first name of the character who calls Miss Gulch by her first name?

A: Almira is Miss Gulch's first name. Aunt Em ("Her name is...uh...Emily," Professor Marvel later guesses; "That's right," Dorothy replies.) calls her Almira ("Almira Gulch! Just because you own half the county doesn't mean you have the power to run the rest of us!").

■

Q: As Dorothy tries to explain her troubles with Miss Gulch, Aunt Em and Uncle Henry are distracted by a crisis and cannot (or will not) pay attention. What has happened?

A: "This old incubator's gone bad, and we're likely to lose a lot of our chicks," Uncle Henry explains as Aunt Em counts.

Clara Blandick was an outside contract player hired by MGM for the part of Aunt Em. May Robson had turned down the part as too brief and undemanding; MGM contract player Sarah Padden had tested for the part on January 31, 1939. On February 1, the role was given to Clara Blandick. Her work on *The Wizard of Oz* took one week. She committed suicide in 1962.

Harlan Briggs had been announced as Uncle Henry on February 1, 1939, but the next week Charley Grapewin, Arthur Freed's first choice for the role, was signed to play Uncle Henry. Grapewin died in 1956.

■

Q: In Munchkinland, Dorothy politely introduces herself. What is her last name?

A: "I'm Dorothy Gale, from Kansas." In L. Frank Baum's *The Wonderful Wizard of Oz*, she is simply Dorothy. Her last name comes from the 1902 stage musical *The Wizard of Oz*, where this punny exchange takes place:

> **DOROTHY:** My name is Dorothy, and I am one of the Kansas Gales.
> **SCARECROW:** That accounts for your breezy manner.

In Baum's third book, *Ozma of Oz* (1907),

Dorothy is called by the last name Gale. And what else would you call a girl who travels on a cyclone?

■

Q: After the Wizard's command to "bring me the broomstick of the Witch of the West," one of the characters jumps out the window of the Wizard's palace. Who?

A: The Cowardly Lion, played by Bert Lahr. In early Freed Unit communications, the Lion is rarely mentioned, as the decision about how to portray him had not been made. Early drafts of the script have the Lion character as an enchanted incarnation of the Prince of Oz. Other discussions involved having the role filled by a real lion—Leo, the MGM trademark. When an April 1938 script draft by Noel Langley described a lion who was just a lion, lyricist Yip Harburg

suggested Bert Lahr. Harburg had worked with Lahr on the revue *Life Begins at 8:40* (1934), and knew that Lahr could balance a broad comic performance with sincerity and pathos. Lahr's casting was announced on July 25, 1938.

By the way, the actual jump out the window was performed not by Lahr but by a stunt double.

■

Q: Obviously, much of *The Wizard of Oz* is built around foreshadowing in the Kansas sequence. Professor Marvel, whose Oz alter ego is the humbug Wizard, drives an elaborate show wagon. Which of Professor Marvel's Kansas talents directly relates to the Oz plot?

A: In addition to juggling and sleight of hand, Professor Marvel's wagon displays one of his talents as "Balloon Exhibitionist." It is in a balloon that the Wizard proposes taking Dorothy back to

From left: Aunt Em (Clara Blandick), Dorothy (Judy Garland), Miss Gulch (Margaret Hamilton), and Uncle Henry (Charley Grapewin).

Among his many talents, the Wizard had been premiere Balloonist par excellence for the Miracle Wonderland Carnival Company.

the land of E Pluribus Unum. A brief exchange between Professor Marvel and Dorothy, where she referred to poppies on the wallpaper of her Kansas bedroom, was cut by the director.

The Wizard in Baum's original book was really much less of a humbug than he was accused of being. For instance, upon his arrival by balloon in this "strange and beautiful country," the Wizard ordered the *building* of the Emerald City "just to amuse myself, and keep the good people busy." According to Baum's *Dorothy and the Wizard in Oz* (1908), the country of Oz bears a name the Wizard brought from his Omaha home—his initials stand for Oscar Zaroster. It seems the Wizard's politician father had a propensity for complicated names—the rest of the Wizard's *nine* initials spell out "pinhead." The Wizard, fearing that the moniker O.Z. P.I.N.H.E.A.D. "might be considered a reflection on his intelligence" shortened it and painted the first two initials on all his belongings, including the circus balloon by which he traveled to the country that would bear those initials as its name.

Much like the Scarecrow, the Tin Woodman, and the Cowardly Lion, the Wizard seems an example of what Oz historian Martin Gardner refers to as "the human tendency to confuse real virtue with its valueless outer symbol."

■

Q: In the forest of the fighting trees, where Dorothy and the Scarecrow first discover the Tin Man, a clever musical underscoring is used. What is it?

A: "In the Shade of the Old Apple Tree." Additional interpolated melodies included Moussorgsky's "Night on Bald Mountain" (in the rescue from the Witch's Castle), the Mendelssohn "Scherzo in E Minor" (Toto's escape—"Run, Toto, run!"), "Happy Farmer" (Kansas sequence), and "Reuben and Rachel" (during the cyclone).

In 1995, Rhino Records and Turner Entertainment released a comprehensive compact disc of this complex musical score, complete with alternate takes and unused music cues. There is also an erudite booklet on the film and its score by Oz expert John Fricke. This CD is a "must" for fans of *The Wizard of Oz*.

Interpolation of existing melodies is both a shortcut and pastiche for movie composers. Much of the inspired lunacy of the Warner Bros. Loony Tunes® came courtesy of composer Carl Stalling, who slyly interpolated traditional and popular melodies to underscore the action on the screen. The Warner cartoon unit had originally created Merrie Melodies® to capitalize on the Warner music library by using its songs in the cartoons.

■

Q: Shortly after Dorothy and the Scarecrow meet the Tin Man, they are confronted by the Wicked Witch as she stands on the roof of the woodcutter's cottage. She threatens to stuff a mattress with the Scarecrow, and use the Tin Man for...what?

A: "I'll use you for a beehive!" the Witch threatens. In the rough-cut script of the film, she did exactly that, for after the Tin Man's retort, "Beehive, bah! Let her try and make a beehive out of me!" the script continues:

TIN MAN: You know—hmm? What's that?
TRICK BEE SHOT —missing—

At this point, a swarm of animated bees was to swirl out of the Tin Man's mouth. It's not clear exactly whether the scene was ever animated, or if it was, why it wasn't used, but by July 6, 1939, the sequence following the Witch's rooftop threat was gone, and the final film had been meticulously restructured to cover the movement of the three characters involved. The scene that immediately preceded it (from the Witch's disappearance to the cut to Dorothy's close-up line "Oh, you're the best friends anybody ever had,") had to be "flopped" (the film negative was duplicated and reprinted on its opposite side) so that the characters would keep continuity with their locations in the following scenes.

■

Q: The Scarecrow tells Dorothy that he's not afraid of anything except...what?

A: The Scarecrow tells Dorothy that, because of his straw-stuffed body, he is afraid of only one thing—a lighted match. The Witch takes advantage of this weakness, initially by hurling a fireball at the Scarecrow, and finally by lighting her broom and asking, "How about a little fire, Scarecrow?" This is her fatal mistake, of course, because Dorothy's attempt to extinguish the Scarecrow results in the Witch's "liquidation."

The Wicked Witch of the West, Margaret Hamilton, was the one who had a truly terrifying experience with fire on the set of *The Wizard of Oz*. The week before Christmas 1938, while shooting her exit from Munchkinland, she was severely burned when the fire effect that hid her trapdoor elevator was tripped too early, resulting in first-degree burns on the right side of her face and chin, and second-degree burns on her hand. Her green makeup was copper-based and the alcohol needed to remove it caused excruciating pain. She was unable to return to work on the picture until mid-February 1939. (An optimistic MGM internal communication dated January 5, 1939, estimated "...she will be able to resume her work in a week or ten days.")

■

Q: Who played The Munchkins?

A: The film credits simply list "The Munchkins," so that answer is correct, as far as it goes. Contemporary promotional material (such as the theatrical trailer) credits The Singer Midgets as The Munchkins. Leo Singer was a German who found and trained his midgets as

Judy Garland in the role that would follow her through her tragically short life.

acrobats, singers, dancers, and wrestlers, and Arthur Freed hired Singer in the summer of 1938 to supply the studio with Munchkins. His own troupe consisted of only eighteen people, so Singer recruited little people from across the country for *Oz*, often paying them far less than the one hundred dollars per week per person that he was being paid by MGM.

The misbehavior of the Munchkins ensconced at the Culver City Hotel has become the stuff of movie legend, and although there were certainly hedonists among the 130 or so little people assembled for *Oz*, it was not the chaotic midget orgy portrayed in popular legend and the Chevy Chase "comedy" *Under the Rainbow* (1981).

Level Two: Not So Easy
The Actors, Artists, & Others

Q: Toto was played by a professional pooch, trained by Carl Spitz. What was Toto's real name?

A: Toto was a female Cairn terrier named Terry. Carl Spitz also trained Buck, the St. Bernard in *The Call of the Wild* (1935) starring Clark Gable; and Prince, the Great Dane in *Wuthering Heights* (1939). Terry was paid $125 a week, the least of the ten major actors in the film. At $500 a week, Judy Garland received the next lowest salary!

■

Q: The casting of *The Wizard of Oz* was rather like a huge game of musical chairs. Legend has it that Loew's (MGM's parent company) chairman Nick Schenck had another choice for Dorothy. Who?

A: Both Shirley Temple and Deanna Durbin are purported to have been suggested by Schenck, but producer Arthur Freed had initially found *Oz* only *after* approaching Louis B. Mayer about developing a vehicle *specifically* for Judy Garland.

Stories about MGM's elaborate star-trading gyrations in an attempt to secure Temple are largely apocryphal, but have been given credence by their inclusion in *That's Entertainment!* (1974) and other Nostalgia Boom media. The popular legend involves a trade of the services of MGM's Jean Harlow and Clark Gable for Fox's Temple. However, Harlow died on June 7, 1937; MGM did not acquire the story rights to *The Wonderful Wizard of Oz* until February 18, 1938. Also, no contemporary trade coverage of *The Wizard of Oz* ever mentions anyone other than Judy Garland for the role of Dorothy.

In 1940, in what many consider a response to *The Wizard of Oz*, Twentieth Century-Fox produced an elaborate Technicolor® fantasy, *The Blue Bird*. Although a visually lavish production, it was a financial disaster, and signaled the downturn of Temple's career.

■

Q: Who was originally cast as the Scarecrow?

A: Buddy Ebsen. In a casting memo from producer Arthur Freed dated January 31, 1938, the role of the Tin Man is given to Ray Bolger, the Scarecrow to Buddy Ebsen. They eventually

Author's Collection. © Turner Entertainment

Ray Bolger was considered in the casting of *The Wizard of Oz* very early on—but not for the role of the Scarecrow.

switched roles, Bolger insisting he was miscast as the rigid Tin Man, and Ebsen not caring much either way: "I wanted to be in the picture because I knew it would be a very big one. And it's always good to be associated with a big project," he recalled in a 1976 interview with Aljean Harmetz. Eventually, the experimental make-up for the Tin Man, which involved an aluminum powder sprayed to a white base, would sideline Ebsen. His lungs were coated with the aluminum powder he had inhaled, and he spent six weeks recovering. He was replaced by Jack Haley. Ebsen, of course, went on to star in TV's "Davy Crockett" (as George Russel), "The Beverly Hillbillies" (as Jed Clampett), and in the title role of "Barnaby Jones."

■

Q: Who was originally cast as the Wicked Witch?

A: An early casting memo shows both Edna Mae Oliver and Fanny Brice as potential "witches" (their ethical orientation is not discussed, wicked or otherwise, but it's not hard to guess the casting). Finally, on August 20, 1938, Gale Sondergaard was announced for the role—a beautiful villain in the style of the evil queen in Disney's *Snow White and the Seven Dwarfs* (q.v.). She did tests for the picture during the last weeks of September 1938, but left by mutual agreement with the producers in early October, when it was decided that the beautiful witch was not acceptable and attempts to hide Sondergaard's beauty in "ugly" make-up seemed ridiculous. The next year she would have the part of Tylette the Cat in *The Blue Bird*.

■

Q: At least four directors were assigned to *The Wizard of Oz*. Name two.

A: **Richard Thorpe** was originally assigned to direct the picture, and began filming on October 13, 1938. He was fired on October 24, after executive producer Mervyn LeRoy expressed disappointment with the work accomplished to date.

George Cukor came in for the week of October 24 to 31, and during his time undid much of Thorpe's "glamorizing" of Dorothy, encouraging Judy Garland to be herself, resulting in a performance that is sincere and vulnerable. He also supervised corresponding revisions to Garland's hair, makeup, and wardrobe. Garland's glamorizing and subsequent simplifying would be echoed fifteen years later by her Esther Blodgett character in the Cukor-directed version of *A Star is Born* (1954). Cukor also supervised a softening of the Scarecrow makeup for Ray Bolger.

Victor Fleming came to Stage 26 at MGM on November 4, 1938, and helmed the body of the picture, but **King Vidor** directed several of the Kansas scenes after Fleming departed *Oz* to direct *Gone With The Wind* (1939) in February 1939. Vidor was actually the director of the famous "Over the Rainbow" number.

■

Q: After their adventure in the Deadly Poppy Field, the four travelers approach the Emerald City gate to an upbeat musical chorus—"You're out of the woods, you're out of the dark, you're out of the night." What is the title of this song?

A: "Optimistic Voices" is the name of the song, and it was sung in the film by a vocal trio called The Debutantes. They also recorded the voices of the Munchkin Lullaby League.

■

Q: The final credits of *Oz* list a character named Nikko, played by Pat Walshe. Who is Nikko?

A: Nikko is the commander of the Flying Monkeys, and the Wicked Witch's henchman, the role apparently the victim of the hundreds of script revisions and editorial decisions made on Oz.

■

Q: As Dorothy and her three companions make their way to the Witch's Castle through the Haunted Forest, the Wicked Witch sends a cadre of Flying Monkeys to capture Dorothy. As the monkeys fly, the Witch tells them that she has "sent a little insect on ahead to take the fight out of them." What is she referring to?

A: The insect that the Witch has sent along is "The Jitterbug," a musical number meant to occur in the picture between the dispatch of the monkeys and their attack on Dorothy and her friends. Although the song was recorded and the sequence filmed, it was cut from the final picture, both in the interest of shortening the running time and because there were those who felt (correctly) that it would date the picture in the future. In the context of the film, the Jitterbug is an insect that produces fear ("jitters"); it was also a popular dance style of the period.

On her weekly TV show in October 1963, Judy Garland and her guest star, Ray Bolger, reminisced about the making of *The Wizard of Oz*, after which they reprised "The Jitterbug" as a TV production number.

In 1989, for the Fiftieth Anniversary video tape and laser disc releases, the cast vocal tracks and orchestration were married to existing black and white stills of the cast and some rare home movies shot on the set of "The Jitterbug" as it was being filmed. The impressive 1995 compact disc release of *The Wizard of Oz* sound track also features "The Jitterbug."

Collection of Craig T. Hyland. © Turner Entertainment

The Tin Man (Jack Haley), Dorothy (Judy Garland), and the Scarecrow (Ray Bolger) enter the disquieting old growth of the Lion's forest.

Q: At the Twelfth Annual Academy Awards® in 1939, *The Wizard of Oz* was nominated for multiple prizes. What were the nominations? What Oscars® did *The Wizard of Oz* win?

A: *Oz* was nominated for Academy Awards in five categories:

Best Picture, along with *Dark Victory*; *Gone With The Wind* (which won); *Goodbye, Mr. Chips*; *Love Affair*; *Mr. Smith Goes to Washington*; *Ninotchka*; *Of Mice and Men*; *Stagecoach*; and *Wuthering Heights*.

Best Art Direction, along with *Beau Geste*, *Captain Fury*, *First Love*, *Gone With The Wind* (again the winner), *Love Affair*, *Man of Conquest*, *Mr. Smith Goes to Washington*, *The Private Lives of Elizabeth and Essex*, *The Rains Came*, and *Stagecoach*.

Best Song, along with "Faithful Forever" from *Gulliver's Travels*, "I Poured My Heart Into a Song" from *Second Fiddle*, and "Wishing [Will Make It So]" from *Love Affair*.

Best Original Score. Also nominated were *Dark Victory*, *Eternally Yours*, *Golden Boy*, *Gone With The Wind*, *Gulliver's Travels*, *The Man in the Iron Mask*, *Man of Conquest*, *Nurse Edith Cavell*, *Of Mice and Men*, *The Rains Came*, and *Wuthering Heights*.

In **Best Special Effects**, a new category that year, *Oz* shared the nomination with *Gone With The Wind*, *The Rains Came* (which won), *Only Angels Have Wings*, *The Private Lives of Elizabeth and Essex*, *Topper Takes a Trip*, and *Union Pacific*.

"Over the Rainbow" won the **Best Song** prize, and Herbert Stothart won the **Best Original Score** award.

Judy Garland won a special Oscar as **Best Juvenile Performer** for her role as Dorothy in *The Wizard of Oz*.

Aren't you glad that the Academy now limits the number of nominations in a given category?

Q: *The Wizard of Oz* achieved its status as an American pop legend only after its initial television broadcasts. When was it first broadcast? On what TV network? Who hosted the broadcast?

A: CBS approached MGM in 1956 about the possibility of airing *Gone With The Wind* on television. The answer was no, so the network asked for *The Wizard of Oz*. It was MGM's first motion picture sale to a TV network, and CBS paid a then-premium fee of $225,000 for each of two broadcasts, with an option for additional airings. The first television showing of *Oz* was hosted by Bert Lahr and Liza Minnelli, and aired on November 3, 1956.

Author's Collection. © Turner Entertainment

Most of Bert Lahr's other work—much like that of his co-stars, Ray Bolger and Jack Haley—would be forgotten in light of the popularity of *The Wizard of Oz*.

Level Three: No Easy Stuff

Minutia & Obscuria

Q: In the first Kansas sequence, Aunt Em chastises one of the farm hands: "I saw you tinkering with that contraption, Hickory! Now you and Hunk get back to that wagon!" What is Aunt Em talking about?

A: In an early (and mercifully edited) draft of the script, Hickory was tinkering with an anticyclone machine. Knowing this, his response to Aunt Em ("Someday they're going to erect a statue to me in this town!") makes a great deal more sense. If his machine had worked, however, there wouldn't have been much of a story.

■

Q: A famous Disney princess makes a brief appearance in *The Wizard of Oz*. Who is she? What is her role?

A: Adriana Caselotti, recently famous as the voice of Snow White in Disney's *Snow White and the Seven Dwarfs* (q.v., 1937), reported to MGM on September 30, 1938, to sing one line. In the song "If I Only Had a Heart," the Tin Man sings "picture me, a balcony, above a voice sings low." Caselotti responds "Wherefore art thou, Romeo?"

■

Q: Another famous Disney character voice makes an appearance in *The Wizard of Oz*. Name him.

A: Pinto Colvig, famed as the voice of Disney's Goofy, went to MGM in December 1938 to work with vocal arranger Ken Darby as a Munchkin (actually, several Munchkins).

Colvig was an itinerant creative talent—actor, musician, and animation story and gag man. Dur-

There's no place like home! Top row, from left: Professor Marvel (Frank Morgan), Uncle Henry (Charley Grapewin), Hunk (Bert Lahr). Bottom row: Dorothy (Judy Garland), Zeke (Ray Bolger), Hickory (Jack Haley), and Aunt Em (Clara Blandick).

ing the 1930s and '40s, he worked on the animation staff at Disney, MGM, and Fleischer Studios. He later gave voice to the original Bozo the Clown.

■

Q: As the Witch and her flying monkey henchman watch Dorothy and her companions being rescued from the Deadly Poppy Field, the monkey hands the Witch what appears to be a gold bag. Although never referred to in the film, fans of the original book will recognize it immediately. What is it?

A: The prop is The Golden Cap. In Baum's *The Wonderful Wizard of Oz*, he describes a Golden

Cap with a circle of diamonds and rubies running around it. This cap had a magic charm, and whoever owned it could call three times upon the Winged Monkeys, who would obey any order they were given.

Apparently a leftover part of an earlier version of the screenplay, in the final film the mighty Golden Cap is just an unnamed (and usually unnoticed) hand prop.

■

Q: The Wicked Witch's sinister hourglass went back to the MGM prop shop at the conclusion of filming. It makes an appearance in another MGM fantasy twenty-five years later. Name the film.

A: *7 Faces of Dr. Lao* (1964). In this George Pal fantasy, the witch's hourglass can be seen during the first sequence hanging on a post inside the circus sideshow tent. As Mrs. Cassan flees the predictions of Appolonius of Tyana, she meets Mrs. Benedict and they have a brief discussion. At this point, the hourglass can be seen right between them. The hourglass was also used in an MGM publicity still for the 1939 Lionel Barrymore picture *On Borrowed Time*.

The hourglass is now owned by a creative executive at Walt Disney Imagineering (Disney's theme park design division). He bought it at the infamous David Weisz MGM Auction in May 1970 for $350.

■

Q What legendary 1930s movie director was announced to supervise the dance sequences for *The Wizard of Oz*?

A Busby Berkeley, famed director of Warner Bros. musicals *42nd Street*, *Gold Diggers of 1933*, and *Footlight Parade* (1933), was announced in the Hollywood trade press on June 20, 1938. Warner Bros. then rushed him into a new pic-

The Wicked Witch of the West (Margaret Hamilton) menaces Dorothy (Judy Garland). Note the sinister hourglass in the left foreground.

ture, *They Made Me a Criminal* (1939), so choreographer Bobby Connolly was brought in by *Oz* executive producer Mervyn LeRoy. Berkeley is sometimes mistakenly credited with the dances in *The Wizard of Oz*.

■

Q: *The Wizard of Oz* has more in common with *Gone With The Wind* than just Victor Fleming and MGM. What else do these two pictures share?

A: The distinctive triangle-brace bridge that Dorothy crosses as she encounters Professor Marvel is also the bridge that Scarlett and the wagon containing Melanie and Prissy hide under in *Gone With The Wind*.

Re-use of sets was common in the days of the studio system. Many of the Columbia Pictures Three Stooges shorts, for instance, were written specifically to re-use existing sets from Columbia A pictures. However, it was rare to find two of the top releases in one year sharing a set, even one as minor as the riverbed and bridge.

It is doubly interesting to note that the set was on a sound stage at Metro-Goldwyn-Mayer Studios, when *Gone With The Wind* was being produced by another company altogether—Selznick International Pictures. MGM's distribution deal and loan-out of Clark Gable resulted in this unusual inter-studio cooperation.

Similarly, the cyclone process footage from *The Wizard of Oz* was later used in *Cabin in the Sky* (1943) and *High Barbaree* (1947).

■

Q: Actor Frank Morgan made a fascinating coincidental discovery during the shooting of the Kansas sequence. What did Morgan find?

A: Morgan's costume as Professor Marvel included a shabby Prince Albert-style coat that had been chosen from a rack of old clothing pur-

chased by the MGM costume department. Morgan turned out the pocket and discovered the name L. Frank Baum sewn into the pocket of the coat. Both Maud Gage Baum, L. Frank Baum's widow, and the Chicago tailor who had made the jacket confirmed that it had, indeed, belonged to the author of *The Wonderful Wizard of Oz*. The coat was given to Mrs. Baum at the conclusion of filming, but the story sounded like such a publicity puff piece that it was rarely related.

■

Q: Although MGM had secured the film rights to *The Wonderful Wizard of Oz*, another famous Hollywood producer held the rights to Baum's subsequent Oz books for years. Who was the filmmaker?

For his role as the Wizard of Oz, beloved character actor Frank Morgan was made up to heighten a resemblance to famed showman P. T. Barnum.

A: Walt Disney acquired the rights to the thirteen subsequent Baum Oz books, and for many years sought to develop a suitable entertainment property based upon them. Attempts included a lengthy Oz segment on the 1958 Fourth Anniversary show of the "Disneyland" television series, featuring the original "Mickey Mouse Club" Mouseketeers. The segment was a tryout of material intended for a long-in-development project called *The Rainbow Road to Oz*, based upon Baum's *Patchwork Girl of Oz* and other Baum material. *The Rainbow Road to Oz* was first announced in 1957 as Disney's premiere foray into live-action musicals. Nothing ever came of the proposed Oz film, and in 1961, *Babes in Toyland* became the first live-action musical to be released by Disney. Development continued on the Oz project, this time as an animated feature, beginning in February 1959. Disney artist Joe Rinaldi created extensive visual concepts for these uncompleted films, as well as a planned Emerald City of Oz for Disneyland. Disneyland Records released a series of Oz albums and storytellers (some with Ray Bolger as the Scarecrow) that incorporated Oz-themed songs by Tutti Camarata and a number of composers. The rights to the Baum books have slipped into the public domain, but the MGM copyrights now owned by Turner Entertainment carefully protect the principal characters of the first book as envisioned in the 1939 film, so the chances of a future Disney Oz project seem unlikely.

In 1985, Disney did produce a sequel of sorts, *Return to Oz*, loosely based on *The Marvelous Land of Oz* and *Ozma of Oz*. It was an odd picture, full of the somber feel and dark mood of the Baum Oz, as well as the spectacular Victorian visual style of Oz illustrator John R. Neill. However, this effective and unique approach was marred by attempts to make plot points from the MGM version mesh with a picture that should have stood on its own.

Q: An animated "sequel" to *The Wizard of Oz* was made. Name it.

A: The soundtrack of *Journey Back to Oz* was recorded in 1964, but the film was not finished and released until 1974. The film is probably most interesting for the peculiarity of its voice casting. A sixteen-year-old Liza Minnelli took the role of Dorothy, Margaret Hamilton played Aunt Em (!), Mickey Rooney was the Scarecrow, Danny Thomas was the Tin Man, Milton Berle was the Cowardly Lion and Ethel Merman played the Witch (!!).

There was a previous cartoon version of *The Wizard of Oz* made in 1933, produced by animator Ted Eshbaugh, but it was never exhibited due to a legal problem with Technicolor. The characters were used for animated framing segments on a 1967–68 ABC anthology series called "Off to See the Wizard" (which generated a wide variety of licensed merchandise, but no second season). An animated television series, "The Wizard of Oz," sanctioned by Turner Entertainment (holder of the copyright to the MGM film) premiered in 1989.

And let's not forget Snagglepuss, the sixties Hanna-Barbera cartoon character with the unmistakable Bert Lahr voice (provided by Daws Butler).

The Wizard of Oz opened at the Fifth Avenue Theater in Seattle, Washington, in early 1940.

Metro-Goldwyn-Mayer presents

A Mervyn LeRoy Production

THE WIZARD OF OZ

Screenplay by Noel Langley, Florence Ryerson, and Edgar Allan Woolf

Adaptation by Noel Langley, from the book by L. Frank Baum

Musical adaptation by Herbert Stothart (and Roger Edens)

Lyrics by E.Y. Harburg

Music by Harold Arlen

Associate conductor George Stoll

Orchestral and vocal arrangements by George Bassman,
Murray Cutter, Paul Marquardt, Ken Darby (Roger Edens)

Musical numbers staged by Bobby Connolly

Photographed in Technicolor®

Directors of photography, Harold Rosson (color), Allen Darby (black and white)

Color direction Natalie Kalmus, associate, Henri Jaffa

Recording director, Douglas Shearer

Art directors, Cedric Gibbons, William A. Horning (associate, Jack Martin Smith)

Set decoration, Edwin B. Willis

Special effects A. Arnold Gillespie; costumes designed by Adrian

Character make-up created by Jack Dawn

Film editor, Blanche Sewell; (associate producer, Arthur Freed)

Produced by Mervyn LeRoy

Directed by Victor Fleming (King Vidor, Richard Thorpe, George Cukor)

Cast

Judy Garland	Dorothy
Frank Morgan	Professor Marvel/The Wizard
Ray Bolger	Hunk Andrews/The Scarecrow
Bert Lahr	Zeke/The Cowardly Lion
Jack Haley	Hickory Twicker/The Tin Man
Billie Burke	Glinda
Margaret Hamilton	Miss Gulch/The Wicked Witch of the West
Charley Grapewin	Uncle Henry
Pat Walshe	Nikko
Clara Blandick	Aunt Em
Terry	Toto

Singin' in the Rain

Singin' in the Rain *was developed under the auspices of the prestigious Freed Unit at MGM, the production group responsible for* The Wizard of Oz, Meet Me in St. Louis, Easter Parade, On the Town, *and a dozen other musicals that are generally regarded as classics. Although financially successful when it was first released,* Singin' in the Rain *hardly raised a critical eyebrow. Perhaps because of the era in which it was released, the film was simply regarded as a good, solid studio product, and nothing more. In the sixties and seventies, the film buffs of the Nostalgia Boom rediscovered* Singin' in the Rain *and were awed by the gem they found. A simple story told with wit and style, captivating stars at the peak of their form, a charming musical score, and breathtaking choreography all united to form a well-made movie that is, above all, just plain fun to watch.*

■

Level One: The Easy Stuff

Story & Characters

Q: *Singin' in the Rain* **opens with a movie premiere. What movie is being premiered? Where?**

A: The silent costume romance *The Royal Rascal*, starring Don Lockwood and Lina Lamont, is having a splashy 1927 premiere at Grauman's Chinese Theater, 6925 Hollywood Boulevard.

Designed by architects Meyer & Hollander and built by showman Sid Grauman, the Chinese opened on May 18, 1927, and immediately became *the* Hollywood movie palace. Famed for its elaborate pseudo-Chinese decor and forecourt of concrete footprints and autographs, the Chinese Theater has seen hundreds of movie premieres, beginning with Cecil B. De Mille's *King of Kings*.

The footage used in the opening effects shot (and in the shot of the later premiere of *The Dancing Cavalier*) is actually from the final sequence of David O. Selznick's *A Star is Born* (1937). This Technicolor footage is of an actual Hollywood premiere, that of *Garden of Allah* (1936). Note the automobiles and you'll see it's definitely not 1927.

The theater interior was replicated for the film on a soundstage at MGM Studios in Culver City, fifteen miles away from the real thing.

Q: **Who is Don Lockwood's best friend? Who plays him?**

A: Cosmo Brown is Don's pal, played by Donald O'Connor.

The child of circus and vaudeville performers, O'Connor made his screen debut at the age of twelve in the Warner Bros. program musical *Melody For Two* (1937). This led to a contract at Paramount for the juvenile O'Connor, where he performed in *Men With Wings*, *Sing You Sinners*, *Tom Sawyer: Detective* (as Huckleberry Finn, 1938), *Beau Geste*, *Million Dollar Legs*, *On Your Toes* (on a loan-out to Warner Bros.), and *Unmarried* (1939).

At age seventeen, O'Connor moved to Universal, where he starred in a dozen light comedies, musicals, and programmers (formulaic, B-type movies) including *Give Out, Sisters*; *Private Buckaroo* (1942); *Bowery to Broadway* (1944); and *Feudin', Fussin' and A-Fightin'* (1948). In 1949, O'Connor was cast opposite a talking mule in *Francis*, which proved so popular that it was followed in short order by *Francis Goes to the Races* (1951) and *Francis Goes to West Point* (1952).

These rather silly movies apparently didn't affect his credibility as a performer. Arthur Freed

"Fit as a Fiddle" Donald O'Connor and Gene Kelly on the Burlesque circuit.

had wanted Oscar Levant as the second banana for *Singin' in the Rain*, but Gene Kelly knew that Cosmo Brown *had* to be a song and dance man—and O'Connor was his choice.

For the next decade, O'Connor kept busy in films and television, appearing in prestigious pictures like *Call Me Madam* (1953), *There's No Business Like Show Business* (1954), and *Anything Goes* (1956); minor pictures like *I Love Melvin* and *Walking My Baby Back Home* (1953); and three more "Francis" pictures. He won an Emmy® as the star of "The Colgate Comedy Hour" on television. In 1957, O'Connor played the great silent comedian in the ambitious but disappointing *The Buster Keaton Story*. He made fewer films in order to concentrate on his composing ("At last I can start suffering and write that symphony"), and in 1956 he conducted the premiere performance of his symphony *Reflections d'un Comique*, with the Los Angeles Philharmonic.

Since then, O'Connor has appeared on television and in occasional film roles. He was featured in *That's Entertainment!* (1974), *The Big Fix* (1978), and *Ragtime* (in a singing and dancing

role, 1981), and the expensive Barry Levinson flop *Toys* (1992).

On stage, he appeared (in the role of Albert Peterson, originated by Dick Van Dyke) in the 1981 four-performance Broadway flop sequel *Bring Back Birdie*, with Chita Rivera, and toured as Cap'n Andy in *Show Boat* in the early 1980s.

O'Connor's then-wife, Gwen Carter, made a cameo appearance in *Singin' in the Rain*, as the young lady Cosmo is "working" at Simpson's party ("Oh, Mr. Brown, do you really think you could get me in the movies?").

■

Q: For which studio does Don Lockwood star? Who heads the studio?

A: Monumental Pictures is the name of the studio, under the benign rule of R. F. Simpson.

The Monumental Pictures gate was just a redressing of an old back lot set at MGM's Culver City studios. The character of R. F. Simpson was actually based on *Singin' in the Rain* producer

Arthur Freed, an inarticulate, gentle giant. It is said that he knew what he wanted, but didn't have the first idea how to ask for it. The creative team on *Singin' in the Rain* poked fun at this Freed characteristic. After the complete "Broadway Ballet" has been "described" by Don (and seen by the audience), R. F.'s response is, "I can't quite visualize it. I'll have to see it on film first."

Simpson was played by Millard Mitchell, who had specialized as tough guys in such films as *Grand Central Murder* (1942), *Kiss of Death* (1947), *Twelve O'Clock High* (1949), *The Gunfighter* (1950), and *The Naked Spur* (1953).

Millard Mitchell died in 1953.

■

Q: **How does Don Lockwood launch his movie career?**

Author's Collection. © Turner Entertainment

Debbie Reynolds (in her nightclub costume) "flaps" with Gene Kelly.

A: Don volunteers to do a movie Western stunt after the villain, Bert (Bill Lewin), is knocked unconscious. He follows this by becoming something of a stuntman-of-all-trades ("Got any other little chores you want done in this picture?"), until the studio chief elevates him to leading man status in a picture with Lina Lamont.

This story is not atypical of the silent and early sound era of filmmaking. Marion Michael Morrison, a former USC football star, became a movie bit player in the late 1920s and rose to stardom as John Wayne. Gary Cooper began playing cowboy extras in Westerns in 1925 and shot to stardom in 1926 when (at the last minute) he replaced actor Harold Goodwin as Abe Lee in *The Winning of Barbara Worth*.

This plot line was probably established early on in the development of *Singin' in the Rain*, when the screenwriters were working with Howard Keel in mind as the hero, on a plot involving a silent Western star who makes the transition to talkies by becoming a singing cowboy.

■

Q: **At the premiere party, the studio boss has "a little surprise" for his guests. What is it?**

A: Cosmo quips, "You gotta show a movie at a party—it's a Hollywood law." What R. F. Simpson shows is a demonstration of a Talking Picture.

Motion pictures had never truly been "silent." The big picture palaces used full orchestras, complete with sound effects. At the very least, a movie palace had a sophisticated pipe organ to do the job. And even tiny neighborhood theaters had a piano player providing musical accompaniment.

Since the earliest days of film, inventors had experimented with synchronized sound for film, but it wasn't until American Telephone & Telegraph subsidiary Western Electric developed the "sound-on-disc" Vitaphone™ system that a workable method was perfected. Warner Bros. decided to adopt the Vitaphone process in 1926, and premiered the new technology at Manhattan's Warner Theater. In addition to Vitaphone short subjects, the feature film *Don Juan* was shown, not with a live orchestra, but with recorded score and sound effects. Only later, in *The Jazz Singer* (1927), was recorded dialogue used as well—and then only occasionally. Warner's *Lights of New York* (1928) was the first "All Talking" picture.

The Vitaphone "sound-on-disc" is the technology that R. F. Simpson is demonstrating to his party guests. The demonstration film in *Singin' in the Rain* features character actor Julius Tannen, and is typical of the awkward, badly-produced demos of the time. The sound quality of the demonstration is pretty accurate, too. Early talkies sounded tinny and had all the surface noise and distortion that is so well-recreated in *Singin' in the Rain*'s demo film.

During the early days of sound film, Fox Film Corporation began to use a "sound-on-film" method, which used a photo-electric cell to convert sound waves into light waves and then record them onto the edge of the film strip. This "optical track" was then "read" by a correlating "exciter lamp" in a sound projector for playback.

What had been considered a novelty and a flash in the pan revolutionized the entire film production and exhibition business within a few short years. Interestingly, before *Singin' in the Rain*, popular films had paid little attention to the high drama and story potential of the sound revolution in movies.

■

Q: **Kathy loses her chorus job because of Lina Lamont. Where has Kathy been performing?**

A: Kathy has been performing at the famous Cocoanut Grove in the Ambassador Hotel in Los Angeles. Opened on April 21, 1921 (four months after the hotel itself), The Cocoanut Grove soon became the height of Hollywood nighttime chic, and remained so well into the 1940s. The Ambas-

sador had originally featured a small club known as the Zinnia Grill, which proved so popular that the management converted the hotel ballroom into the 1,000-seat Cocoanut Grove. Legend has it that the decor for the club was taken from the set of Valentino's *The Sheik*, papier-mâché coconuts and stuffed monkeys with electrically-lighted eyes hanging from artificial palms in the faux-oasis on Wilshire Boulevard.

Mack Sennett discovered Bing Crosby crooning onstage at "The Grove"; a starlet named Lucille Le Sueur—later known to the world as Joan Crawford—was a frequent winner of dance contests there. Freddy Martin and a vocalist named Merv Griffin, Guy Lombardo, Phil Harris, and Rudy Vallee helped spread the fame of The Cocoanut Grove across the country when big bands broadcast live from the Cocoanut Grove in the thirties and forties.

"The Grove" is the same nightclub where Esther Blodgett and The Glen Williams Orchestra perform after the Shrine Auditorium benefit in *A Star is Born* (1954). Norman Maine is too late to catch up with Esther and scans the room for a companion. Later in the same film, the Academy Awards presentation takes place at the Cocoanut Grove (the event had actually taken place there from 1930 to 1936).

In 1964, a little-known New York-based vocalist named Barbra Streisand gave her first Los Angeles concert at the famous club. The Cocoanut Grove became chic again in the 1970s with the help of several young performers weaned on its legends, including Sonny and Cher, Sammy Davis Jr., and Diana Ross.

The Ambassador Hotel and The Cocoanut Grove closed in 1988. Donald Trump planned an office tower for the site but withdrew his bid. The Los Angeles Unified School District developed a plan for a "performing arts academy" on the site, but failed to put the necessary funding in place. The Ambassador and The Cocoanut Grove sit vacant on Wilshire Boulevard today, available for rentals, private parties, and film locations. Recent films shot there include *Defending Your Life* (1991), *L.A. Story* (1991), *Guilty by Suspicion* (1991), *Mr. Saturday Night* (1992), and *The Mask* (1994).

■

Q: Cosmo tries to cheer the downhearted Don with a song and dance. Name it.

A: "Make 'Em Laugh," a comic acrobatic song-and-dance, is performed by the seemingly indestructible Cosmo Brown in an attempt to cheer his pal.

One of the reasons for his casting had been O'Connor's unique comic and athletic abilities. His parents had been circus performers and then vaudevillians, and the years O'Connor had spent with them had taught him many tricks of the trade.

When it came time to choreograph O'Connor's specialty number there was really nothing in the Freed-Brown music catalogue that was suitable for the number that O'Connor and the directors had in mind. They approached Arthur Freed and told him that they needed another song, something befitting the knockabout comedy dance that was planned, and suggested that it should be like the famous Cole Porter song "Be a Clown." Freed and Brown more than complied, they pretty much duplicated "Be a Clown" and delivered "Make 'Em Laugh" to the filmmakers. Although it was obvious to everyone concerned that subconscious—or conscious—plagiarism had taken place, no one had the courage to bring it up to Freed personally. Irving Berlin, one of Cole Porter's close friends, is reported to have visited the set while the number was being shot, and sputtered angrily at Freed about the song's suspect origins. Porter himself, although aware of the song, never mentioned it.

O'Connor had ad-libbed much of the number, looking around the MGM scenery dock and prop shop for appropriate items, including the head-

less dummy that he flirts with. He also wears a very concealing costume during this number, to disguise the amount of protective padding he is wearing—he appears to have gained about twenty-five pounds since his previous scene. Naturally the athletics of the number were taxing. O'Connor experienced bumps, bruises, and even carpet burns from the rigors of the number. The day after it was filmed, O'Connor spent the day in bed recuperating. The following day, a grim Gene Kelly approached O'Connor with the news that the film from the day's shoot had been fogged and was unusable—he'd have to do the number again.

O'Connor, ever the trouper, did—and spent the following three days confined to his bed.

■

Q: Don proclaims his love for Kathy in a unique way. How?

A: On an empty soundstage, Don serenades Kathy ("You Were Meant for Me") in a setting he has created with the tools of movie-making magic: a beautiful sunset, mist from the distant mountains, colored lights in a garden, moonlight, a soft summer breeze, and even 500,000 kilowatts of stardust.

The screenplay had originally outlined this number as a song-and-dance medley to take place in five different back lot sets around MGM: a Paris boulevard, a London street, and even a jungle. The filmmakers finally considered this sequence too self-conscious, cumbersome, and lacking in romance.

By the time the number was to be filmed, the screenwriters had long since departed MGM and were in Philadelphia working on the out-of-town tryouts for a revue they were involved with. They were called on for a solution and delivered the finished scene as filmed. Simple, romantic, meaningful, and yet still tied to the key setting of a busy movie studio.

easy

Q: To make *The Duelling Cavalier* a talkie, microphones must be hidden to record dialogue. Where do we see them hidden?

A: The microphones are hidden, with varying degrees of success, in a potted plant, on Lina's costume bodice at the breast, and finally on her shoulder.

The screenwriters had interviewed several old-timers at MGM who had worked on films during their painful transition to sound. Many of the anecdotes they related were translated into situations and gags in *Singin' in the Rain.* Costumer Walter Plunkett verified the accuracy of the "hidden microphone," as well as noting that the early mikes would indeed pick up sounds like Lina's necklace.

Plunkett also reported that he had to be careful in costuming early talkies because of the sensitive mikes. Bugle beads, he recalled, "clanked like chain mail," and had to be covered with fine mesh to restrict their movement and muffle the noise. For *Rio Rita* (1929), Plunkett remembered having made a paper fan for star Bebe Daniels. When she opened it, it sounded like a thunderstorm, so he had to remake it out of silk.

■

Q: "Fellas, I feel this is my lucky day!" Don crows. What day is Don's lucky day?

A: At first, Don thinks it's March 23, but Cosmo reminds him that it's 1:30 A.M.—it's the morning of March 24, leading to the exuberant "Good Morning" number.

"Good Morning" was originally scripted to take place in a restaurant after the disastrous preview of *The Duelling Cavalier.* After the number in the restaurant, all three principles were going to burst into the stormy street for the title number. It was decided that this breezy trio was too reminiscent of Kelly, Phil Silvers, and Rita Hayworth and the "Make Way for Tomorrow" number in *Cover Girl* (1944), which begins in a nightclub after hours and dances out into a Brooklyn street. "Good Morning" was relocated to Don's Hollywood mansion, and "Singin' in the Rain" was relocated to the street outside Kathy's apartment building after the star drops off his young love…where it became perhaps the most famous solo dance number ever put on film.

Author's Collection. © Turner Entertainment

The iconic moment from perhaps the most famous solo dance number in any movie musical.

medium

Q: Who plays Lina Lamont? The part was written with whom in mind?

A: Jean Hagen plays the dim blond movie star who believes all her own publicity. Born Jean Shirley Verhagen in Chicago, Hagen graduated from Northwestern University with a major in drama. She went to New York, where she worked as a radio actress (and as a theater usherette), and began her stage career on Broadway. She was put under contract by MGM in 1949, made her screen debut in *Adam's Rib* (1949), and continued to work there on pictures such as *Ambush* and *Side Street* (1949). Only *The Asphalt Jungle* (1950) and *Singin' in the Rain* seemed to take full advantage of her versatile talent. From 1953 to 1957 she played Danny Thomas' wife in "The Danny Thomas Show" (a.k.a. "Make Room for Daddy").

She continued to work in film, making appearances in *Arena*, *Half a Hero*, *Latin Lovers* (1953), *The Big Knife* (1955), *Spring Reunion* (1957), *The Shaggy Dog* (1959), *Sunrise at Campobello* (1960), *Panic in Year Zero* (1962), and *Dead Ringer* (1964).

The screenwriters had created the role of Lina Lamont with Judy Holliday in mind; she had performed with them in their cabaret act in New York. Holliday had perfected the character of a shrill, dumb, wisecracking Brooklyn blond, a persona that she took to the stratosphere in the stage and screen versions of *Born Yesterday*. By the time *Singin' in the Rain* started production (June, 1951), Holliday was too big a star to be considered for the part. Nina Foch, Gene Kelly's co-star in *An American in Paris* (1951), was tested, but was found unsuitable for the role. Then, among MGM's contract players, Jean Hagen was found. Hagen had appeared in a touring company of *Born Yesterday*, in the part originated by Judy Holliday.

Hagen died of throat cancer at the age of fifty-four in 1977.

Q: The score of *Singin' in the Rain* features the songs of what composing team?

A: The score is (mostly) from the trunk of Arthur Freed and Nacio Herb Brown, including "Broadway Melody," "The Wedding of the Painted Doll," and "You Were Meant for Me" from *The Broadway Melody* (1929); "Singin' in the Rain" from *Hollywood Revue of 1929*; "Should I?" from *Lord Byron of Broadway* (1929); "Beautiful Girl" used in both *Stage Mother* and *Goin' Hollywood* (1933); "Temptation," from *Goin' Hollywood*; "All I Do Is Dream of You" from *Sadie McKee*; "I've Got a Feelin' You're Foolin'," "You Are My Lucky Star," and "Broadway Rhythm" from *The Broadway Melody of 1936* (1935); "Would You" from *San Francisco* (1936); and "Good Morning" from the film *Babes in Arms* (1939).

Freed and Brown had first met in 1921, and, together with King Zany, they wrote "When Buddha Smiles" and "Take Me in Your Arms." Both were recorded by Paul Whiteman, at that time the premier white American jazz band leader.

Freed went to California, working at Famous Players-Lasky as an assistant director and—shades of Cosmo Brown—playing piano "mood music" on the shooting stages of the studio.

Brown and Freed collaborated again, writing songs for the stage revue *Hollywood's Music Box Revue of 1927*. With the advent of sound pictures, MGM production head Irving Thalberg decided to make a musical, and at a meeting with Thalberg, Freed and Brown presented the best of what they had in their trunk, along with "The Broadway Melody," "The Wedding of the Painted Doll," and "You Were Meant for Me." They got the job, writing music for *The Broadway Melody*, *The Broadway Melody of 1936*, and *The Broadway Melody of 1938* (1937).

Freed and Brown stayed on at Metro. Freed

eventually became the legendary producer of musical films.

It's easy to see why *Singin' in the Rain* was probably dear to the heart of Freed—not just because of his songs, but because it evoked the epoch and experiences that he remembered so personally and well.

∎

Q: One of the *Singin' in the Rain* cast appeared not only in this great screen musical, but in the film versions of *The King and I* (1956) and *West Side Story* (1961), too. Who?

A: Rita Moreno, as Monumental Pictures ingenue Zelda Zanders. Born Rosita Dolores Alverio in Humacao, Puerto Rico, Moreno made her motion picture debut at age fourteen in *A Medal for Benny* (1945). Other of her early films are *Pagan Love Song*; *So Young, So Bad*; *The Toast of New Orleans* (1950); *Cattle Town*; *The Fabulous Senorita*; and *The Ring* (1952) before her appearance in *Singin' in the Rain*.

Her subsequent film efforts included such diverse titles as *Fort Vengeance*, Jack London's *Tales of Adventure*, *Latin Lovers*, *Ma and Pa Kettle On Vacation* (1953), *Garden of Evil*, *Jivaro*, *The Yellow Tomahawk* (1954), *Seven Cities of Gold*, and *Untamed* (1955).

In 1956, she appeared as Tuptim in the Twentieth Century-Fox film adaptation of Rodgers & Hammerstein's *The King and I*.

Again, after a big prestige picture, Moreno got back to the grind, appearing in *The Lieutenant Wore Skirts*, *The Vagabond King* (1956), *The Deerslayer* (1957), *This Rebel Breed* (a.k.a. *Three Shades of Love*, 1960), and *Summer and Smoke* (1961).

She assumed the film role of Anita in *West Side Story* (Broadway's Anita, Chita Rivera, was unavailable, being was under contract to the original New York company of *Bye Bye Birdie*). Moreno's fun, fiery, and poignant performance earned her the Academy Award for Best Supporting Actress.

Moreno was, in fact, the first person ever to earn the Oscar, Emmy, Tony®, and Grammy® awards.

She made only a dozen more films, most notably *Marlowe* (1969) and *Carnal Knowledge* (1971); and gave hilarious performances in both *The Ritz* (1976, in which she had won the Tony Award for her stage portrayal of Googie Gomez) and *The Four Seasons* (1981). She starred in a subsequent TV series based on *The Four Seasons*.

In the mid-1970s, Moreno had a recurring guest role with *Marlowe* co-star James Garner on "The Rockford Files," as whore-with-a-heart-of-gold Rita Capkovich (for which she won an Emmy). She was also one of the cast members of the PBS educational series for kids, "The Electric Company" (she won her Grammy for the concurrent "The Electric Company" children's record).

Most recently, she has been seen on "The Cosby Mysteries" as Cosby's feisty, health-obsessed "housekeeper," Angie Corea.

∎

Q: What famed team created the story and screenplay of *Singin' in the Rain*?

A: Betty Comden and Adolph Green supplied the story and screenplay for *Singin' in the Rain*. They had begun their show business careers in 1938 in a group called The Revuers, which featured Comden, Green, Judy Holliday (née Judy Tuvim), Alvin Hammer, and John Frank. They performed in a cabaret called Max Gordon's Village Vanguard in Greenwich Village. The group became quite popular, moving on to the Rainbow Room at Rockefeller Center and Café Society both Uptown and Downtown. They went to Hollywood (without John Frank) and appeared at the Trocadero on the Sunset Strip, where their act was signed by Twentieth Century-Fox for *Greenwich Village* (1944, from which their scene was cut!). Judy Holliday was offered a film contract and the group split. Comden and Green returned to New York, reworked their act, and began appearing as a duo at Max Gordon's Blue Angel cabaret.

Their friends Jerome Robbins and Leonard Bernstein told them of a ballet they were working out together, called *Fancy Free*. The dance vignettes told the story of three sailors on leave, and in *Fancy Free* Comden and Green saw the source of a Broadway musical comedy. They pitched the idea to Broadway director George Abbott, who signed them to write the show with Leonard Bernstein as composer and Jerome Robbins as choreographer. *On the Town* opened scarcely six months after the premiere of *Fancy Free*, on December 28, 1944, with Comden and Green in the roles of Claire and Ozzie. In 1945, they wrote the Broadway musical *Billion Dollar Baby* with composer Morton Gould.

Hollywood called Comden and Green, and they arrived at the Freed Unit at MGM, where they wrote a new screenplay, as well as some new songs (with Roger Edens), to the 1927 chestnut *Good News* (1947). This was followed by *The Barkleys of Broadway* (1948) and the film version of *On the Town* (1949). They followed *Singin' in the Rain* with *The Band Wagon* (1953), another highly-regarded original musical comedy, and *It's Always Fair Weather* (1955).

They adapted Jerome Lawrence and Robert E. Lee's 1956 Broadway comedy *Auntie Mame* to the screen in 1958, as well as their own 1956 Broadway musical comedy *Bells Are Ringing* (1960), which starred Judy Holliday. They later wrote the screenplay for the black-comedy/musical *What a Way to Go!* (1964), which co-starred Gene Kelly.

Comden and Green also continued to perform on stage and in concert (notably *Follies in Concert* in 1985) and act in films. Adolph Green played television producer Leo Silver in the 1982 comedy *My Favorite Year*. Betty Comden played the reclusive Greta Garbo in the underrated *Garbo Talks* in 1984.

Q: At the premiere, Don is interviewed by a "radio columnist." Who? Who plays the columnist?

A: Dora Bailey, played by Madge Blake. Dora is based on Louella O. Parsons (born Louella Oettinger in 1893), an influential and feared Hollywood gossip columnist, syndicated in Hearst newspapers. Like her colleague and rival Hedda Hopper, she was a real power in manipulating the public opinion. Also like Hopper, Parsons appeared in several films (although Hopper had actually begun her career as an actress), including *Hollywood Hotel* (1937), *Without Reservations* (1946), and *Starlift* (1951). Parsons wrote two autobiographies, *The Gay Illiterate* (1944) and *Tell It to Louella* (1961). Parsons died in 1972.

MGM bosses were afraid of the Parsons send-up, no matter how loving it was—Parsons was a publicity force to be feared, publicity departments worked overtime to accommodate Louella. Gene Kelly recalled that "one was never sure with these ladies, and we knew in *Singin' in the Rain* that we were all taking a chance. Fortunately, Louella adored it, and only said flattering things about us."

Madge Blake was born in 1900, but didn't begin acting until her sons were grown and she had reached her fortieth year. She began acting on stage at the famed Pasadena Playhouse, but her career was truly launched when she was "discovered" by Fanny Brice. By the time of her death in 1969, she had appeared in more than two hundred films and television shows. She was Mrs. Mondello, Larry's mother, on "Leave It to Beaver," spent six seasons as Flora MacMichael on "The Real McCoys" (1957–63), and appeared as Mrs. Barnes on "The Joey Bishop Show" (1961–62).

Blake was made immortal to generations of TV viewers as Bruce Wayne's dotty Aunt Harriet Cooper in the 1966–1969 "Batman" series and the 1966 feature film based on the series.

Q: Who was Gene Kelly's co-director and co-choreographer on *Singin' in the Rain*?

A: Stanley Donen had been a chorus dancer in the Broadway cast of *Pal Joey*, in which Gene Kelly had risen to stardom. The two became fast friends, and Kelly brought Donen to Hollywood as his assistant in 1942. Eventually, the pair co-directed, beginning with *On the Town* and *Take Me Out to the Ball Game* (1949). Donen's solo directing debut was *Royal Wedding* (1951), and he re-teamed with Gene Kelly for *Singin' in the Rain*. Donen went on to direct several prominent films, including *Seven Brides for Seven Brothers* (1954), *Funny Face*, *The Pajama Game* (1957), *Damn Yankees* (1958), *Charade* (1963), *Two for the Road* (1967), *Lucky Lady* (1975), *Saturn 3* (1980), and *Blame It On Rio* (1984).

Donen's directorial technique in his films with Kelly features direct, simple, and straightforward staging of dialogue scenes, economical and unencumbered by inconsequential flash. This style is coupled with a creative use of camera in dance scenes, where Donen leaned toward sweeping motion and/or vividly styled visuals.

Donen was briefly married to his (and Kelly's) dance assistant Jeanne Coyne (who Kelly later married). Donen married actress and trivia quiz/word game favorite Yvette Mimieux in 1972.

■

Q: The basic plot that Cosmo cooks up for *The Dancing Cavalier* is a satirical lift from an actual Broadway show (and subsequent film). Which one?

A: "We throw a modern section into the picture. The hero's a young hoofer in a Broadway show, right?...And he sings and he dances, right?...But one night backstage he's reading *The Tale of Two Cities* between numbers, see? And a sandbag falls and hits him on the head, and he dreams he's back during the French revolution, right?...Well, this way we get the modern dancing numbers—

Charleston-Charleston—but in the dream part we can still use the costume stuff!"

Cosmo's idea to save *The Duelling Cavalier* would be just as ridiculous as it sounds—if it hadn't been pretty much lifted from *DuBarry Was a Lady*. Ethel Merman and Bert Lahr starred in this 1939 Cole Porter musical, which ran for 408 performances on Broadway. The plot concerned a nightclub men's room attendant (Lahr) in love with the club's star performer (Merman). Lahr wins a sweepstakes and buys the club in a bid to woo Merman, then accidentally drinks a Mickey Finn which he has

Author's Collection. © Turner Entertainment

Debbie Reynolds and Gene Kelly in a vintage publicity shot for *Singin' in the Rain*.

intended to slip to Merman's beau. He passes out and dreams that he is King Louis XIV and Merman is Madame DuBarry, and he spends the balance of the show in vain comic attempts to compromise her virtue. At the end, Lahr comes to and nobly loses his lady love to her sweetheart.

A much-reworked *DuBarry Was a Lady* was filmed by MGM in 1943, starring Red Skelton in the Bert Lahr role (changed to a cloakroom attendant) and Lucille Ball in the Merman role. As Ball's love interest and Skelton's adversary (known as The Black Arrow in the dream section), a young hoofer named Gene Kelly made his third screen appearance.

■

Q: In the film plot, Kathy Selden dubs Lina's voice. In reality, who dubbed whom in *Singin' in the Rain*?

A: When Kathy is seen dubbing Lina's *dialogue* for *The Dancing Cavalier*, that's not Debbie Reynolds' voice, it's actually Jean Hagen's. Hagen had theater background and vocal training, while Reynolds' voice had a quality that Stanley Donen called "that terrible western noise." In the context of *The Dancing Cavalier*, Reynolds' voice coming from Hagen's noblewoman would have sounded almost as jarring as Lina Lamont's. What the movie audience gets was described by film historian and critic Peter Wollen as "the unveiling of a mystery which subverts its own appearance of authenticity."

Lina Lamont's *singing* voice ("Would You?") and some of Debbie Reynolds' singing (high notes and her final duet of "You Are My Lucky Star" with Gene Kelly) was dubbed by Betty Noyes. Noyes had performed the poignant vocal of "Baby Mine," the Oscar-nominated best song in Disney's *Dumbo* (1941).

■

Q: What famous early talkie star plays Lina Lamont's hairdresser?

A: Mae Clarke was the young lady in *The Public Enemy* who got the grapefruit in the kisser from James Cagney. When Lina complains, "Gee, this wig weighs a ton," it is hairdresser Clarke who clucks, "Honey, you look just beautiful." Mae Clarke was born Mary Klotz in 1907, the daughter of a movie theater organist. She began dancing in cabarets at sixteen, and went on to perform in stage musicals and dramas. In 1929 she made her first film, *Big Time*, and was a leading lady for more than a decade in prestigious pictures like *Frankenstein*, *The Front Page*, *Waterloo Bridge* (1931), and *The Lady Killer* (again with Cagney, 1933). As her career status declined, Clarke was reduced to supporting and bit parts and occasional leads in B pictures.

She did keep working, though, turning up in *Annie Get Your Gun* (1950), *The Great Caruso* (1951), *Magnificent Obsession* (1954), *A Big Hand for the Little Lady* (1966), *Thoroughly Modern Millie* (1967), and *Watermelon Man* (1970), among dozens of others.

Mae Clarke died in 1992.

■

Q: How many Academy Awards did *Singin' in the Rain* win?

A: None. The film that Pauline Kael has called "just about the best Hollywood musical of all time" did well at the box office (it grossed $7,665,000 on a budget of $2,540,000), but it won no Oscars, made no critic's "year's best" list. Audiences began to warm to the greatness of *Singin' in the Rain* when it was re-released as part of an MGM classics package in 1958. It was nominated for the 1952 Academy Award in only two categories:

Supporting Actress: *Singin' in the Rain* (Jean Hagen), *The Bad and the Beautiful* (the winner,

Gloria Grahame), *Moulin Rouge* (Colette Marchand), *Come Back, Little Sheba* (Terry Moore), and *With a Song in My Heart* (Thelma Ritter).

Music Scoring Awards (Scoring of a Musical Picture): *Singin' in the Rain* (Lennie Hayton), *The Jazz Singer* (an interesting coincidence, this remake of what is considered the first

talkie starred Jean Hagen's future TV co-star Danny Thomas; Ray Heindorf and Max Steiner were the nominees), *Hans Christian Andersen* (Walter Scharf), *The Medium* (Gian-Carlo Menotti), and *With a Song in My Heart* (the winner, Alfred Newman).

Author's Collection. © Turner Entertainment

Film critic Pauline Kael called *Singin' in the Rain* "just about the best Hollywood musical of all time."

Level Three: No Easy Stuff

Minutia & Obscuria

Q: How many songs in the *Singin' in the Rain* score are not by Arthur Freed and Nacio Herb Brown?

A: Two. "Fit as a Fiddle" has a *lyric* by Arthur Freed, but the music is by Al Hoffman and Al Goodhart. "Moses" was written by Betty Comden and Adolph Green, with music by Roger Edens (and is vaguely reminiscent of the Comden-Green-Edens "French Lesson" from the 1947 *Good News*).

Edens was born in 1905, in Hillsboro, Texas, and earned his B.A. at the University of Texas. He studied music in Paris and went to New York in 1929, where he worked for George Gershwin and was Ethel Merman's nightclub and vaudeville accompanist for four years. He arrived in Hollywood in 1933, and worked at Samuel Goldwyn as composer, arranger, and music supervisor on the Eddie Cantor/Ethel Merman vehicle *Kid Millions* (1934); after that he spent time at Para-

mount writing special material for Ethel Merman's subsequent films. He was providing his musical talents to the Rudy Valee radio show in 1935 when he was brought to MGM, where he became a musical jack-of-all-trades—musical supervisor, composer, and arranger. He worked a great deal with young Judy Garland (he wrote the new lyrics for "You Made Me Love You," which Garland sang as "Dear Mr. Gable"), and was certainly a primary influence in the definition of her musical persona.

Edens went to work for the Freed Unit in the early 1940s, and became an associate producer to Freed as well as composing, scoring, and arranging many classic MGM musicals such as *The Wizard of Oz* (q.v.), *Babes in Arms* (1939), *Meet Me in St. Louis* (1944), *The Harvey Girls* (1946), *An American in Paris* (1951), and *The Band Wagon* (1953). It has been said that Edens was truly the "style and taste" of the Freed Unit, but was content to remain uncredited for much of the accom-

Author's Collection. © Turner Entertainment

The name of MGM's parent company, Loew's, is prominently on display in the "Broadway Ballet."

plishment that was incorrectly credited to Freed and others.

As one of Judy Garland's frequent collaborators and stalwarts, Edens was seemingly one of the few associates who understood the fragility of her special gifts. He stuck by her through most of her difficult life, working with her long after her 1950 termination from MGM; on her legendary live shows at the London Palladium and the New York Palace, and as composer, arranger, and music supervisor on her landmark "comeback," *A Star Is Born* (1954). Their final rift came in 1961. They never worked together again.

Edens was nominated for a dozen Academy Awards, and won the Oscar for his work on *Easter Parade* (1948), *On the Town* (1949), and *Annie Get Your Gun* (1950).

His last notable film projects were *Funny Face* (1957), *The Unsinkable Molly Brown* (1964), and *Hello, Dolly!* (q.v., 1969). Edens died in 1970.

■

Q: To prepare for her transition to talkies, Lina sees a diction coach. What is the coach's name? Who played her?

A: Phoebe Dinsmore is Lina's diction coach, played by Kathleen Freeman. Kathleen Freeman is one of those terrific, ubiquitous character actors that pop up on the screen and feel like an old friend. Her career in Hollywood spans nearly fifty years, and includes *The Fly* (1958), *North to Alaska* (1960), *The Blues Brothers* (1980), *Innerspace, Dragnet* (1987), *FernGully: The Last Rain Forest* (1991), and *Hocus Pocus* (1993). She also did *ten* Jerry Lewis films, including *The Nutty Professor* (1963), *The Disorderly Orderly* (1964), and *Three on a Couch* (1966). In essence, she was Lewis's Margaret Dumont. It's a treat to watch Kathleen Freeman trying not to break up in the face of Lewis's hyperactive clowning.

Her television roles have included stints on "Nurses," "Doogie Howser, M.D.," "Major Dad,"

"Matlock," "L.A. Law," "The Golden Girls," "Murphy Brown," "The Dick Van Dyke Show," and "The Lucy Show." She appeared on stage in *Annie* (as Miss Hannigan) and *Deathtrap*. Not surprisingly, she is also a respected acting coach.

Don Lockwood also goes to a diction coach, but naturally has more success at it than Lina. He has more fun, too. He and Cosmo break into the "Moses" number, and proceed to generally abuse Don's poor, passive teacher, played by Bobby Watson.

In Woody Allen's *Radio Days* (1986), aspiring actress Sally White, played by Mia Farrow, goes to a voice class to improve her career opportunities. Sally's interpretation of the phrase, "Hark, I hear the cannon's roar," owes a great deal to Lina Lamont's "An' I can't stan 'im!"

■

Q: The basic plot of "Broadway Ballet" was lifted and used in another musical two years after *Singin' in the Rain*. What film flattered the "Broadway Ballet" plot line by imitation?

A: *A Star is Born* (1954). The "Born in a Trunk" sequence is an extended musical number at the end of the film's first act. It's a musical sequence ostensibly from Vicki Lester's screen debut, as seen by a sneak preview audience. The sequence was an afterthought, and was pulled together in answer to the need for a first-act finale and the lack of a "big number" for Judy Garland. It has the feeling of being an addition, since it does little for the plot other than give a tangible demonstration of why Vicki Lester becomes an overnight sensation with the moviegoing public.

The "Broadway Ballet" in *Singin' in the Rain* was originally intended as a duo for Gene Kelly and Donald O'Connor, but commitments to "The Colgate Comedy Hour" television program made O'Connor unavailable, so Kelly became the sole focus of the ballet story. The sequence was shot

hard

after the completion of principle photography on the picture proper. The ballet was rehearsed for a month and shot for two full weeks.

The similarity in story lines has a simple explanation—Roger Edens. The associate producer of *Singin' in the Rain* was also a talented musical arranger. Many times when "pastiche" numbers show up in MGM musicals, Edens is behind them ("Good Morning" is a good example of his musical vignettes). Who came up with the story line for the "Broadway Ballet?" Edens and Kelly, it would seem. What uncredited person put together the "Born in a Trunk" number (and wrote the music for it)? Roger Edens.

Gene Kelly is a naive young hoofer and Cyd Charisse is a chic chanteuse in the celebrated "Broadway Ballet."

Q: Two musical scenes were cut from *Singin' in the Rain*. Can you name them?

A: A version of "All I Do Is Dream of You" sung by Gene Kelly was deleted from the final cut of *Singin' in the Rain*. It takes place after R. F. Simpson's party, when all Don can think of is the chorus girl who has stolen his heart.

Also cut is a rendition of "You Are My Lucky Star," sung by Debbie Reynolds. It takes place after Don has serenaded Kathy on the empty soundstage. Kathy runs across the studio lot, where she sees a billboard of Monumental Pictures' two top stars, Don Lockwood and Lina Lamont, and she sings to the billboard image of her new love.

The deleted number contains a patter segment at the bridge that is strongly reminiscent of Judy Garland's "Dear Mr. Gable," which should come as no surprise—both patter segments were written by, again, Roger Edens.

The latter segment is part of the 1991 MGM/UA laser disc release of *Singin' in the Rain* and was part of the "lost" footage in *That's Entertainment III* (1994).

■

Q: At the end of the "Singin' in the Rain" solo dance number, Kelly gives his umbrella to a passing pedestrian. Who is the grateful recipient of Kelly's bumbershoot?

A: Snub Pollard. Born Harold Fraser in Australia in 1886, Pollard spent most of his life in the motion picture business, beginning in the silent days in slapstick comedy shorts. He continued to work as a bit player after the advent of sound made such broad visual comedy passé, all the way up to his death from cancer in 1962. Pollard's film appearances include *The Crime Patrol* (1936), *The Perils of Pauline* (1947), *Miracle on 34th Street* (1947), *Pete Kelly's Blues* (1955), and *Man of a Thousand Faces* (1957).

His last picture was Frank Capra's *Pocketful of Miracles* (1961).

■

Q: Scenes from the Lockwood and Lamont premiere *The Royal Rascal* are actually clips from what MGM costume picture?

A: *The Three Musketeers* (1948), which starred Gene Kelly as D'Artagnan. During *The Royal Rascal*, Kelly is attacked by a guard with a spear, which lodges in a door. The door opens and briefly reveals Lana Turner, who played Lady de Winter in *The Three Musketeers*. A quick cut later it's Jean Hagen in the same doorway. The athletic fight scenes are from the 1948 swashbuckler; the final scene (with Jean Hagen) was simply staged on the same back lot set as had been used in *The Three Musketeers*.

As for the physical world of *Singin' in the Rain*, the titanic film factory at MGM had just about every bit of its history in storage, and what it didn't have it could easily duplicate. Randall Duell, Edwin Willis, and Jacque Mapes found or duplicated dozens of filmmaking artifacts of twenties vintage—film production hardware like Cooper-Hewitt lights, the "icebox" sound booths, and camera "blimps." They even renovated a glass-walled shooting stage on the studio lot that had been used in the silent era (in 1951 it was being used as a studio machine shop).

Many of Walter Plunkett's costume designs were also duplicates of designs he had done earlier—in all seriousness—for stars like Lilyan Tashman and Pola Negri, who represented the height of twenties glamour. In the premiere scene that opens the picture, the "vamp" Olga Mara wears a Walter Plunkett costume based on an original design he had created thirty years earlier for Negri.

This level of research, detail, and basis in factual events gives *Singin' in the Rain*, in the words of historian Peter Wollen, "a depth which is belied by its surface frothiness."

Q: Don Lockwood and Lina Lamont are based on real movie stars. Who?

A: Screenwriters Comden and Green were silent movie aficionados, and during the course of writing *Singin' in the Rain* they spent a great deal of time with the old-timers on the MGM lot, learning anecdotes about the tumultuous epoch when Hollywood "learned to talk."

Although Don and Lina aren't based on any *specific* stars, incidents drawn from reality are incorporated into both characters. Don's dislike of his florid dialogue and his replacement of it with the comic repetition of "I love you, I love you, I love you" are said to be based on an early John Gilbert talkie disaster, *His Glorious Night* (1929). It is said that John Gilbert's reportedly high-pitched voice was the death of his career, but that was probably not as difficult to take as the broad pantomime acting style and purple

Author's Collection. © Turner Entertainment

The "Broadway Ballet" was originally planned as a duo for Donald O'Connor and Gene Kelly, but TV commitments made O'Connor unavailable.

prose of the awkward early sound films.

The character of Lina Lamont is reportedly an amalgam of Clara Bow, Norma Talmadge (both reportedly had thick Brooklyn accents that belied their screen images), and foreign-born stars like Pola Negri (who had a thick Polish accent).

As stated before, *Singin' in the Rain* was one of the few films to use this tumultuous era for its plot. George S. Kaufman and Moss Hart had used the era as the basis for their stage comedy *Once in a Lifetime*, which was filmed in 1932. An obscure 1948 French melodrama called *Star Without Life* involved a star (Mila Parely) whose career is threatened because of her voice. Her lover (Marcel Herrand) arranges for her singing in a film to be dubbed by a hotel maid (Edith Piaf). When the star's deception is discovered, she kills herself.

■

Q: *Singin' in the Rain* has something in common (besides being a musical) with Disney's *Beauty and the Beast*. What is it?

A: Both popular films were adapted into successful Broadway stage shows.

The Broadway musical version of *Singin' in the Rain* opened on July 2, 1985, at the Gershwin Theater. It starred Don Correia as Don Lockwood, Mary D'Arcy as Kathy Selden, and Faye Grant as Lina Lamont. It closed the following May. (*Singin' in the Rain* had actually premiered as a stage musical in London in 1984, starring Tommy Steele as Don Lockwood, Roy Castle as Cosmo Brown, and Danielle Carson as Kathy Selden. The version that appeared on Broadway was a radical reworking of the London show.)

Disney's Beauty and the Beast: A New Musical opened on April 19, 1994, at the Palace Theater in New York.

The usual transition is from Broadway hit to film adaptation, with varying degrees of success. *Seven Brides for Seven Brothers*, *Gigi*, and *Meet Me in St. Louis* have all gone from film to Broadway musical versions, with none achieving the success on the stage as had been attained by the film original.

■

Q: Kathy's automobile has a famous "previous owner." What movie character drove the car before Kathy Selden?

A: Kathy drives a jalopy that once tooled through the small mid-American town of Carvel, with a young character named Andy Hardy at the wheel.

Mickey Rooney first appeared as all-American boy Andy Hardy in *A Family Affair* (1937), with Lionel Barrymore as his father, Judge Hardy. The film's popularity spawned a sequel, *You're Only Young Once* (1938), this time with Lewis Stone as Judge James Hardy and Fay Holden as Andy's mother. There were a dozen more Andy Hardy pictures between 1938 and 1946. Over the course of the series, MGM used the Hardy films to showcase contract players and new talent like Kathryn Grayson, Lana Turner, Esther Williams, Donna Reed, and Judy Garland.

In 1958, MGM tried the Hardy formula one more time in *Andy Hardy Comes Home*, which failed. A special Oscar was given to MGM in 1942 for the Andy Hardy series, "for its achievement in representing the American Way of Life."

Beyond Andy Hardy's jalopy, a lot more of MGM's history is on display in *Singin' in the Rain* than most people know. On the first day of filming *The Duelling Cavalier*, Don Lockwood steps out of a portable dressing room that once belonged to Norma Shearer. He meets Lina Lamont, who is wearing Norma Shearer's costume from *Marie Antoinette* (1938), as well as Shearer's wig, which apparently weighs a ton. Even Don Lockwood's house and furnishings are from the 1927 MGM John Gilbert picture *Flesh and the Devil*.

Q: Comden and Green had another ending in mind for *Singin' in the Rain*. What happened at the end of their "first draft"?

A: As millions of fans of *Singin' in the Rain* know, the film ends with Don and Kathy in a simple embrace in front of the billboard for their film, *Singin' in the Rain*.

According to film historian Ron Haver, another Hollywood premiere was originally in store for the finale—presumably the premiere of *Singin' in the Rain* from Monumental Pictures (as portrayed on the billboard seen in the final shot as filmed), duplicating the premieres already seen in the film. Don Lockwood would roll up with his new wife, Monumental Pictures' new star, Kathy Selden.

The next car would carry the head of the Monumental Pictures music department, Cosmo Brown, accompanied by *his* new wife—Lina Lamont! If the original ending had been filmed, one of the great unanswered questions of cinema would be answered: "What happened to Lina Lamont?" As it stands, the mortified star actually *disappears* from the stage of the Chinese Theater between cuts. After Cosmo assumes the "dubbing" chores from Kathy, Lina turns and moves to the right of frame. Then there is a cut to show Don rushing onstage from frame left, panning across the theater stage—but there's no Lina. She apparently *sprinted* off stage in embarrassment.

The romance between Kathy Selden and Don Lockwood was further developed by two musical numbers that were cut after initial showings of *Singin' in the Rain*.

Metro-Goldwyn-Mayer presents
SINGIN' IN THE RAIN
Story and Screenplay by Adolph Green and Betty Comden

Suggested by the Song "Singin' in the Rain"

Songs: Lyrics by Arthur Freed, Music by Nacio Herb Brown

("Moses" by Betty Comden, Adolph Green, and Roger Edens
"Fit as a Fiddle" lyric by Arthur Freed, music by Al Hoffman and Al Goodhart)

Musical Direction Lennie Hayton

Musical Numbers Staged and Directed by Gene Kelly and Stanley Donen
(Dance Assistants Jeanne Coyne and Carol Haney)
(Stunt Doubles for Gene Kelly Russ Saunders, Dave Sharpe)

Color by Technicolor®

Director of Photography Harold Rosson, ASC

(Camera Operator Frank Phillips)

Technicolor Color Consultants Henri Jaffa, James Gooch

Art Directors Cedric Gibbons and Randall Duell

Film Editor Adrienne Fazan, ACE

Recording Supervisor Douglas Shearer

Orchestrations by Conrad Salinger, Wally Heglin, and Skip Martin

Vocal Arrangements by Jeff Alexander

Set Decorations by Edwin B. Willis, Jacque Mapes

Special Effects Warren Newcombe, Irving G. Reis, ASC

Costumes Designed by Walter Plunkett

Hair Styles Designed by Sydney Guilaroff

Make-Up Created by William Tuttle

(Associate Producer Roger Edens)

Produced by Arthur Freed

Directed by Gene Kelly and Stanley Donen

No MPAA Rating. Running Time: 103 Minutes

Cast

Gene Kelly	Don Lockwood
Donald O'Connor	Cosmo Brown
Debbie Reynolds	Kathy Selden
Jean Hagen	Lina Lamont
Millard Mitchell	R. F. Simpson
Rita Moreno	Zelda Zanders
Douglas Fowley	Roscoe Dexter
Cyd Charisse	Dancer
Madge Blake	Dora Bailey
King Donavan	Rod, Public Relations Man
Kathleen Freeman	Phoebe Dinsmore, Diction Coach
Bobby Watson	Diction Coach
Tommy Farrell	Sid Phillips, Assistant Director
Jimmie Thompson	Male Lead, "Beautiful Girl" Number
Dan Foster	Assistant Director
Margaret Bert	Wardrobe Woman
Mae Clark	Hairdresser

Judy Ladon .... Olga Mara

John Dodsworth .... Baron de la Bouvet de la Toulon

Stuart Holmes .... J. Cumberland Spendrill, III

Dennis Ross .... Don as a Boy

Bill Lewin .... Bert, Villain in Western

Richard Emory .... Phil, Cowboy Hero

Julius Tannen .... Man in Sound Demonstration Film

Dawn Addams .... Teresa, Lady-in-Waiting

Elaine Stewart .... Second Lady-in-Waiting

Carl Milletaire .... Villain in *The Duelling Cavelier* and "Broadway Ballet"

Ben Strombach .... Pilot in Flying Film

Tommy Walker .... Footballer in Film Sequence

Jac George .... Orchestra Leader

Wilson Wood .... Rudy Vallee Impersonator

Brick Wood .... Cop in Title Number

Snub Pollard .... Pedestrian in Title Number

Paul Maxey .... Skeptical Party Guest

Dorothy Patrick, William Lester, Joi Lansing .... Audience Members

Charles Evans .... Irritated Audience Member

Dave Sharpe, Russ Saunders .... Fencers

Patricia Denise, Jeanne Coyne, Joyce Horne,
Bill Chatham, Ernest Flatt, Don Hulbert, Robert Day .... Dancers

David Kasday .... Kid

Robert B. Williams .... Traffic Cop

Ray Teal .... Employee

Chapter Three

Guys and Dolls

Guys and Dolls *was the biggest deal Broadway had ever seen when it premiered in 1950, and because of this stage success, the 1955 film version was bound to disappoint many. Although reasonably faithful to its source, and with a shrewd script and direction, for many people the film version of* Guys and Dolls *doesn't measure up to the stage original. No matter that this criticism is unfair to the film, and that most people who criticize the film have never seen* Guys and Dolls *performed on any stage, let alone the Broadway original. Examined on its own merits,* Guys and Dolls *is a much better film musical than it is often credited with being. It benefits from an intelligent adaptation that alludes to its literary roots, a skilled and attractive cast, and a behind-the-camera team that was tops in its field.* Guys and Dolls *is an amiable, jocular, and creditable adaptation of the stage show, and can more than stand on its own as a movie musical.*

■

Level One: The Easy Stuff
Story & Characters

Q: Where does Guys and Dolls take place? In what era?

A: *Guys and Dolls* is all about the denizens of Times Square, New York City. The film version is chronologically indeterminate, but probably intended to be current to 1955, although Times Square is depicted on film with such whimsy-whamsy that it doesn't very much matter. The story from which *Guys and Dolls* springs was published in *Collier's* magazine in 1933.

When *Guys and Dolls* opened on Broadway in 1950, New York was at a post-war peak, and the show was a valentine to the life and spirit of Manhattan. The population of the city at the time was nearly eight million. Construction of office space and housing was at an all-time high. The city had three major league baseball teams (Yankees, Dodgers, and Giants). By contemporary accounts, the city was extremely livable, assuming that one was employed and had a moderate income, which most New Yorkers were and did.

The New Yorkers represented in *Guys and Dolls* are certainly idealized; the petty larcenists, hoods, and tarts are presented with a sub-cultural acceptance and an embracing affection. Broadway librettist Abe Burrows recalled, "Damon Run-

yon's characters were very much like the characters we had on 'Duffy's Tavern.' The people on that show were New York muggs, nice muggs, sweet muggs, and, like Runyon's muggs, they all talked like ladies and gentlemen."

In retrospect, *Guys and Dolls* seems like a guileless tribute to a fleeting epoch of New York City's life.

■

Q: How did Sky Masterson get his name?

A: Because he is "the highest player of them all." As related in the film:

> **NATHAN:** Why do you think they call him Sky? Once with my own eyes I saw him bet five thousand bucks that one raindrop would beat another raindrop down the window. Another time, he was sick and would not take penicillin, because he bet his fever would go to a hundred and four—always makes crazy bets like that.
> **NICELY:** Did he win?
> **NATHAN:** Him and his crazy bets—he got lucky, it went to a hundred and six.

In the libretto to the stage musical, the story is a little different:

> **NATHAN:** Why do you think they call him Sky? I once saw him bet five thousand dollars on a

caterpillar race. And another time he was sick, and he wouldn't take penicillin on account he had bet ten G's that his temperature would go to 104.

NICELY: Did it?

NATHAN: Did it? He's so lucky, it went to 106. Good old Sky.

And still a different version is told by Damon Runyon, who presents Sky as somewhat less of a quixotic charmer betting on propositions and more of a…well…cheat. "The Sky" (as he is known in the original story) bets after a ball game that he can throw a peanut from second base to home plate. He does, but The Sky has also loaded the peanut with lead. In Mindy's restaurant, The Sky bets that he can go to the restaurant cellar and catch a live rat with his bare hands. Earlier, The Sky has planted a tame rat there.

This version of Sky (or The Sky) exhibits—more than somewhat—the stage and screen characteristics of Nathan Detroit. It's Nathan who's fond of the "rigged proposition," first betting Sky on the amount of cheesecake and strudel sold in Mindy's (after having sent his touts to find out), then setting it up so that Sky unwittingly bets that he can take "the Mission Doll" to dinner in Havana.

Sky's real name is Obediah Masterson.

■

Q: What is the name of the club where Adelaide works?

A: Miss Adelaide is the headliner at The Hot Box. Here she performs the near-risqué musical

The Goldwyn Girls as the Hot Box Girls. From left: Madelyn Darrow, June Kirby, Larri Thomas, Barbara Brent, Pat Sheehan, and Jann Darlyn.

numbers typical of this type of Manhattan joint in the twenties, thirties, and forties.

The composer of *Guys and Dolls* had worked in the early 1930s as a singer and piano player at The Back Drop on 52nd Street. Much of The Hot Box is derived from the experience and idiom of the hard-shelled but soft-hearted crooks and tarts he had met at The Back Drop.

The Hot Box Girls (a.k.a. "Miss Adelaide and her Alley Kittens" and "Miss Adelaide and her Debutantes") are played by "The Goldwyn Girls." The Goldwyn Girls had been created by Samuel Goldwyn, inspired by one of the "secrets" of the successful Florenz Ziegfeld and his Ziegfeld Follies: the glorification of the woman. A fresh-faced line of radiant and well-scrubbed maidens were a fixture of many Goldwyn productions, including the Eddie Cantor vehicles *Whoopee!* (1930), *The Greeks Had a Word for Them*, *Palmy Days* (1932), and *Roman Scandals* (1933); as well as *The Goldwyn Follies* (1938), *The Princess and the Pirate*, *Up in Arms* (1944), and *The Secret Life of Walter Mitty* (1947).

The Goldwyn Girls of *Guys and Dolls* were Larri Thomas, Madelyn Darrow, June Kirby, Barbara Brent, Pat Sheehan, and Jann Darlyn. Virginia Mayo, Betty Grable, Jean Howard, Paulette Goddard, Virginia Bruce, and Lucille Ball all put in time as Goldwyn Girls before moving out of the chorus line to stardom.

Q: Nathan Detroit runs a floating crap game. What the hell is that?

A: According to Lieutenant Brannigan, it's "a crap game that moves to a different spot every night so the police can't find it and break it up."

Craps is the most popular modern dice game. Its origin is in an older and more complex French dice game known as hazard. In craps, each player puts down a bet, and the "shooter" (the holder of the dice) can "cover" (match) any or all bets. The shooter then "throws" (rolls) the dice. If the shooter rolls 7 or 11, this is called a "natural," and the shooter wins. If they come up 2, 3, or 12, this is "craps"—the shooter loses. Any other number becomes the shooter's "point." The shooter keeps rolling until he shoots the point (the shooter wins), or throws a 7 (the shooter loses).

Dice, and hence dice games, are thought to be nearly as ancient as humankind. There is no known human culture which has not known and used dice. The first dice were pebbles, or bone. The use of dice is mentioned in the Indian classic *The Rig Veda*, and dice were popular in Ancient Rome and during the Middle Ages.

Q: Where does Nathan wish to hold his game? Where does he wind up holding it?

A: Some of the locations Nathan has considered include the Gym at Public School 84, the stockroom behind McClosky's Bar, and even the back of the Police Station. The Biltmore Garage seems to be Nathan's last hope, but Joey Biltmore wants a thousand dollars up front, a grand that Nathan doesn't have. The Oldest Established Permanent Floating Crap Game in New York winds up taking place in an unusually large subterranean New York City sewer service access.

Although *Guys and Dolls'* underground is pure fancy, the actual New York underground is stranger than fiction. Manhattan is honeycombed with viaducts, tunnels, caves, tubes, and burrows; many date back more than a hundred years. In 1980 in Brooklyn, a twenty-two-year-old "urban archaeologist" discovered a long-abandoned and long-forgotten 1840s railroad tunnel. Hailed as an important find, the tunnel is now considered the first subway tunnel (the first acknowledged subway system was built in London twenty years later). It is twenty-one feet wide and supported by a brick archway eighteen

Nathan's floating crap game goes "underground."

feet high. The New York City Transit Authority estimates that there are twenty-three abandoned subway stations and five and a half miles of unused tunnels in the city.

Nathan Detroit isn't the only New Yorker to have found an alternate use for the underground. Columbia University uses a network of old coal delivery tunnels for building access and new utility systems; rioting students used the tunnels to invade the university in 1968. A four-block-long aqueduct of unknown lineage beneath the Metropolitan Museum facility is now used for general storage, and the city uses one of those abandoned subway stations for a transit museum.

Nathan's subterranean crap game ("The Crapshooters Dance") was one of the choreographed set pieces (along with the opening "Runyonland" ballet and the rhythmic "Cuban Nightclub Dance") brought to the screen by Michael Kidd. Production notes mention that Kidd was dissatisfied with the authenticity of the dancers' dice throwing technique, and that

he imported half a dozen professional crap shooters from Las Vegas to appear in the dance and "Luck Be a Lady" numbers.

■

Q: A popular young actor of the time was cast—much against type—in the role of Sky Masterson. Who?

A: Marlon Brando. At the time of production, the then thirty-year-old Brando had already been nominated for four Academy Awards and had won one, Best Actor, for *On the Waterfront* (1954). He had become, as described in *Baseline's Encyclopedia of Film*, "the unappointed spokesman for his generation, identified with a character in revolt against something he could not comprehend." For youth of the time, he represented a nonconformist prototype; for older filmgoers, he was a threatening antisocial. Brando spent the greater portion of his film career trying to break the stereotypes established by four of his first films: *The Men* (1950), *A Streetcar Named Desire* (1951), *On the Waterfront*, and *The Wild One* (1954).

He had studied at the Dramatic Workshop of the New School for Social Research (The New School) and at Actors Studio, where he became an exponent of "the method," a style based on the teachings of Stanislavsky. He performed on Broadway in *I Remember Mama* (1944), *Truckline Cafe*, and *Candida* (1946), and shot to stardom as Stanley Kowalski in Tennessee Williams's *A Streetcar Named Desire* (1947).

After his Oscar win, Brando's performances ranged hither, thither, and even yon; Napoleon Bonaparte in *Désirée* (1954), Sky Masterson in *Guys and Dolls*, and Fletcher Christian in *Mutiny on the Bounty* (1962). In his attempt to divorce himself from his early and popular persona, he failed to establish himself anywhere else. Subsequent roles, varied in both style and quality, include *The Ugly American* (1963), *Bedtime Story* (1964), *Reflections in a Golden Eye* (1967), and *Burn!* (1969).

He regained his stature with his portrayal of Don Corleone in *The Godfather* (1972), another performance so skilled and precise that it became the subject of seemingly endless parody. Brando was awarded a second Oscar for this performance, which he refused to accept to protest the plight of Native Americans. He followed *The Godfather* with the equally well-regarded *Last Tango in Paris* (1973).

Since then, Brando has been more famous for his bizarre behavior and the scandalous deaths of his son and daughter than for his spotty motion picture work. These films include The *Missouri Breaks* (1976), *Superman* (1978), *Apocalypse Now* (1979), *The Formula* (1980), *The Freshman* (1990), and *Christopher Columbus: the Discovery* (1992). Brando earned another Oscar nomination for *A Dry White Season* (1989), and turned in a charming and sexy performance in *Don Juan de Marco* (1995).

Some of the...interesting...casting ideas for *Guys and Dolls* make Brando look like a winning compromise: Gene Kelly (MGM refused to loan him), Tony Martin, Kirk Douglas, Robert Mitchum, and Burt Lancaster were considered; both Bing Crosby (who reportedly hungered to play Sky) and Clark Gable (through his agent) lobbied for the part. Goldwyn considered pursuing Dean Martin as Sky with Jerry Lewis as Nathan. Luckily, the director protested.

The director also put up a fight *for* Brando, considering him a consummate actor.

■

Q: Arvide Abernathy, Sarah Brown's mission Brother, is related to her. Who is he?

Author's Collection. © The Samuel Goldwyn Company

A classic studio portrait of character great Regis Toomey.

A: In the film, Arvide Abernathy is Sarah Brown's uncle. In the stage musical, Arvide is her grandfather, and sings the lovely ballad "More I Cannot Wish You" to his granddaughter.

Why the character change? Only speculation, but it's an extra song and an extra level of relationship for an already highly-populated show. If the character was removed from his truly paternal role and relegated to "uncle-hood," the song doesn't make much sense. If the song was deleted for the sake of timing and tightening, it makes sense to have removed the character of Arvide from such a close relationship with Sarah.

It's sort of a pity, since the actor playing Arvide is such a charming one, and brings off what little he has to do with the aplomb of a seasoned vet. And a seasoned vet Regis Toomey was.

He began his career on the stage in the early 1920s, appearing in, among others, the Broadway company of *Rose Marie*. He made his film debut in 1929, in "the first all-talking melodrama," *Alibi*, and continued to work in film and series television until he was in his seventies.

Some of the more than 150 pictures in which Toomey appeared were *Union Pacific* (1939), *His Girl Friday* (1940), *Meet John Doe*, *They Died With Their Boots On* (1941), *Spellbound* (1945), *The Big Sleep* (1946), *The Bishop's Wife* (1947), *The Boy With Green Hair* (1948), *Mighty Joe Young* (1949), *Show Boat* (1951), *Voyage to the Bottom of the Sea* (1961), *Change of Habit* (1969), and *The Carey Treatment* (1972). His last film was *God Bless Dr. Shagetz* (1977).

Toomey was also featured in dozens of TV shows, including recurring appearances in the series "Dante's Inferno," "Richard Diamond," and "Burke's Law." Regis Toomey died in 1992 at the age of ninety.

■

Q: Nathan and his cronies are in distress, for someone is turning up the heat very hot. Who is it?

A: Lieutenant Brannigan is turning up the heat very hot. Brannigan is an ineffectual and somewhat lovable authority/threat, much like Simon Oakland's Lieutenant Schrank in the film *West Side Story* (1961).

Brannigan is played by veteran character actor Robert Keith, who made his stage debut in 1914 in stock, and went on to appear in Broadway productions and silent films. In 1927, he authored the Broadway play *The Tightwad*, then went to Hollywood as a dialogue writer for Columbia and Universal, also acting in several films. He went back to Broadway, where in 1932 he wrote another play, *Singapore*, and appeared in dozens of others. Keith created the role of Doc in *Mister Roberts* on Broadway (1948), after which he returned to California and appeared in many well-known pictures such as *The Wild One* (1954), *Love Me or Leave Me* (1955), *My Man Godfrey* (1957), and *Cimarron* (1960).

Not only all of that, but he is also the father of actor Brian Keith. Robert Keith died in 1966, at the age of sixty-eight.

■

Q: In the finale scene, one of Nathan's henchman has apparently converted. Which one?

A: Nicely-Nicely Johnson is wearing the mission uniform. The screenwriter changed the original direction of the Broadway musical here. On stage, it is *Sky* who shows up in the finale beating the mission drum! "We know Sky is going to be a good husband and father, but he wouldn't be a brass-buttoned, uniformed Save-A-Soul-er," the screenwriter asserted. "He's not the type. It just wouldn't happen." So, more to type, Nicely-Nicely beats the drum of salvation at story's end.

The role of Nicely-Nicely had been created on the Broadway stage by Stubby Kaye, who was brought to Hollywood to recreate the part of the tout described by Damon Runyon as "short and fat and very good-natured and a wonderful eater even when he is not hungry."

Born in 1918, Kaye was a winner of the Major Bowes Amateur Hour radio program in 1939. This success led to tours in the waning days of vaudeville, and USO tours during WW II.

His film debut came in 1953 with the Dan Dailey vehicle *Taxi,* followed by *Guys and Dolls* in 1955. Kaye was a featured player in *Li'l Abner* (as Marryin' Sam, 1959), *Forty Pounds of Trouble* (1963, a remake of Damon Runyon's *Little Miss Marker*), *Sex and the Single Girl* (1964), *Cat Bal-* *lou* (as the Sunrise Kid, 1965), *The Way West* (1967), *Sweet Charity* (1969), *Cockeyed Cowboys of Calico County* (1970), *The Dirtiest Girl I Ever Met* (1973), and *Six-Pack Annie* (1975).

Kaye will be remembered by a whole different generation as the patty-cake playing cartoon executive R. K. Maroon, in *Who Framed Roger Rabbit* (1988).

In the 1937 Runyon tale "A Piece of Pie," the character is named Nicely-Nicely *Jones.*

Several souls saved, and all is well in Runyonland. Mary Alan Hokanson and Stubby Kaye.

Level Two: Not So Easy
The Actors, Artists, & Others

Q: The film *Guys and Dolls* is adapted from what source?

A: The multiple-award-winning Broadway musical comedy *Guys and Dolls* was the source property for the film. In turn, the stage musical had been freely adapted from a 1933 short story by Damon Runyon, "The Idyll of Miss Sarah Brown," with characters from other Runyon stories rounding out the roster.

Jo Swerling, a well-known screenwriter who had lent his talents to *Platinum Blond* (1931), *Pennies from Heaven* (1936), *Pride of the Yankees* (1942), and *It's a Wonderful Life* (1946) wrote the first libretto for the stage musical, which the producers found wanting. Swerling's name stayed on the show's billing because of a contractual agreement, and it is rumored that ten other writers had a crack at the script before Abe Burrows apparently supplied the missing ingredients. Burrows was a gag man who had achieved prominence as head writer of the "Duffy's Tavern" radio program. The director of *Guys and Dolls* was George S. Kaufman, a renowned playwright and "show doctor" whose specific influence on the script was never publicly documented, but inevitable.

Guys and Dolls opened at the Forty-Sixth Street Theater in November 1950, to overwhelming critical praise and popularity. Abe Laufe, in his authoritative book *Broadway's Greatest Musicals*, summed up the critical response: "Conservative critics called *Guys and Dolls* an excellent show; more effusive critics hailed it as the greatest musical ever presented on the Broadway stage."

Guys and Dolls won the Critics' Circle Award, the Donaldson Award, the Antoinette Perry Award ("The Tony"), the Outer Circle Critics' Award, The Aegis Theater Club Award, and The Show of the Month Award as the best musical produced in the 1950–51 season.

Q: Who composed the musical score for *Guys and Dolls*?

A: Frank Loesser had been a songwriter since the age of six, when he wrote "The May Party" about the parade of children he saw in Central Park. Loesser's father, Arthur, was an accomplished pianist and music critic who frowned on popular songs. Young Frank rejected a formal music education, dropping out of City College after only a year. "I wasn't in the mood to learn," he recalled. He moved to New Rochelle, New York, at the age of eighteen, where he was city editor of the local newspaper. On his days off, he wrote material for vaudeville acts. He moved through a series of jobs during the Depression: process server, jewelry salesman, waiter; finally he was put under contract as a lyricist by the music publisher Leo Feist. He performed as a pianist and singer in a Manhattan nightclub, and had five songs in a 1936 flop Broadway revue called *The Illustrator's Show*. In 1936, he went to Hollywood under a brief contract to Universal Pictures, after which he worked with Burton Lane in the music department at Paramount, where he plied his trade on such forgettable fare as *Blossoms on Broadway* (1937), *College Swing*, *Sing You Sinners*, and *Thanks for the Memory* (1938).

Loesser continued working in pictures through World War II, as a composer and/or lyricist on such varied films as *Destry Rides Again*, *St. Louis Blues* (1939), *Beyond the Blue Horizon*, *Sweater Girl* (1942), *Something for the Boys* (which starred Vivian Blaine, 1944), *The Perils of Pauline* (1947), and *Neptune's Daughter* (1949).

Along the way, several Loesser songs became standards, including "I Don't Want To Walk Without You, Baby" (with Jule Styne), "Two Sleepy People," "Jingle, Jangle, Jingle," "Slow Boat to China," "Praise the Lord and Pass the Ammunition," "They're Either Too Young or Too

Old" (written with Arthur Schwartz for Bette Davis), "Small Fry," "Spring Will Be a Little Late This Year," and "Baby, It's Cold Outside," for which he won an Oscar in 1949.

Cy Feuer and Ernest Martin asked Loesser to provide the music and lyrics for their first Broadway show in 1948, after which he returned to pictures only once, aside from film adaptations of his own hit stage shows.

His music publishing company developed novice talent, among them *The Pajama Game* and *Damn Yankees* team Adler and Ross, and Meredith Willson of *The Music Man* (q.v.) and *The Unsinkable Molly Brown*.

A lifelong smoker, Loesser died in 1969 at the age of fifty-nine, reportedly with a respirator and a pack of cigarettes.

■

Q: Who directed the film *Guys and Dolls*? Who wrote the screenplay?

A: Two questions, one answer. Goldwyn entrusted his expensive picture to Joseph L. Mankiewicz, who admittedly had absolutely no experience in the musical-comedy idiom.

Born in Wilkes-Barre, Pennsylvania, in 1909, Mankiewicz graduated from Columbia University after which he moved to Berlin, ostensibly for further education, but securing a job with UFA (the government-backed German mega-studio) writing English subtitles for German films instead. Here Mankiewicz served as a stringer for *Variety* and a copy boy in the *Chicago Tribune*'s Berlin office. On his return to the States, Joseph, like his brother Herman, found work as a film scenarist, lending his talents to *Skippy* (1931), *If I Had a Million, Million Dollar Legs* (1932), and *Manhattan Melodrama* (1934).

Author's Collection. © The Samuel Goldwyn Company

Jean Simmons and Joseph L. Mankiewicz confer on the *Guys and Dolls* set.

Mankiewicz became a producer at MGM in 1936, generating such varied fare as Fritz Lang's *Fury* (1936), *A Christmas Carol*, *Three Comrades*, *The Shopworn Angel* (1938), *The Philadelphia Story* (1940), and *Woman of the Year* (1942).

After ten years of producing, Mankiewicz became a director, helming *Backfire* (1946), *The Ghost and Mrs. Muir* (1947), *A Letter to Three Wives* (1949, Academy Award for Best Screenplay and Best Director), *House of Strangers* (1949), *All About Eve* (1950, Academy Award for Best Screenplay and Best Director), and *Julius Caesar* (1953, in which he directed Marlon Brando as Marc Antony).

Mankiewicz approached *Guys and Dolls* straightforwardly, telling Goldwyn, "My primary, almost only, objective in this writing has been to tell the story as warmly and humanly as possible—and to characterize our four principals as fully as if their story were going to be told in purely dramatic terms." Feeling that the book of the stage musical lacked weight, he wrote an entire script that could have played without any music—with songs, the running time would have been close to four hours! Goldwyn liked the approach, though, particularly the development of the characters and the earnest love story.

The benefit of this approach is that the dramatic romance of Sky and Sarah is shaded, their characters are well-defined, and their dialogue crackles with real sexual tension. For the comic characters, the dialogue becomes closer to the style of Runyon the author. On the whole, the entire effort is given the kind of intimate realism required of a motion picture. The disadvantage is that the physical production treats the entire effort with fantasy and broad strokes, and the two styles are never really comfortable together, much in the same way that, no matter the beauty of his acting, Marlon Brando is never at ease when he's singing.

Orson Welles saw the film of *Guys and Dolls*, and reported to Broadway librettist Abe Burrows that "they put a tiny turd on every one of your lines." Even Burrows tacitly admitted that this wasn't really accurate, calling Welles' comment an "amusing exaggeration."

Mankiewicz was later brought to the troubled Twentieth Century-Fox megaproduction *Cleopatra* (1963) to replace Rouben Mamoulian. His efforts on the elephantine spectacular couldn't save it—*Cleopatra* was a notorious and embarrassing flop, and proved to be a career debacle for Mankiewicz. He only made four more films: director, producer, and screenwriter on *The Honey Pot* (a.k.a. *It Comes Up Murder*, 1967), director of *King: A Filmed Record—Montgomery to Memphis* (1970), director/producer of *There Was a Crooked Man* (1970), and director of *Sleuth* (1972).

Joseph L. Mankiewicz died in 1993.

■

Q: Of the principal cast, only one had appeared in the stage musical *Guys and Dolls*. Who?

A: Vivian Blaine had created the role of Miss Adelaide in the 1950 Broadway production of *Guys and Dolls*, and had traveled to London to play the role in that company in 1953.

Blaine had begun her career as a band and nightclub singer, and had seen minor success in musicals and unmemorable films at Twentieth Century-Fox such as *Girl Trouble* (1942), *Jitterbugs* (with Laurel and Hardy, 1943), *Something for the Boys* (1944), and *State Fair* (1945); and at MGM in *Skirts Ahoy!* (1952). After her success in the stage and screen versions of *Guys and Dolls*, Blaine made few film appearances. She was briefly married (1959 to 1961) to the president of Universal Pictures and Decca Records, Milton Rackmill. In the 1970s, she appeared on the TV series "Mary Hartman, Mary Hartman." Vivian Blaine died in December, 1995, at the age of 74.

Several supporting players in the film had been imported from the Broadway cast, including Stubby Kaye (Nicely-Nicely Johnson), Johnny

Silver (Benny Southstreet), Dan Dayton (Rusty Charlie), and B. S. Pully (Big Jule). The payroll office at Samuel Goldwyn Studio reported that B. S. Pully had filled out his payroll deduction slip with five dependents listed: a wife, a child, and three bookies. Hmmm…any guesses as to what B. S. stands for?

■

Q: The song "Woman in Love" is performed in the film how many times? By whom?

A: The inclusion of "Woman in Love" no fewer than *seven* times in the film score seems a pretty blatant attempt to "create" a love theme and a pop standard.

Vivian Blaine seems annoyed and ready to attack with—no kidding—a mink flyswatter.

Often, when stage hits have been translated to the screen, one or more new songs are added to the score (usually in place of an original song) in an attempt to "freshen" the material, or because the source material has been so completely reworked from the stage original. The ancillary reason is to create new pop hits for publicity value and/or to obtain an Academy Award nomination for an original song. Some other examples include *The Music Man* (q.v., 1962), *The Sound of Music* (1965), *Funny Girl* (1968), *Hello, Dolly!* (q.v., 1969), *Cabaret* (1972), *Grease* (1978), and *Annie* (1982).

"Woman in Love" is first heard under the opening credits. Then, as Sky and Sarah go to Havana, "Woman in Love" becomes a leit motif for the developing romance between the two. In the church plaza, Reuben de Fuentes sings a plaintive, simple, Spanish translation of the song. As Sky and Sarah regroup in a Havana bar, a guitar and vocal trio take up the refrain. As they move to a nightclub, the song goes, too; this time in a sensual, melodic instrumental version that segues into the underscore of Sarah's declaration to Sky and their first kiss. As the pair have dinner, Renee Renor sings an upbeat, Latin-rhythm, Spanish version of the tune that leads into a dance number and a brawl. As the two return to the mission, the song is reprised as a duet. And finally, a processional version is heard during the Times Square wedding finale.

■

Q: Who was the eccentric independent producer behind the film version of *Guys and Dolls*?

A: Feisty and pugnacious, with such style and taste that pundits dubbed it "The Goldwyn Touch," and so prone to malapropisms that the term "Goldwynisms" was created, Samuel Goldwyn was one of the most fascinating of Hollywood's founding fathers. Born Schmuel Gelbfisz in Warsaw, Poland, in 1882, Goldwyn went from penniless immigrant into the garment trade, and (as Samuel Goldfish) into the infant motion picture business in 1912. He was affiliated with the founding of three motion picture studios that still operate today. Goldfish founded the Jesse L. Lasky Feature Play Company with his father-in-law, impresario Jesse Lasky, and Cecil B. De Mille. The studio made the first feature film shot entirely in the sunny hamlet of Hollywood, California, *The Squaw Man*, in 1914. In 1916 they merged with Adolph Zukor's Famous Players, forming Famous Players/Lasky, precursor to Paramount Pictures.

Disagreements in management pushed Goldfish out, so, partnered with Edgar Selwyn, he founded Goldwyn Pictures Corporation (a combination of their names—the alternative would have been "Selfish"). Goldfish, much to the consternation of his business partners, adopted the company name as his own, and was henceforth known as Samuel Goldwyn.

He was forced out of his own company in 1922, but he must have taken a lifetime of satisfaction that when his former company merged with Marcus Leow, Metro Pictures, and Louis B. Mayer Studios, the enterprise was named Metro-Goldwyn-Mayer. The most prestigious studio in Hollywood had Sam Goldwyn's name forever attached to it.

The indomitable Goldwyn started again, this time founding his own studio, Samuel Goldwyn Inc. His new studio (today known as The Samuel Goldwyn Company and headed by his son, Samuel Goldwyn, Jr.) stayed completely independent and privately held. Goldwyn was the single studio head, with no board of directors. Over the next thirty-five years, Goldwyn produced dozens of classic films, including *Dodsworth* (1936), *Dead End*, *Stella Dallas* (1937), *Wuthering Heights* (1939), *Ball of Fire*, *The Little Foxes* (1941), *The Pride of the Yankees* (1942), *The Best Years of Our Lives* (1946, Oscar winner, Best Picture), *The Bishop's Wife*, *The Secret Life of Walter Mitty* (1947), and *Hans Christian Andersen* (1952). Goldwyn's final picture was the extrava-

gant screen version of Gershwin's *Porgy and Bess* (1959).

During his long career, Goldwyn was associated with productions of high quality and good taste—fewer pictures, but better ones. He was instrumental in the careers of stars such as Eddie Cantor, Ronald Colman, Gary Cooper, Will Rogers, David Niven, Danny Kaye, and Merle Oberon.

Although definitely predisposed to malapropism, Goldwyn simply didn't say some of his most famous mangled maxims. For a time, gag writers and columnists had a field day making up "Goldwynisms." Some of the most famous of these are: "A verbal agreement isn't worth the paper it's written on," "Include me out," "Anyone seeing a psychiatrist should have his head examined," and "I can answer you in two words. Im possible."

Also a beloved philanthropist, Goldwyn was a founder and proponent of the Permanent Charities Committee of the Motion Picture Industry. Goldwyn died in 1974, at the age of ninety-two.

■

Q: Who dubbed the singing voices of Marlon Brando and Jean Simmons?

A: A trick question, since Brando provided his own breathy baritone, Simmons her own thready soprano. Casting non-singers in a musical was pretty risky stuff, but as has been stated before, the director was interested in the romantic drama between the characters of Sky and Sarah and the songs were secondary.

Brando and Simmons make "I'll Know" sizzle on its content, not its melody, and the strong dialog scenes that lead up to it help, too. Simmons admirably performs the comic "If I Were a Bell," again *because* she is an actress, not a singer. Their duet of "Woman in Love" is, once again, charged by their performances, but pales compared to the "chemistry" exhibited earlier in "I'll Know."

Brando's weakest moment is "Luck Be a Lady"; even though he acts with aplomb, the number requires a high energy and gusto that he simply doesn't muster. This is Sky's strong moment of conviction, emotional and moral, and since it is communicated in song, Brando isn't really up to the task.

■

Q: Which *Guys and Dolls* cast member went on to become a powerful and respected producer of series television?

A: Sheldon Leonard. Sheldon Leonard Bershad was born in New York in 1907 and raised on the mean streets of the East Bronx. Leonard was an

Author's Collection. © The Samuel Goldwyn Company

SG-7400-18

B. S. Pully, Frank Sinatra, and Sheldon Leonard.

intelligent and scholarly man—he graduated from Syracuse University in 1929 with an honors degree in sociology. Leonard's external characteristics—his distinctive accent and inflection, his physical stature, and his truculent attitude—were all actually the antithesis of his personal character. These external characteristics made him a popular character actor on stage, radio, and the screen from the 1930s to the 1950s.

His notable films include *Another Thin Man* (1939), *Lucky Jordan*, *Tortilla Flat* (1942), *To Have and Have Not* (1944), *The Gangster* (1947), *Money From Home* (1953), Frank Capra's *Pocketful of Miracles* (1961, based on the Damon Runyon Story *Madame La Gimp*), and *The Brink's Job* (1978, as J. Edgar Hoover). One of his best-remembered roles is Nick the bartender in Frank Capra's *It's a Wonderful Life* (1946), "Ou'chyoo two pixies go, out da door or out da winda!"

In the early fifties, he became a director (later a producer) on the long-running "Danny Thomas Show," which led to many directing assignments in television. In 1960, Leonard introduced the character of small-town sheriff Andy Taylor in an episode of "The Danny Thomas Show." This appearance by Andy Griffith as the homespun lawman led to the gigantically successful Leonard-produced "Andy Griffith Show." He continued producing TV hits like "The Dick Van Dyke Show" and "I Spy."

In 1993, Leonard was inducted into the Academy of Television Arts and Sciences Hall of Fame.

■

Q: Brando and Simmons had appeared in a film together prior to *Guys and Dolls*. What was the film?

A: Brando had starred as a brooding Napoleon Bonaparte opposite Jean Simmons in *Désirée* (1954), a widescreen historical costume romance made by Twentieth Century-Fox.

Pauline Kael caught the flavor of this silly project as well as the "chemistry" between Brando and Simmons that shows up in *Guys and Dolls*:

> A ridiculously simpleminded costume picture—ten-ton romantic fluff, with some campily enjoyable scenes…The two stars play together with conspiratorial charm; doubtless they knew they were trapped in a joke and tried to have as good a time as possible. Brando makes one laugh out loud when his Napoleon elevates his sisters to royal rank by rapping them on their heads—hard. And he's quite funny when he grabs the crown and crowns himself.

■

Q: How many Academy Awards were won by *Guys and Dolls*?

A: None. *Guys and Dolls* was only nominated in four categories:

Art Direction/Set Decoration (Color) *Guys and Dolls* (Oliver Smith, Art Direction; Joseph C. Wright, Art Direction; Howard Bristol, Set Decoration), *Daddy Long Legs* (Lyle Wheeler, Art Direction; John De Cuir, Art Direction; Walter M. Scott, Set Decoration; Paul S. Fox, Set Decoration), *Love Is a Many Splendored Thing* (Lyle Wheeler, Art Direction; George W. Davis, Art Direction; Walter M. Scott, Set Decoration; Jack Stubbs, Set Decoration), *Picnic* (the winner, William Flannery, Art Direction; Jo Mielziner, Art Direction; Robert Priestley, Set Decoration), and *To Catch a Thief* (Hal Pereira, Art Direction; Joseph McMillan Johnson, Art Direction; Sam Comer, Set Decoration; Arthur Krams, Set Decoration).

Cinematography (Color) *Guys and Dolls* (Harry Stradling), *Love Is a Many Splendored Thing* (Leon Shamroy), *A Man Called Peter* (Harold Lipstein), *Oklahoma!* (Robert L. Surtees), and *To Catch a Thief* (the winner, Robert Burks).

Costume Design (Color) *Guys and Dolls* (Irene Sharaff), *Interrupted Melody* (Helen Rose), *Love Is a Many Splendored Thing* (the winner, Charles LeMaire), *To Catch a Thief* (Edith Head), and *The Virgin Queen* (Charles

LeMaire, Mary Wills).

Music Scoring Awards (Scoring of a Musical Picture) *Guys and Dolls* (Jay Blackton, Cyril J. Mockridge), *Daddy Long Legs* (Alfred Newman), *It's Always Fair Weather* (Andre Previn), *Oklahoma!* (the winner, Robert Russell Bennett, Jay Blackton, Adolph Deutsch), and *Love Me or Leave Me* (Percy Faith, George Stoll).

1955 was sort of a "generation gap" year for the Academy—intimate, character- and issue-driven pictures like *Marty* and *Rebel Without a Cause* were being lauded above films that were perceived as "old-fashioned," like *Guys and Dolls*. Even *Guys and Dolls* lead Frank Sinatra was nominated for Best Actor—but for his dramatic turn as a heroin addict in *The Man With the Golden Arm*, which lost out to Ernest Borgnine as *Marty*.

Author's Collection. © The Samuel Goldwyn Company

"Yeah, chemistry!" Marlon Brando and Jean Simmons exhibit their chemistry on their excursion to Havana.

Level Three: No Easy Stuff
Minutia & Obscuria

Q: The characters in *Guys and Dolls* speak a distinct dialect. What is it called? Describe one of its characteristics.

A: The dialogue style has been dubbed "Runyonese," after the celebrated writer who reveled in its rhythm and made it famous. One key characteristic of Runyonese is its courtly tone; another is its deliberate avoidance of contractions. Unlike the language of common hoods, Runyonese is multisyllabic and rather elegant.

A good way to demonstrate Runyonese is to read a passage rendered in American English, followed by the same tale in Runyonese:

> On the day I left home, my father took me aside. "Son," he said, "I'm sorry I don't have the necessary cash to start you off. Instead I'm going to give you some valuable advice. Someday, a man will show you a brand new deck of cards. This man will then offer to bet you that he can make the Jack of Spades jump out of the deck and squirt cider in your ear. But son, don't accept the bet, because you'll get an earful of cider.

Lacks poetry, doesn't it? Here's the same story, as told by Sky Masterson in the film *Guys and Dolls*, after Nathan Detroit has offered him a sucker bet:

> On the day when I left home to make my way in the world, my daddy took me to one side. "Son," my daddy says to me, "I am sorry I am not able to bankroll you to a very large start, but not having the necessary lettuce to get you rolling, instead I am going to stake you to some very valuable advice. One of these days in your travels a guy is going to show you a brand new deck of cards on which the seal is not yet broken. Then this guy is going to offer to bet you that he can make the Jack of Spades jump out of this brand new deck and squirt cider in your ear. But son, you do not accept this bet, because as sure as you stand there you are going to get an earful of cider.

A promotional booklet for *Guys and Dolls* even provided a "Slanguage Glossary" of "Damon Runyonisms" used in the picture:

A GUY: A Guy is a male who, no matter how terrible he seems, you can never be sure that some girl won't go for him. When a Guy shoots the works it's better than even money that he's only doing it for some Doll.

A DOLL: A Doll is an unmarried female, pleasing in appearance to one and all. Some say that all Dolls are the same, and are something to have around only when they come in handy, like cough drops. Others think that Dolls are a necessity, for if a Guy does not have one, who would holler at him?

ACTION: Action among Guys of sporting inclination is a term designating a game of chance, usually played with dice or cards, sometimes even in a city sewer. With players addicted to such pastimes, the craving for action can become insatiable.

CHUMP: A chump is one who accepts a foolish wager, or one in which impossible odds are stacked against him. Being a chump is like losing your citizenship. A chump is an outsider, a yokel who will buy anything with varnish on it.

FLOATING CRAP GAME: A floating crap game is a form of gambling played with two dice by two or more players that moves to a different spot every night, so that the police can't find it and break it up.

HEALTHY: (See Loaded)

HIGH PLAYER: A high player is a gambler who plays for high stakes. The Guy they call Sky Masterson is one.

BUNDLE OF LETTUCE: A player's bankroll, especially one that consists of coarse notes (i.e. currency of large denominations). Sometimes called a nice head of cabbage

LOADED: (See Well Heeled)

MARKER: A marker is a promise to pay. Not, however, just a piece of paper that says I.O.U. A marker is the one pledge a Guy cannot welch on, never. It is like not saluting the flag.

RUN-DOWN: A run-down is a statement of the conditions, vis., weights and ages, past performance, post positions and profitable odds—as in a horse race.

PROPOSITION: A proposition is the point at issue in sporting wagers, such as are always coming up among citizens who follow games of chance for a living. Some citizens will sit up all night making up propositions to offer other citizens the next day.

SUCKER BET: A sucker bet is reserved for suckers. For a gambler to get suckered into such a bet is most humiliating. But to lose it means you are marked, for a long time, as a sucker.

WELL HEELED: (See Healthy)

■

Q: How much did Samuel Goldwyn pay for the film rights to *Guys and Dolls*?

A: *Variety* first reported on April 8, 1953, that preliminary talks had been held with Samuel Goldwyn and others regarding the film rights to the Broadway hit, and that the producers "may hold back on a pic deal pending further clarification" concerning production of the picture in 3D, the presentation technology flavor-of-the-month at the time.

The next day, *The Hollywood Reporter* announced that Frank Loesser and producers Feuer and Martin had bought out Paramount's 15 percent interest in the film rights for $75,000. Paramount held the rights to the source story for *Guys and Dolls*. This effectively removed the competitive edge of the built-in "first look deal" such film rights would have guaranteed to Paramount.

On February, 18, 1954, *The Hollywood Reporter* related that producer William Goetz had made a $300,000-against-10-percent-of-gross deal for the film rights to *Guys and Dolls*, which he would produce as his first picture under a production deal with Columbia Pictures. Other studios cried foul, saying that The Dramatists Guild had no right to sell the stage property for films without engaging in open bidding. It was reported in the same article that the deal had been negotiated by the Guild at the behest of Frank Loesser, and that Abe Burrows, Jo Swerling, Cy Feuer, Ernie Martin, and others connected with the stage musical were similarly up in arms over the Goetz "deal."

The following day, *Variety* reported bids from MGM for $600,000 and Samuel Goldwyn for

$650,000, indicating that the Goetz deal was far from done.

Finally, the sale of the film rights to *Guys and Dolls* was announced on March 4, 1954. Samuel Goldwyn secured the rights for $1,000,000 in cash. He spent a further $4,500,000 bringing the finished product to the screen.

In 1976, *Variety* reported that Samuel Goldwyn, Jr. was planning a remake of *Guys and Dolls* with an all-black cast (an all-black Broadway revival was then a big hit). He reportedly came very close to finalizing a deal with Bob Fosse to direct and choreograph when Fosse became unavailable—the film that would become his masterpiece, *All That Jazz*, had been green-lighted.

When the musical was successfully revived on Broadway in 1992, the junior Goldwyn revealed to Robert Osborne in *The Hollywood Reporter* that he was "giving some very serious thought to doing a new movie version of [*Guys and Dolls*]." Several days later, columnist Liz Smith suggested that he cast Marky Mark (Mark Wahlberg) as Sky Masterson, Luke Perry as Nathan Detroit, Winona Ryder as Sarah Brown, and Madonna as Miss Adelaide. Which on the face of it seems bizarre, but on closer inspection is not a bad cast, particularly the female roles.

■

Q: Many people felt that the character of Sky Masterson was better suited to what musically-talented actor?

A: It has been stated time and again, and by people who should know better, that Frank Sinatra was better suited to the role of Sky Masterson than was Marlon Brando. This is all pretty subjective stuff, and really depends on what the individual regards as the important traits or definitive incarnation of Sky. Does Sky need to be a crooner the caliber of Sinatra? Not really. According to Damon Runyon's own description,

Author's Collection. © The Samuel Goldwyn Company

Although annoyed to this day at his "miscasting" in *Guys and Dolls*, Sinatra is an adept Nathan Detroit (seen here with Johnny Silver).

Sky Masterson is "maybe thirty years old, and is a tall guy with a round kisser and big blue eyes, and he always looks as innocent as a little baby." Sinatra at the time of *Guys and Dolls* was forty years old, slight and small, most definitely not baby-faced, and certainly—and probably most important to the film—not the kind of smooth, sexy, and sophisticated sinner that had been created for Sky's film incarnation.

Sinatra, of course, is simply a legend, coming to pop idol fame as a "boy singer" with the Harry James and Tommy Dorsey orchestras. This celebrity led naturally to a film career, which included some impressive affiliations with MGM musicals such as *Anchors Aweigh* (1945), *Till the Clouds Roll By* (1946), *It Happened in Brooklyn*

(1947), *On the Town*, and *Take Me Out to the Ball Game* (1949).

He suffered a career setback in the early 1950s, hemorrhaged vocal chords and bad press ending the first phase of his career. So Sinatra sought out non-singing parts, his versatility and stubborn resolve (and rumored mob ties—his fall and comeback allegedly served as the basis for the Johnny Fontane character in *The Godfather*) leading to an acclaimed "comeback" as Maggio in *From Here to Eternity* (1952), for which he won the Best Supporting Actor Oscar.

After regaining his vocal powers, Sinatra performed in a range of material from musicals like *Guys and Dolls* and *High Society* (1956) to breezy romantic comedies like *The Tender Trap*

(1955) to substantial dramatic roles in Otto Preminger's *The Man With the Golden Arm* (1955, Academy Award nominee for best actor) and in *The Manchurian Candidate* (1962).

Sinatra's resilience and versatility made him a show business institution: pop star, movie star, Las Vegas nightclub legend, film producer, and television guest star. (One of the gentlemen responsible for the orchestrations of the *Guys and Dolls* score, Nelson Riddle, would go on to a heady creative collaboration in popular recording with Sinatra).

In 1964, Sinatra got the chance to create his own incarnation of Sky Masterson in the musical *Robin and the 7 Hoods*, which he also produced. It takes place in a fairy-tale 1920s Chicago, filled with golden-hearted, well-mannered gangsters and tinhorns. One musical number, "Mr. Booze," involves a series of confessions at a prayer meeting—any of this sound familiar?

■

Q: Composer Frank Loesser was no stranger to Samuel Goldwyn and his studios. Why?

A: Loesser had written the music and lyrics for Samuel Goldwyn's 1952 musical *Hans Christian Andersen*, starring Danny Kaye. Samuel Goldwyn had nursed the idea of a musical based on the famed teller of fairy tales since the late 1930s, and had even talked with Walt Disney about collaborating on an animated version of the tale in the 1940s. By the time Goldwyn seriously revisited *Hans Christian Andersen* in 1951, he owned no fewer than thirty treatments of the potential film. He first approached Rodgers and Hammerstein about contributing an original score, but was turned down.

Frank Loesser had written the theme song for Goldwyn's *Roseanna McCoy*, a Romeo and Juliet story about the famous feuding Hatfields and McCoys, and *Guys and Dolls* was in the second year of its Broadway run. An approach to Loesser

seemed the next logical step.

Loesser and screenwriter Moss Hart worked to create some order out of the completely fictive tale of the storyteller, combined with retellings of his most beloved stories.

No matter that the resulting storyline was utterly ridiculous. (Farley Granger, who—under duress—played the ballet master in the film, summed it up: "Look at that plot," he said, "Boy meets girl; boy loses girl; boy gets boy.") The finished film scored six Academy Award nominations and was a box office bonanza for Goldwyn, and Loesser's score delivered the goods with such standards as Oscar nominee "Thumbelina," "Wonderful Copenhagen," "No Two People," "Anywhere I Wander," and "Inchworm."

■

Q: Five songs were cut from the Broadway musical in its transition to film. Three songs were added. Which were cut? Which were added?

A: Technically, the first musical casualty of the film version of *Guys and Dolls* is "Follow the Fold," which has been cut in half, but that doesn't constitute a real "cut."

"A Bushel and a Peck," Adelaide's first number at The Hot Box, was replaced with "Pet Me, Poppa," although an instrumental version of "A Bushel and a Peck" can be heard in the background while Nathan is on the dressing room pay phone just prior to "Pet Me, Poppa."

"My Time of Day," Sky's personal anthem, is gone, but shows up as a melancholy underscore upon Sky and Sarah's return from Havana.

"I've Never Been in Love Before," Sky and Sarah's love ballad, has been replaced by "A Woman in Love."

"More I Cannot Wish You," Arvide's loving "charm song" is cut, as is an awkward pairing of Adelaide and Sarah, "Marry the Man Today."

Added is a song apparently written for the

stage musical *Guys and Dolls*, "Adelaide." According to Abe Burrows, Frank Loesser had written four songs for the character of Nathan, but the actor who originated the role on Broadway, Sam Levene, couldn't sing. The creative team all agreed to live with this, since Levene was so perfect for the role in every other regard. Levene struggled through "Sue Me," but was even asked to mouth the words to the ensemble numbers, because if he sang he ruined the harmony. "To this day, every actor who gets to play the part of Nathan Detroit wonders why he has only one song to sing," Burrows said. "He has to be told the sad saga of Sam Levene's singing."

Naturally, when Sinatra was cast, songs for Nathan *had* to be added. Not only does Frank sing Nathan's standard "Sue Me" and the added "Adelaide," but he also joins Johnny Silver and Stubby Kaye in the title song, "Guys and Dolls," and joins the ensemble in "The Oldest Established" and "Luck Be a Lady."

■

Q: **Name at least three other films based on the writings of Damon Runyon.**

A: *Lady for a Day* (1933, remade as *Pocketful of Miracles*, 1961); *Little Miss Marker* (1934 and 1980, also remade as *Sorrowful Jones*, 1949); *The Lemon-Drop Kid* (1934, remade in 1951); *A Slight Case of Murder* (1938, remade as *Stop, You're Killing Me*, 1953); *Straight, Place and Show* (a.k.a. *They're Off*, 1938); *The Big Street* (1942); *Johnny One-Eye* (1950); *Bloodhounds of Broadway* (1952, remade in 1989); and *Money From Home* (1953).

■

Q: **Name two of Frank Loesser's other Broadway hits.**

A: Loesser provided the music and lyrics for *Where's Charley?* (1948), which starred Ray Bolger and featured the songs "Once in Love with Amy" and "My Darling, My Darling." The stage musical ran 792 performances at the St. James Theater. Warner Bros. made a movie version with Bolger in 1952.

Loesser's post-*Guys and Dolls* hit was *The Most Happy Fella* (1956), for which he wrote a complex, varied, and near-operatic score that had only about fifteen minutes of spoken dialogue. This "abundance of abundance" ran 676 performances at the Imperial Theater. This is also the musical that Lucy, Ricky, Fred, and Ethel run in and out of on the 1957 "I Love Lucy" episode, "Lucy's Night in Town."

How to Succeed in Business Without Really Trying (1961) was Loesser's last hit show, run-

Author's Collection. © The Samuel Goldwyn Company

Jean Simmons' shiny Sister Sarah Brown.

ning 1,417 performances at the Forty-Sixth Street Theater, and starring Robert Morse and Rudy Vallee. The show won dozens of awards, including the Pulitzer Prize for Drama. United Artists and Mirisch Pictures collaborated on a well-regarded film version of *How to Succeed in Business Without Really Trying*, released in 1967.

■

hard

Q: Now, name two of Frank Loesser's musical flops.

A: Although it featured a gentle and lovely score, *Greenwillow* (1960) was doomed by a gentle and lovely book, based on the novel by B. J.

Chute. This fascinating musical failure featured Anthony Perkins (!), Cecil Kellaway, and Pert Kelton (Widow Paroo of *The Music Man*, q.v.), and was directed by George Roy Hill (*Butch Cassidy and the Sundance Kid*, *The Sting*, *The World According to Garp*). It ran only 97 performances at the Alvin Theater. *Greenwillow* is a lovely score to listen to, even if it doesn't hang together as a show.

Pleasures and Palaces (1965) was Loesser's final musical, which closed on the road. Again, it seems the show was sunk by a bad book. *Pleasures and Palaces* was based on a flop 1961 play called *Once There Was a Russian*—it had a one-performance run on Broadway. Even with choreography and direction by Bob Fosse and performances by Broadway stalwarts John McMartin and Phyllis Newman, the show's weak score and origin in a failure doomed it. Boston and Broadway openings were canceled, and *Pleasures and Palaces* closed in Detroit.

■

Q: Many musicals have a component known as an "Eleven O'Clock Spot." What is that? What is the Eleven O'Clock Spot in *Guys and Dolls*?

A: The "Eleven O'Clock Spot" is a high energy musical number placed close to the end of a show, but not at the finale. The purpose is simplicity itself. The audience has been sitting for nearly three hours, and the "Spot" will jolt and invigorate the sedate spectators, readying them for the actual finale.

The Eleven O'Clock Spot in *Guys and Dolls* is "Sit Down, You're Rockin' the Boat," perhaps the best example of the Spot in musical theatre history.

Other examples of the Eleven O'Clock Spot include "Get Me to the Church on Time" in *My Fair Lady*, "Shall We Dance?" in *The King and I*, and "That's How Young I Feel" in *Mame*.

■

Stubby Kaye catches up on the sport of kings while waiting for "The Eleven O'Clock Spot."

Q: Name the three *characters* who sing the racetrack anthem "Fugue for Tin Horns." What's a tinhorn?

A: Nicely-Nicely Johnson (Stubby Kaye), Rusty Charlie (Dan Dayton), and Benny Southstreet (Johnny Silver) perform "Fugue for Tin Horns."

Frank Loesser had written the trio for a spot in the initial libretto of *Guys and Dolls* by Jo Swerling. When Abe Burrows rewrote this abortive first script, he couldn't find a plot point for the "Fugue." He simply placed it at the opening of the show, establishing the mood, setting, and vocabulary of the characters.

According to Webster, a *tinhorn* is slang for a person pretending to have money, ability, or influence, though actually lacking these; cheap and showy. It derives from *tin horn gambler*, named from the use of metal dice-shakers in chuck-a-luck games, scorned as petty by faro dealers.

■

Q: What do the following have in common: *Guys and Dolls*, *Brigadoon*, *Mary Poppins*, and *Victor/Victoria*?

A: That they're all musicals would be correct, but not where this is headed. It's not that they're all based on hit Broadway shows, since *Mary Poppins* and *Victor/Victoria* are original film musicals. Here's the truly obscure answer: Each of these movie musicals was shot completely indoors!

Even such sound-stage-bound musicals as *Singin' in the Rain* (q.v.) and *Seven Brides for Seven Brothers* have location footage and/or sequences filmed on studio back lots. The musicals listed above, interiors and exteriors, were shot completely within the confines of sound stages.

In fact, the Times Square set for *Guys and Dolls* took up an entire twenty-seven-thousand-square-foot sound stage, Goldwyn's largest. The set streets were paved with real asphalt, due to the fact that real automobiles would be traversing them, and typical set materials like linoleum or plywood wouldn't have held up through the shooting schedule. Because the paving of Times Square was too big a job for the Goldwyn Studio staff construction crew, the task was contracted to a Los Angeles road builder, Holman & Powell Paving Company.

Joseph Mankiewicz even insisted that the set be littered with real New York newspapers.

Samuel Goldwyn presents

GUYS AND DOLLS

In CinemaScope®

Based upon the play *Guys and Dolls*; book by Jo Swerling and Abe Burrows
from a Damon Runyon Story

Produced on the stage by Cy Feuer and Ernest H. Martin

Music and Lyrics by Frank Loesser

Director of Photography Harry Stradling, ASC

Dances and Musical Numbers staged by Michael Kidd

Production Design by Oliver Smith; Costumes Designed by Irene Sharaff

Music Supervised and Conducted by Jay Blackton
Background Music Adapted by Cyril J. Mockridge
Orchestrations: Skip Martin, Nelson Riddle, Alexander Courage, Al Sendrey

Film Editor Daniel Mandell, ACE; Color Consultant Alvord L. Eiseman
Special Photographic Effects Warren Newcombe

Sound: Fred Lau, Roger Heman, Vinton Vernon

Assistant Director Arthur S. Black, Jr.

Art Director Joseph Wright

Set Decorations by Howard Bristol

Make-up Ben Lane; Hair Stylist Annabell

Photographed in Eastman Color; Recorded in Perspecta Stereophonic Sound

Released by Metro-Goldwyn-Mayer in November, 1955

Passed by the National Board of Review. Running time: 149 minutes

Cast

Marlon Brando	Sky Masterson
Jean Simmons	Sarah Brown
Frank Sinatra	Nathan Detroit
Vivian Blaine	Adelaide
Robert Keith	Lieutenant Brannigan
Stubby Kaye	Nicely-Nicely Johnson
B. S. Pully	Big Jule
Johnny Silver	Benny Southstreet
Regis Toomey	Arvide Abernathy
Sheldon Leonard	Harry the Horse
Dan Dayton	Rusty Charlie
George E. Stone	Society Max
Mary Alan Hokanson	Agatha
Veda Ann Borg	Laverne
Kathryn Givney	General Cartwright
Joe McTurk	Angie the Ox
Kay Kuter	Calvin
Stapleton Kent	Mission Member
Renee Renor	Cuban Singer
Reuben de Fuentes	Church Plaza Singer
Johnny Indrisano, Jack Perry, Tommy Herman, Kid Chissell	"The Runyon Characters"
The Goldwyn Girls	Larri Thomas, Madelyn Darrow, June Kirby, Barbara Brent, Pat Sheehan, and Jann Darlyn

Chapter Four

My Fair Lady

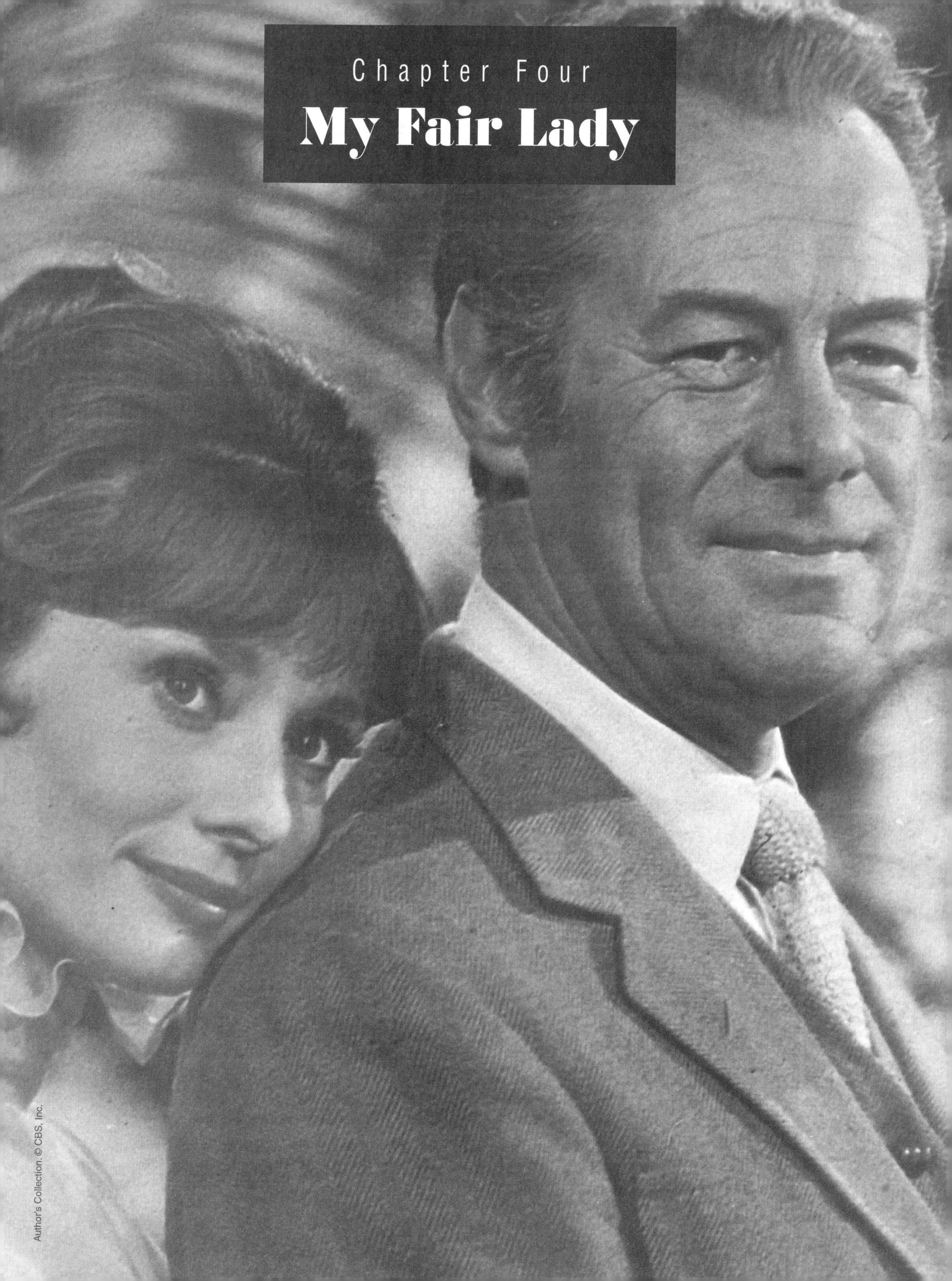

My Fair Lady *is one of the most faithful adaptations of a successful Broadway musical ever to come to the screen. Produced in the waning days of the powerful studios, and in what would become the declining era of the movie musical,* My Fair Lady *is an endearing but odd amalgam of the art of cinema and the art of theatre. For many purists of the stage, it represents the finest work that Hollywood can do in translating a hit stage musical to film. For many cinephiles, it is a dully-realized, stagebound "repackaging" of a stage show for the mass audience. Both assesments are true to a degree, but as the years go by,* My Fair Lady *seems to nestle happily in the center of those opinions. It remains a conscientious, handsome, and genial film, with the benefit of a strong cast of actors, including the original Broadway lead joyously re-creating his role for posterity. Whether you think it's stodgy and stagebound or faithful and felicitous, at the very least* My Fair Lady *is solid musical theatre turned into enjoyable cinema.*

■

Level One: The Easy Stuff
Story & Characters

Q: In what year does *My Fair Lady* take place? In what locale?

A: 1912, in London, England, and environs, all realized on the sound stages and back lot of the Warner Bros. studio in Burbank, California.

The producer of *My Fair Lady*, Jack L. Warner, might possibly have been the inspiration for this time-honored Hollywood tale: A young director approaches the powerful studio head with the vision for his new film. It entails taking the company on location to capture the serene beauty of the Vermont woods, or the Virginia coast, or the mighty forests of the Pacific Northwest (it varies from telling to telling). The unflappable studio executive looks at the director with a combination of confusion and disdain. "A tree's a tree. A rock's a rock. Shoot it in Griffith Park."

Not only did Warner like the bottom line savings of shooting entirely on the studio lot, but one can assume that, a consummate showman, he liked the publicity advantages. One can also assume that, a consummate studio chief, Warner liked the control of having the entire company of a big production like *My Fair Lady* firmly established on his Burbank turf.

Thus, Covent Garden, Wimpole Street, and Ascot were built indoors on Warner's sound stages. "With a Little Bit of Luck" was shot on the redressed Tenement Street back lot set.

■

Q: What is Henry Higgins' profession? What is his hobby?

A: Higgins' profession, as well as his hobby, is "simple phonetics, the science of speech." He makes not just a living at phonetics, but "quite a fat one." He is also the author of *Higgins' Universal Alphabet*.

Higgins is played by the creator of the musical version of the role on Broadway, Rex Harrison. Reginald Carey Harrison was born in 1908, in Huyton, England. He made his stage debut with the Liverpool Repertory Theatre in 1924, and his London stage debut in 1930. The same year, Harrison made his film debut, and appeared for the next five years in British films such as *The Great Game*, *School For Scandal* (1930), *Get Your Man*, *Leave It to Blanche* (1934), and *All at Sea* (1935).

Harrison's Broadway debut came in 1936, in *Sweet Aloes*. Later that year, he became a star in London, in *French Without Tears*. He continued

A street scene of Covent Garden, by way of Burbank, California.

in British films as well, including *Men Are Not Gods* (1936), *Over the Moon, School For Husbands, Storm in a Teacup* (1937), *The Citadel* (1938), *St. Martin's Lane* (a.k.a. *Sidewalks of London*, 1938. This film was adapted for the musical stage in 1995 under the title *Busker Alley*, starring Tommy Tune.), *Continental Express* (a.k.a. *The Silent Battle*), *Missing Ten Days* (a.k.a. *Ten Days in Paris*, 1939), *Night Train to Munich* (a.k.a. *Night Train*, 1940), and George Bernard Shaw's *Major Barbara* (1941).

Harrison served in World War II as flight lieutenant in the RAF, but resumed his stardom quickly afterward in the films *Blithe Spirit* and *The Rake's Progress* (a.k.a. *Notorious Gentleman*, 1945). He made his American film debut in a fullbodied performance as the King in *Anna and the King of Siam* (1946), followed by equally strong performances in the romantic fantasy *The Ghost and Mrs. Muir* (1947) and the Preston Sturges comedy *Unfaithfully Yours* (1948).

Harrison's film work in the 1950s included *The Long Dark Hall* (UK, 1951), *The Four Poster* (1952, adapted for the musical stage in 1966 as *I*

Do! I Do!), *Main Street to Broadway* (1953), *King Richard and the Crusaders* (1954), and *The Constant Husband* (UK, 1955).

In 1954, Harrison and then-wife Lilli Palmer were appearing together in *Bell, Book and Candle* in the West End, when Harrison was offered the role of Henry Higgins in the still-untitled musical adaptation of Shaw's *Pygmalion*. Harrison was intrigued, and began vocal lessons to exercise his vocal cords and tempi. The role of Higgins was never expected to be a "singing" role per se, and was "sung" through a combination of Harrison's faultless sense of rhythm and ability to speak absolutely on pitch.

On March 15, 1956, Harrison made his debut in the role with which he would thereafter be identified: Henry Higgins in the musical now entitled *My Fair Lady*. The show was a smash hit and won nine 1957 Tony awards, including Best Musical—and Best Actor in a Musical for Harrison.

The prolific Harrison returned to film in 1958, in *The Reluctant Debutante*, which was followed by *Midnight Lace* (1960), *The Happy Thieves* (1962), *Cleopatra* (1963), and the film version of

My Fair Lady, for which he was again named Best Actor, this time winning an Oscar.

Following this latest Harrison-as-Higgins triumph, he starred (as Pope Julius II) in *The Agony and the Ecstasy*, and in *The Yellow Rolls-Royce* (1965).

Naturally, Hollywood had been trying almost constantly since the success of *My Fair Lady* to get Harrison into another musical role, an effort which was realized in the elephantine Twentieth Century-Fox musical *Doctor Dolittle*, in which Harrison played a charming Henry Higgins knock-off, a veterinarian who can talk to his patients. The film was a misfire, to say the least,

but the resilient Rex Harrison followed it with *The Honey Pot* (1967), *A Flea in Her Ear* (1968), *Staircase* (1969), *Prince and the Pauper* (a.k.a. *Crossed Swords*), *Shalimar* (a.k.a. *Deadly Thief*, 1978), *Ashanti*, *The Fifth Musketeer* (1979), and his final film, *A Time to Die* (which was made in 1979, but not released until 1983).

Harrison was knighted in 1989, was married six times (no wonder he was often snickeringly called "Sexy Rexy"), and wrote two books: the 1974 autobiography *Rex*, and an analysis of the art of comedy called *A Damned Serious Business*, which was published posthumously in 1990.

■

Q: Higgins mentions that he had intended to go to India. Why?

A: To meet the author of *Spoken Sanskrit*, Colonel Hugh Pickering, played by Wilfrid Hyde-White.

Hyde-White, who replaced Broadway original Robert Coote in the role of Pickering, was born in 1903 in Bourton-on-the-Water, England.

Hyde-White graduated from the Royal Academy of Dramatic Arts, and appeared on stage and in film from 1936. He was a popular character actor both in his native Britain and in the United States. He often played pompous or befuddled authority figures—or characters perceived as being such—with an underpinning of wry humor and mischief.

Among Hyde-White's dozens of films, the best known are *Elephant Boy* (1937), *The Winslow Boy* (1948), *The Third Man* (1949), *No Highway in the Sky* (a.k.a. *No Highway*, 1951), *Betrayed* (1954), *Let's Make Love* (1960), *In Search of the Castaways* (1962), *The Magic Christian* (1969), *Battlestar: Galactica* (1979), *Oh God! Book II*, cult favorite *Xanadu* (1980), and the Richard Pryor/Jackie Gleason vehicle *The Toy* (1982).

One of Hyde-White's last projects was the 1979–80 situation comedy "The Associates,"

Collection of Craig T. Hyland. © CBS, Inc.

The quintessential Henry Higgins, Rex Harrison.

which starred Alley Mills and Martin Short as two young law school graduates who get jobs at a big Wall Street law firm. The senior partner of the firm was played in that crazy-like-a-fox way by Hyde-White. Wilfrid Hyde-White died in 1991.

While studying at RADA, Hyde-White reportedly once consulted George Bernard Shaw himself for direction on a line reading from a Shaw play. Shaw is said to have replied, "Read them, young man, as I expect all my lines to be read…in such a manner that people in the audience will exclaim: 'Only George Bernard Shaw could have written those lines!'" Hmmm.

In the opening scenes of *My Fair Lady*, Hyde-White had the opportunity to carry his lucky umbrella. He had used said brolly in eighteen of his films at the time of *My Fair Lady*.

■

Q: **What is Henry Higgins' address?**

A: When Pickering tells Higgins he's staying at the Hotel Carlton, Higgins rejoins, "No you're not, you're staying at 27A Wimpole Street!"

On a research trip to London, the *My Fair Lady* production designer had taken the film's director to number 75 Wimpole Street, the home of his own physician, Dr. Gottfried. In a 1964 book about the making of *My Fair Lady*, he recalled that "Many of these houses, with their decorative windows of frosted glass and individual doorways of no accepted style, could certainly have belonged to Professor Higgins. So entirely suitable for our purpose did this house appear that we decided to copy it in almost all essentials. Permission was granted to photograph and measure every detail from the servants' basement to attic bedrooms."

■

Q: **As *My Fair Lady* begins, elegantly dressed patrons are exiting the Opera House. What opera have they just seen?**

A: The grandly-wardrobed extras are leaving the Covent Garden Opera House and a production of Charles Gounod's *Faust*, probably the most famous version of Goethe's tale of a man who sells his soul to the Devil to regain his lost youth.

The reference is a subtle in-joke, since *My Fair Lady* and its source are, in the words of Keith Garebian, an integration of "Faustian legend with Cinderella fairy-tale."

■

Q: **Higgins and Pickering are doing their phonetics thing like two greedy babies, when a taxi deposits an unexpected visitor. Who?**

Well, I'm dashed! Wilfrid Hyde-White escorts Audrey Hepburn to the races at Ascot.

easy

A: Miss Eliza Doolittle, who has come to see the "pro-fessor" about helping her learn to talk like a "lie-dee." Audrey Hepburn played Eliza. Hepburn was born Edda van Heemstra Hepburn-Ruston (no kidding) in 1929, in Brussels, Belgium.

She studied ballet at Arnhem Conservatory, and became a poised and successful model. Hepburn made her film debut in 1951, with a small role in *Laughter in Paradise*, which was followed by a walk-on in *The Lavender Hill Mob* the same year.

French author Colette saw Hepburn while she was shooting an obscure film called *Nous irons à Monte Carlo* (1951), and was convinced that Hepburn should play *Gigi* in the Broadway production then being assembled. Hepburn toured with this production, arriving in Los Angeles in 1953. She was immediately approached with film offers, and her star truly ascended with the film *Roman Holiday* (1953), for which she won the Best Actress Academy

Award. This was followed by hit after career-building hit, including, *Sabrina* (1954), for which she was again Oscar-nominated, *War and Peace* (1956), *Funny Face, Love in the Afternoon* (1957), *Green Mansions, The Nun's Story* (1959, another Oscar nomination), *The Unforgiven* (1960), *Breakfast at Tiffany's* (1961, yet another Academy Award nomination), *The Children's Hour* (1962), and *Charade* (1963).

Taking the role of Eliza Doolittle in the film version of *My Fair Lady* was a challenge for Hepburn. First, she would be working with the well-rehearsed Broadway principals Rex Harrison and Stanley Holloway. Second, Hepburn was not known for her singing ability—a disadvantage when about to tackle one of the most popular Broadway song scores in history. Finally, she faced a backlash for replacing the original Broadway lead in the role of Eliza.

Hepburn stood up well alongside her Broad-

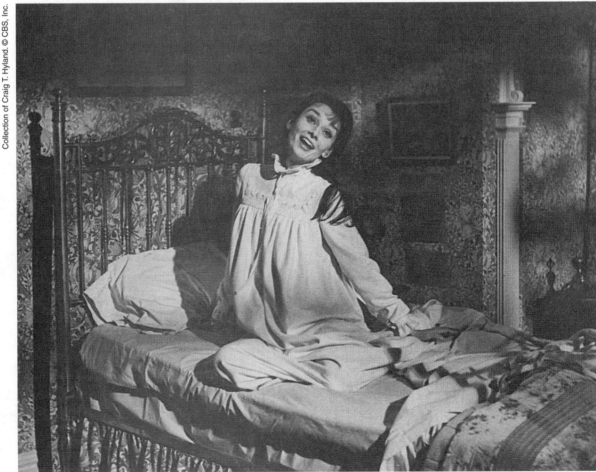

Bright and beautiful, but never really a "squashed cabbage leaf," Audrey Hepburn.

way-honed co-star, delivering a performance of depth and strength that inspired compassion. Her vocals were, for the most part, dubbed by a soprano vocalist, and Hepburn acted the songs well. She worked for two months with a diction coach to develop Eliza's Cockney screech, and with the Warner Bros. makeup and wardrobe experts to suitably sully her elegant appearance.

In the final analysis, her Eliza is strong, graceful, well-defined, and, above all, well-acted; Hepburn more than stands up to the strengths of her co-stars. But Hepburn had been born an aristocrat (her father was an English banker, her mother a Dutch baroness) and therein lies the basic problem of her Eliza. While there is no doubt that there is a duchess in Hepburn's guttersnipe, there is very little guttersnipe in her duchess.

No matter, since her Eliza was highly regarded, and Hepburn continued in film, following *My Fair Lady* with *Paris When It Sizzles* (1964), *How to Steal a Million* (1966), *Two for the Road*, and *Wait Until Dark* (1967), for which she snagged her last Oscar nomination.

Hepburn left films for nearly a decade, returning as an aging Maid Marian opposite Sean Connery's Robin Hood in *Robin and Marian* (1976), followed by *Bloodline* (a.k.a. *Sidney Sheldon's Bloodline*, 1979) and Peter Bogdanovich's *They All Laughed* (1981).

She acted infrequently due to her commitment to the United Nations Children's Fund (UNICEF), to which she served as a Special Ambassador. Hepburn focused her time on publicizing the plight of children in famine-plagued and war-torn countries.

Her final film role was, appropriately enough, that of an angel, in the 1989 Steven Spielberg romantic fantasy *Always*.

Audrey Hepburn died on January 20, 1993, at her home near Lausanne, Switzerland.

■

Q: **What does Eliza Doolittle's father do for a living?**

A: Alfred P. Doolittle is "a common dustman," the British equivalent of a trash collector, portrayed by the decidedly uncommon Stanley Holloway. London-born in 1890, Holloway had begun his career as a boy soprano in English music-halls, becoming a baritone by the time of his first big success, *The Co-Optimists*, in 1921, in which he had a six-year run (and which was revived for several more seasons beginning in 1929). He continued in music-hall, becoming a popular star, and then moved into musical comedy with *Hit the Deck* (1927) and *Song of the Sea* (1928).

Holloway became a staple of British film over the next three decades in widely varied screen roles, beginning with *The Rotters* (1921) and the film version of *The Co-Optimists* (1930), followed by *The Bride of the Lake* (a.k.a. *Lily of Killarney*), *Sing As We Go* (1934), *Squibs* (1935), and *The Vicar of Bray* (1936).

Holloway appeared in the 1941 film version of Shaw's *Major Barbara* (with Rex Harrison), and in *Brief Encounter* (1945), Shaw's *Caesar and Cleopatra* (1946), as Vincent Crummles in *Nicholas Nickleby* (a.k.a. *The Life and Adventures of Nicholas Nickleby*, 1947), and as a gravedigger in *Hamlet* (1948).

He appeared, with Wilfrid Hyde-White, in the British standard *The Winslow Boy* (1948), and in *The Lavender Hill Mob* (1951) and *The Beggar's Opera* (as Lockit, 1953), among dozens of other films.

Author and theatre historian Keith Garebian adeptly describes Holloway: "A favourite with working-class Englishmen as much as with the country's royal family, Holloway seemed quintessentially Old English 'roast beef,' solid and hearty but not to be taken for granted."

In October 1954, Holloway was in New York appearing in the Old Vic production of *A Midsummer Night's Dream* when he was intrigued and excited to hear rumors of a musical production of *Pygmalion*. Several months later, back in London over lunch at Claridge's, Lerner and Loewe confirmed the rumor by asking Holloway to play Alfred Doolittle in their upcoming production. Holloway played Doolittle on Broadway, for which he was nominated for a Tony as Best Supporting Actor, as well as in the London company.

Holloway returned to film in *An Alligator Named Daisy* (1957), *No Trees in the Street* (1958), *Hello London* (1959), *No Love for Johnnie* (1961), and the film version of *My Fair Lady*, for which he was nominated for the Best Supporting Actor Oscar. He followed this with *In Harm's Way* (1965); Agatha Christie's *Ten Little Indians* (1966); *Mrs. Brown, You've Got a Lovely Daughter* (1968); *Target: Harry* (a.k.a. *How to Make It*, 1969); Billy Wilder's *The Private Life of Sherlock Holmes* (1970); *Flight of the Doves* (1971); *Up the Front* (1972); and his last film, *Journey Into Fear* (1975).

In 1967, Holloway's autobiography, *Wiv a Little Bit O' Luck*, was published.

Stanley Holloway died in 1982.

■

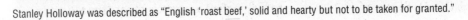

Stanley Holloway was described as "English 'roast beef,' solid and hearty but not to be taken for granted."

Collection of Craig T. Hyland. © CBS, Inc.

Courtesy of Fox Video. © CBS, Inc.

Zoltan Karpathy (Theodore Bikel) is baffled by Eliza Doolittle at the Embassy Ball.

Q: At the Embassy Ball, Higgins is accosted by whom?

A: Higgins is greeted vociferously by his "first, greatest, best pupil," the Hungarian Zoltan Karpathy, played by Theodore Bikel.

Bikel was born Meir Bikel in Vienna, Austria, in 1924, but emigrated to Palestine in his teens. There he made his stage debut at the Habimah Theater in Tel Aviv in *Tevye the Milkman*. Bikel studied at the Royal Academy of Dramatic Art, and made his London stage debut in 1948. His New York debut was in 1955.

Bikel began appearing in films in the early 1950s, and has typically played suspicious "foreigners." His films have included *The African Queen* (1951), *The Little Kidnappers* (1953), *The Enemy Below*, *The Pride and the Passion* (1957), *The Defiant Ones* (for which he received an Oscar nomination for Best Supporting Actor, 1958), *The Blue Angel*, *A Dog of Flanders* (1959), *Sands of the Kalahari* (1965), *The Russians Are Coming! The Russians Are Coming!* (1966), *My Side of the Mountain* (1969), *Two Hundred Motels* (1971), *Prince Jack* (1984), *Shattered*

(1991), and *The Assassination Game* (1992).

Most recently, Bikel returned to Tevye the Milkman, playing the role in a touring production of *Fiddler on the Roof*.

Of course, a great irony of *My Fair Lady* is the fact that non-singers abound in singing roles—Rex Harrison, Audrey Hepburn, Jeremy Brett, even Wilfrid Hyde-White (who sings a few lines of "You Did It")—while Bikel, who had not only originated the role of Captain von Trapp in the original Broadway cast of *The Sound of Music* (1959), but had also established himself as a prominent folk singer and guitarist by the time of *My Fair Lady*, has a non-singing role.

■

Q: How does Higgins "ruin" Alfred Doolittle?

A: By "delivering him into the hands of middle-class morality."

An American philanthropist, Ezra Wallingford, has been pestering Higgins to lecture to his Moral Reform Society. As a joke, Higgins writes to Wallingford, suggesting that "the most original moralist in England" is the unscrupulous Alfred P. Doolittle.

Wallingford dies, leaving Doolittle four thousand pounds a year in his will. The wealth, Doolittle maintains, has ruined the structure of his life. "Who asked him to make a gentleman outta me?" Doolittle laments. "I was happy, I was free, I touched pretty nigh everyone for money when I wanted it, same as I touched 'im. Now I'm tied, neck and 'eels, and everybody touches me. Ooh, I 'ave to live for others now, not for m'self."

The joy of Doolittle's existence had been living by his wits and exercising his vices at the expense of society. By virtue of his new-found wealth, Doolittle is still able to excercise his drunkenness and philandering, but has himself become the exploited.

■

Q: To whom does Eliza turn for solace after she walks out on Henry Higgins?

A: To Higgins' mother, played with delicate imperiousness by Gladys Cooper. Cooper was born in 1888, in Lewisham, England, had entered the theatre as a chorine at the age of sixteen, and became famous as a favorite pin-up girl during World War I.

Cooper worked in silent films such as *Dandy Donovan* (1914), *Masks and Faces* (1917), and *Bohemian Girl* (1922). She became a British stage star in the 1920s, and, for a time, managed London's Playhouse Theatre.

Her screen career became truly established upon her relocation to Hollywood in 1940, where she spent the next thirty years playing dignified Brits. Her numerous Hollywood films included *Kitty Foyle*; *Rebecca* (for which she received an Oscar nomination for Best Supporting Actress, 1940); *The Black Cat*; *That Hamilton Woman* (a.k.a. *Lady Hamilton* 1941); *Now, Voyager* (another Oscar nomination for Best Supporting Actress, 1942); *Mr. Lucky*; *The Song of Bernadette* (1943); *Mrs. Parkington* (1944); *The Bishop's Wife*; *Green Dolphin Street* (1947); *The Pirate* (1948); *Madame Bovary*; *The Secret Garden* (1949); *Separate Tables* (1958); and *The List of Adrian Messenger* (1963). She wrote her autobiography, *Without Veils*, in 1953.

After *My Fair Lady*, for which she was again nominated for the Academy Award for Best Supporting Actress, Cooper made only a few more films, including *The Happiest Millionaire* (1967) and *A Nice Girl Like Me* (1969). She also appeared in the 1964–65 NBC-TV series "The Rogues." Gladys Cooper died in 1971.

Her Mrs. Higgins is wonderfully intolerant of her son's eccentricities, a mother who knows just what a spoiled baby her son is and will have none of it, and who makes no apologies for telling him so. Her performance, however, lacks the warmth a mother might actually exhibit for her son, however nasty he may have turned out—but that's probably splitting hairs.

Her delivery of the line "Of course, dear. What did you expect?" is a gem of a reading.

Level Two: Not So Easy
The Actors, Artists, & Others

Q: What is the source material for *My Fair Lady*?

A: The facile answer is the 1956 Tony Award-winning Lerner and Loewe Broadway musical *My Fair Lady*. Which is correct, as far as it goes.

My Fair Lady, of course, had been based on the 1914 George Bernard Shaw play *Pygmalion*. Shaw was not particularly proud of *Pygmalion*, calling it one of his "shameless potboilers" written to oblige theatre managers or aspiring players. Shaw labelled it "intensely and deliberately didactic," with a subject he thought dry. The success of *Pygmalion* was, in Shaw's opinion, proof that "great art can never be anything [but didactic]."

The genesis of the Shaw play is in the classical myth of Pygmalion, a woman-hating sculptor whose only true love is his art. Having made a beautiful ivory statue of a woman, Pygmalion falls in love with it and prays to Aphrodite to give the statue life. *Pygmalion* also has roots in W. S. Gilbert's 1871 *Pygmalion and Galatea*. Shaw's play is aptly described by author Keith Garebian as an Edwardian reworking of the Pygmalion myth with an emphasis on themes of linguistic and class distinctions.

The popular Shaw play had been brought to the movie screen in 1938 by flamboyant Rumanian producer Gabriel Pascal. Shaw wrote the screenplay, Leslie Howard starred as Higgins and co-directed with Anthony Asquith, and Eliza was played by Wendy Hiller. Pascal went on to film *Major Barbara* (1941) and *Caesar and Cleopatra* (1945), neither of which had the critical or commercial success of *Pygmalion*.

Pascal actually initiated the idea of a musical version of *Pygmalion*, but died in 1954, before the concept came to fruition.

Q: The prolific director of *My Fair Lady* had made only five movie musicals before. Who was the director? What were the musicals?

A: The director was the revered George Cukor. Of his fifty films, his entire musical output was *One Hour with You* (1932, directed by Ernst Lubitsch and Cukor), *A Star Is Born* (1954), *Les Girls* (1957), *Let's Make Love*, *Song Without End* (1960), *My Fair Lady*, and *The Blue Bird* (1976).

New York-born in 1899, George Dewey Cukor began his career in the theatre as a stage manager. By the mid-1920s he had become one of the top directors on Broadway. With the advent of sound pictures, Cukor went to Hollywood to work as a dialogue coach. He co-directed three films before his first solo directing credit with *Tarnished Lady* (1931).

Cukor gained a reputation as a "woman's director," apparently because many of his films featured strong, independent, intelligent women playing strong, independent, intelligent women. Cukor gained the respect of actors, writers, technicians, and crew (male and female alike) through a style that embraced the collective nature of the theatre.

Cukor's significant films include *A Bill of Divorcement*, *What Price Hollywood?* (1932, the original version of *A Star is Born*, to which he would return in 1954), *Dinner at Eight*, *Little Women* (1933), *David Copperfield* (1935), *Romeo and Juliet* (1936), *Camille* (1937), *The Women* (1939), *The Philadelphia Story* (1940), *Gaslight* (1944), *A Double Life* (1947), *Adam's Rib* (1949), *Born Yesterday* (1950), *Pat and Mike* (1952), *The Chapman Report* (1962), and *Travels With My Aunt* (1972). Cukor had been nominated for the Best Director Academy Award five times, for *Little Women*, *The Philadelphia Story*, *A Double Life*, *Born Yesterday*, and the one for which he finally won, *My Fair Lady*.

Cukor's final project with Katharine Hepburn was *Love Among the Ruins* (1975), for which he won an Emmy. In 1981 he directed his fiftieth and final film, *Rich And Famous*. George Cukor died in 1983, at the age of eighty-four.

■

Q: Who played Eliza Doolittle on Broadway?

A: Julie Andrews originated the role of Eliza in the Broadway production. Andrews was born Julia Elizabeth Wells in Walton-on-Thames, England, in 1935. Andrews began her career in musical revues with her mother and stepfather, and had made a hit in *The Boy Friend* in 1954, which led to her being cast as "the squashed cabbage

Collection of Craig T. Hyland. © CBS, Inc.

Rex Harrison, Audrey Hepburn, and Stanley Holloway, arriving at the Embassy Ball.

leaf of Covent Garden" in the stage version of *My Fair Lady*.

Andrews appeared in an original TV musical *High Tor* (1956) with Bing Crosby, the Rodgers and Hammerstein original TV musical *Cinderella* (1957), and originated the role of Guenevere in *Camelot* (1960). Her film debut came in *Mary Poppins* (1964), a role she accepted only after being passed over for the role of Eliza Doolittle.

"To be honest, I didn't hold out that much hope that I was going to get the role," Andrews recalled. "I wished for it, and wanted it, but I don't think I thought I would get it. So it wasn't as desperately awful a disappointment as people think that it might have been."

Any anguish Andrews suffered over the loss of the role was short-lived, as she won the Academy Award for Best Actress that year for *Mary Poppins*. Audrey Hepburn wasn't even nominated for *My Fair Lady*. On the same evening that Andrews was awarded her Oscar, Rex Harrison was presented with his Best Actor trophy—by Audrey Hepburn. He diplomatically acknowledged them both by professing his "deep love to—uh—well, *two* fair ladies."

Andrews next appeared in the black comedy *The Americanization of Emily* (1964), and her star was assured after appearing in the blockbuster musical *The Sound of Music* (1965), for which she was again nominated for the Best Actress Oscar. She attempted to vary her roles with appearances in *Hawaii* and *Torn Curtain* (1966), but followed these with *Thoroughly Modern Millie* (1967) and the less successful musical spectaculars *Star!* (1968) and *Darling Lili* (1970).

Though somewhat encumbered by her popularity as a wholesome musical star, Andrews work over the next two decades was varied, and showcased her skills at drama and comedy in such films as *The Tamarind Seed* (1974), *10* (1979), *S.O.B.* (1981), *The Man Who Loved Women* (1983), *Duet for One* (1986), *That's Life!* (1986), and *A Fine Romance* (1992).

Under the name Julie Edwards, she has written well-received children's books.

In 1995, Julie Andrews returned to Broadway with an adaptation of her Oscar-nominated 1982 film hit *Victor/Victoria*.

■

Q: Name two other Lerner and Loewe musicals.

A: The first teaming of Alan Jay Lerner and Frederick Loewe was *Life of the Party*, which played for nine weeks in Detroit in 1942.

Their first Broadway success was the 1943 production *What's Up?*, followed by *The Day Before Spring* in 1945.

Their next effort was *Brigadoon*, which premiered on Broadway at the Ziegfeld Theater in March 1947 and ran for 581 performances. It was made into a CinemaScope® film by MGM, released on September 8, 1954. The film was directed by Vincente Minnelli and starred Gene Kelly, Van Johnson, and Cyd Charisse.

The fifth Lerner and Loewe collaboration was *Paint Your Wagon*, which premiered on Broadway in 1951. *Paint Your Wagon* was made into a film starring Clint Eastwood, Lee Marvin, Jean Seberg, Ray Walston, and Harve Presnell. The stage libretto was chucked, and half the songs were discarded as well—Alan Jay Lerner and Andre Previn wrote five new tunes for the film. *Paint Your Wagon*, a legendary film flop, was released in 1969.

Their sixth collaboration was *My Fair Lady*, which premiered at the Mark Hellinger Theater on March 15, 1956. The original Broadway production ran for a staggering 2,717 performances (more than six years).

The seventh Lerner and Loewe collaboration, their first for the movies, was the MGM CinemaScope film *Gigi*, which was released in May 1958. *Gigi* won eight Academy Awards, including Best Picture, Best Song ("Gigi"), and Best Musical Scoring.

Camelot was the eighth Lerner and Loewe

musical. It opened at the Majestic Theater in December 1960, and ran 873 performances. It starred Richard Burton, Julie Andrews, and Robert Goulet. The Warner Bros. film version was released in October 1967, with Richard Harris, Vanessa Redgrave, and Franco Nero in the leads.

The Little Prince was the final Lerner and Loewe collaboration. The musical film, directed by Stanley Donen and starring Richard Kiley, Gene Wilder, and Bob Fosse was released in 1974.

■

Q: The costume designer for *My Fair Lady* had won the Oscar for Best Costume Design for another Lerner and Loewe musical. Who was the designer? What was the other musical?

A: Cecil Beaton had won the 1958 Costume Design Academy Award for *Gigi*. Beaton was born in 1904, and educated at Harrow and Cambridge. He initially gained renown as a photographer of British royalty and entertainment celebrities, notably Greta Garbo.

He went on to design opera, ballet, and stage sets in both London and New York, as well as to create costume designs for the films *Anna Karenina*, *An Ideal Husband* (1948), *Doctor's Dilemma* (1958), and *On a Clear Day You Can See Forever* (1970).

Beaton authored and illustrated a number of books, including *The Glass of Fashion* and a journal of the making of *My Fair Lady*, *Cecil Beaton's 'Fair Lady.'* Beaton was knighted in 1972. He died in 1980.

Although Beaton is credited with the overall production design of *My Fair Lady*, it was recently revealed in a documentary on the making of *My Fair Lady* that his billing was contractual. Although Beaton did design the costumes, coifs, and hats, and helped establish the overall look of *My Fair Lady*, veteran designer Gene Allen was the instrumental production designer for the film.

medium

"Just You Wait," one of the few firing-line executions in a major film musical.

Q: The actor who played Freddy Eynsford-Hill gained prominence in the nineties on another famous street. Who was the actor? What was the street?

A: Jeremy Brett was the actor. In the smarmy bio statement in the original *My Fair Lady* program, Brett is described as a "a shiny, clear-eyed young Englishman [who] abandoned the London theatre to come to Hollywood…[winning] his role of Freddie…over some forty other shiny young Englishmen." Geez, did Brett piss off someone in the Warner Bros. publicity department?

In the late 1980s, the famous street Brett traversed was Baker Street. He played the title role in "Sherlock Holmes" on British television, broadcast in the United States over PBS, The Disney Channel, and the A&E Network.

In 1995, Brett, one of the few surviving cast members of the film, hosted a marvelous documentary about *My Fair Lady*, *More Loverly Than Ever: The Making of My Fair Lady*, which was released with the Thirtieth Anniversary home video and aired on The Disney Channel.

Jeremy Brett died in September 1995.

Q: Who dubbed Audrey Hepburn's singing voice?

A: Soprano Marni Nixon doubled Hepburn's vocals on "Wouldn't It Be Loverly," parts of "Just You Wait," "The Rain in Spain," "I Could Have Danced All Night," "Show Me," and "Without You." Hepburn sang the reprise of "Just You Wait" herself.

Marni Nixon was a singer and voice double who had dubbed Deborah Kerr in *The King and I* and *An Affair to Remember*, and Natalie Wood in *West Side Story*. She had a small part in *The Sound of Music* as Sister Sophia. In the late 1970s, Nixon was the host of a successful and highly-regarded children's program called "Boomerang," which originated from KOMO-TV in Seattle, Washington.

Jeremy Brett's vocal of "On The Street Where You Live" was dubbed by Bill Shirley. Shirley's most famous role had been the voice of Prince Philip in the Disney animated feature *Sleeping Beauty*.

Q: Who inspired "I've Grown Accustomed to Her Face"?

A: Alan Jay Lerner's wife, actress Nancy Olsen, revealed the origin of Higgins' love song. According to Olsen, Lerner was puzzled by how to create an expressive love ballad for a die-hard bachelor like Higgins.

Lerner recalled what Maxwell Anderson called the "recognition scene," "that scene wherein the hero or heroine recognizes the nature of his problem, be it external or internal, and either conquers it or is conquered by it. We felt that Higgins must have a recognition scene in which he recognizes the nature of his problem, albeit obliquely and slightly astigmatically."

Freddy's dewy-eyed love had inspired "On the Street Where You Live," but that kind of childish infatuation was completely inappropriate to Higgins. Higgins' appreciation of Eliza actually had to be more selfish than loving.

At the height of his dilemma, Olsen left Lerner to his writing, offering to bring him a cup of tea. As she later descended the stair with the tea tray, Lerner gazed at Olsen and said, "You know, Nancy, you really are a very pretty girl." Olsen was rather nonplused by his remark, but Lerner explained, "I wake up with you every morning, I see you every day, I've grown accustomed to you. I've grown accustomed to your face."

medium

Collection of Craig T. Hyland. © CBS, Inc.

The elegant choreography of the Embassy Ball.

Seizing inspiration firmly by the throat, Lerner picked up legal pad and pencil, and began writing the love song for a cynic, "I've Grown Accustomed to Your Face."

■

Q: Who put the "dance" in "I Could Have Danced All Night"?

A: Hermes Pan was the choreographer of *My Fair Lady*. Born in Nashville, Tennessee, in 1910, Pan was a respected film choreographer for more than thirty years. He is especially well-known for his collaborations with Fred Astaire on *Flying Down to Rio* (1933), *The Gay Divorcee* (1934), *Roberta*, *Top Hat* (for which he was nominated for an Oscar, 1935), *Follow the Fleet*, *Swing Time* (another Dance Direction Oscar nomination, 1936), *A Damsel in Distress* (for which he won the Dance Direction Oscar), *Shall We Dance* (1937), and *Carefree* (1938).

Pan was also a favorite of Betty Grable, working with the pin-up girl on *Moon Over Miami* (1941), *Footlight Serenade*, *Song of the Islands*, *Springtime in the Rockies* (1942), *Coney Island*, *Sweet Rosie O'Grady* (1943), *Pin Up Girl* (1944), and *Diamond Horseshoe* (a.k.a. *Billy Rose's Diamond Horseshoe*, 1945).

Other films from what might be called Pan's Prolific Period include *Rise and Shine*, *Sun Valley Serenade*, *That Night in Rio*, *Week-end in Havana* (1941), *My Gal Sal* (1942), *Irish Eyes Are Smiling* (1944), *Blue Skies* (1946), *I Wonder Who's Kissing Her Now* (1947), and *That Lady in Ermine* (1948).

Pan came to MGM in 1949 for *The Barkleys of Broadway*, which reunited him with Fred Astaire and Ginger Rogers. Other MGM musicals he choreographed included *Three Little Words* (1950), *Kiss Me Kate* (1953), *The Student Prince* (1954), and *Hit the Deck* (1955).

For the rest of his career, Pan worked mainly on film adaptations of Broadway musicals, including *Pal Joey*, *Silk Stockings* (1957), *Porgy and Bess* (1959), *Can-Can* (1960), *Flower Drum Song* (1961), *My Fair Lady*, and *Finian's Rainbow* (1968). Pan also served as dance director for *Cleopatra* (1963) and *Darling Lili* (1970)

Pan's last film work was the bizarre choreography for the equally bizarre Ross Hunter musical version of *Lost Horizon* (1973). In 1980, Pan was presented with a National Film Award for Achievement in Cinema. The Joffrey ballet presented him with a special award in 1986. Pan died in 1990.

■

Q: How many Academy Awards did *My Fair Lady* win?

A: *My Fair Lady* took eight Academy Awards in 1964, including:

Best Picture: Other nominees were *Becket*, *Dr. Strangelove or: How I Learned to Stop Worrying and Love the Bomb*, *Mary Poppins*, and *Zorba the Greek*.

Best Actor: Rex Harrison. Other nominees were *Becket* (Richard Burton), *Zorba the Greek* (Anthony Quinn), *Becket* (Peter O'Toole), and *Dr. Strangelove* (Peter Sellers).

Best Director: George Cukor. Other nominees were *Zorba the Greek* (Michael Cacoyannis), *Becket* (Peter Glenville), *Dr. Strangelove* (Stanley Kubrick), and *Mary Poppins* (Robert Stevenson).

Art Direction/Set Decoration (Color): Cecil Beaton, Gene Allen, Art Direction; George James Hopkins, Set Decoration. Other nominees were *Becket* (John Bryan, Maurice Carter, Art Direction; Patrick McLoughlin, Robert Cartwright, Set Decoration); *Mary Poppins* (Carroll Clark, William H. Tuntke, Art Direction; Emile Kuri, Hal Gausman, Set Decoration); *The Unsinkable Molly Brown* (George W. Davis, Preston Ames, Art Direction; Henry Grace, Hugh Hunt, Set Decoration); and *What a Way to Go!* (Jack Martin Smith, Ted Haworth, Art Direction;

Walter M. Scott, Stuart A. Reiss, Set Decoration).

Cinematography (Color): Harry Stradling. (Stradling had also photographed the 1938 film version of *Pymalion*!) Other nominees were *Becket* (Geoffrey Unsworth), *Cheyenne Autumn* (William H. Clothier), *Mary Poppins* (Edward Colman), and *The Unsinkable Molly Brown* (Daniel L. Fapp).

Costume Design (Color): Cecil Beaton. Other nominees were *Becket* (Margaret Furse), *Mary Poppins* (Tony Walton), *The Unsinkable Molly Brown* (Morton Haack), and *What a Way to Go!* (Edith Head and Moss Mabry).

Sound: George R. Groves, Warner Bros. Studio Sound Department. Other nominees were *Becket* (John Cox, Shepperton Studio Sound Department), *Father Goose* (Waldon O. Watson, Universal City Studio Sound Department), *Mary Poppins* (Robert O. Cook, Walt Disney Studio Sound Department), and *The Unsinkable Molly Brown* (Franklin E. Milton, Metro-Goldwyn-Mayer Studio Sound Department).

Music Scoring Awards (Scoring of Music Adaptation or Treatment): Andre Previn. Other nominees were *A Hard Day's Night* (George Martin), *Mary Poppins* (Irwin Kostal), *Robin and the 7 Hoods* (Nelson Riddle), and *The Unsinkable Molly Brown* (Robert Armbruster, Leo Arnaud, Jack Elliott, Jack Hayes, Calvin Jackson, Leo Shuken).

Nominations *My Fair Lady* didn't win were:

Best Supporting Actor: *My Fair Lady* (Stanley Holloway), *Becket* (John Gielgud), *Seven Days in May* (Edmond O'Brien), *The Best Man* (Lee Tracy), and *Topkapi* (the winner, Peter Ustinov).

Best Supporting Actress: *My Fair Lady* (Gladys Cooper), *The Chalk Garden* (Edith Evans), *The Night of the Iguana* (Grayson Hall), *Zorba the Greek* (the winner, Lila Kedrova), and *Hush… Hush, Sweet Charlotte* (Agnes Moorehead).

Writing (Best Screenplay based on Material from Another Medium): *My Fair Lady* (Alan Jay Lerner), *Becket* (the winner, Edward Anhalt), *Dr. Strangelove* (Stanley Kubrick, Peter George, Terry Southern), *Mary Poppins* (Bill Walsh & Don DaGradi), and *Zorba the Greek* (Michael Cacoyannis).

Film Editing: *My Fair Lady* (William Ziegler), *Becket* (Anne V. Coates), *Father Goose* (Ted J. Kent), *Hush…Hush, Sweet Charlotte* (Michael Luciano), and *Mary Poppins* (the winner, Cotton Warburton).

Level Three: No Easy Stuff
Minutia & Obscuria

Q: Who first attempted to musicalize *Pygmalion*?

A: The owner of the rights to *Pygmalion*, Gabriel Pascal, suggested to Lawrence Langner of the Theatre Guild that they produce a musical version of the Shaw play. Pascal had obtained the rights from the Shaw estate, and the Guild had successfully adapted two shows, *Green Grow the Lilacs* and *Liliom*, into the musicals *Oklahoma!* and *Carousel*.

The composers who had adapted those plays were approached first about creating a musical version of *Pygmalion*. Richard Rodgers and Oscar Hammerstein II determined that such an adaptation was impossible. "It can't be done," Hammerstein told Alan Jay Lerner, "Dick and I worked on it for a year and gave it up."

Gabriel Pascal died in 1954, and Alan Jay Lerner and Frederick Loewe secured the rights to work on a musical *Pygmalion* from both the Pascal and Shaw estates.

■

Q: How much did Warner Bros. pay for the film rights to *My Fair Lady*?

A: It was announced on February 6, 1962, that Warner Bros. had secured the motion picture rights to *My Fair Lady* for the staggering sum of $5,500,000. The production itself was budgeted at a further $12,084,000. It was the highest amount paid to that time for the movie rights to a Broadway show.

And these rights were only temporary—they contractually reverted to the owner, CBS (CBS had financed the Broadway show) after only ten years, in 1972.

■

Q: Which director was originally considered by Jack Warner for *My Fair Lady*?

A: According to his 1978 autobiography, *Movie Stars, Real People and Me*, Joshua Logan was initially approached by Warner to direct the film.

Logan was a famed director of Broadway successes like *By Jupiter* (1942), *Annie Get Your Gun* (1946), *Mister Roberts* (1948), *South Pacific* (1949), *Picnic* (1953), and *Fanny* (1954); and hit films like *Picnic*, *Bus Stop* (1956), *Sayonara* (1957), *South Pacific* (1958), and *Fanny* (1961).

According to Logan, "He was crazy for me to direct *My Fair Lady* until I said, 'Sure, Jack, I'll do it, but I do hope we can shoot some of it in England.' I never heard from Jack Warner again, and before I knew it George Cukor was doing the picture—on the back lot."

Ironically, when Logan directed *Camelot* for Warner in 1967, he contributed much to its visual richness by shooting location footage at Castle Coca and Castle Alcazar in Spain. Warner agreed grudgingly to what he considered an unnecessary extravagance, because it enabled production of *Camelot* to commence before the end of the fiscal year, saving Warner Bros. millions of dollars.

■

Q: Who was originally offered the role of Henry Higgins?

A: Although there is a revisionism that would have us believe that the part was developed especially for Rex Harrison, initial casting ideas for the stage were Noël Coward, Michael Redgrave, George Sanders, and John Gielgud. It is believed that Coward suggested Rex Harrison for the role.

Jack L. Warner was rumored to want Cary Grant as Henry Higgins and James Cagney as Alfred Doolittle in the film version. A well-known story tells of Grant responding to Warner that not only would he not *play* Henry Higgins, but if

Rex Harrison didn't play the professor, Grant wouldn't even *see* the film.

Luckily for posterity, Rex Harrison and Stanley Holloway were allowed to reprise their Broadway roles in the film.

■

Q: A film and television technology we take for granted today got a trial run on *My Fair Lady*. What was it?

A: Rex Harrison recorded his musical numbers "live" on-set, using a prototype wireless microphone.

Typically in musicals, songs are pre-recorded, and the actors "sing along" on camera—they don't just move their lips, they have to sing in synch to make it look real.

Army Archerd reported in *Variety* on September 16, 1963, that Rex Harrison had refused to lip-synch to playback, claiming that he had "never sung any one of the songs the same." For the first time, Warner Bros. sound department rigged a wireless microphone in his cravat.

The other actors who sing in the film used the "pre-record and playback" method, or were synching to someone else's vocals. In one case, "Wouldn't It Be Lovely," Audrey Hepburn had actually recorded and synched to her own vocals, and Marni Nixon came in *after* the fact and looped a new voice track!

Collection of Craig T. Hyland. © CBS, Inc.

Rex Harrison is singing "live" in "The Rain in Spain."

hard

Q: The credits list a Technical Advisor named Peter Ladefoged. Who was he? What did he do?

A: Peter Ladefoged was an associate professor of English at the University of California at Los Angeles. He worked with the *My Fair Lady* company over the course of pre-production and production. Among his tasks as dialogue coach and phonetics consultant, Ladefoged helped rough up Audrey Hepburn's Cockney speech for the film. Ladefoged even advised on (and helped secure) the various set dressings and props that fill Higgins' house: phonics charts and machines, dimensional models, and recording devices.

■

Q: A near-disaster involving *My Fair Lady* occurred in 1994. What was this disaster?

A: The physical condition of the remaining prints of *My Fair Lady* was so poor that the complete loss of the film was imminent. CBS Video had planned a Thirtieth Anniversary Edition of *My Fair Lady*, but during the process of remastering, it was discovered that more than one-third of the original camera negative was missing. What remained was in several thousand cans, many unlabeled, in a half-dozen locations. Most of these cans were in piles on film vault floors as a result of the January 1994 Northridge earthquake. Pieces of the film were scratched, torn, or dirty; some had disintegrated.

Ken Ross of CBS Video ordered a full-scale restoration, a meticulous frame-by-frame process. Ross called in Bob Harris and Jim Katz, who had gained notoriety for their acclaimed restorations of *Lawrence of Arabia* and *Spartacus*.

So many prints had been struck for the initial release of *My Fair Lady* that the negative had suffered unusual wear. Much of it fell apart as it was removed from cans. The color separations had suffered differential shrinkage, and could not be used to restore many scenes.

Harris and Katz were able to use the latest computerized digital technology to effect several repairs to original flaws, as well as to color correct the finished output to stable Technicolor dye transfer samples. The restoration team also had the input of Gene Allen, the film's art director, and John Burnett, an assistant film editor, both of whom were very familiar with *My Fair Lady*.

There were myriad audio problems. The original music tracks had not survived. The only tracks available were heavily worn. Due to the manner in which they were recorded, Rex Harrison's song vocals had a brittle, tinny quality that was more harsh than the other tracks in the film. The team was able to re-mix and upgrade the soundtrack through state-of-the-art digital recording and Dolby™ Stereo technology. They were even able to solidify the originally flawed Harrison audio track to match the aural quality of the rest of the film.

The restoration of *My Fair Lady* took eight months and cost $750,000.

■

Q: One song in the *My Fair Lady* score is not by Lerner and Loewe. Which one?

A: "Glorious Beer," by Steve Leggett and Wil Godwin. Legal clearance of the drinking song that Alfred Doolittle spontaneously sings (early in the film, after he has secured the funds for a little "liquid protection" from his noble daughter, Eliza) was entrusted to the music department at Warner Bros. The international rights, for use of not more than sixteen bars of "Glorious Beer," were secured from the copyright owner, Harms Music Incorporated, for $750.

■

Q: The lyricist/librettist of *My Fair Lady* was about to begin a new collaboration at the time of his death. With whom? On what project?

A: According to composer Andrew Lloyd Webber, Alan Jay Lerner had agreed to collaborate with him on *The Phantom of the Opera*. They had discussed working on the opulent "Masquerade" number, but had gotten no further when Lerner became ill in 1986.

It's a pity this collaboration didn't happen, since Lerner's literate and witty touch could certainly have outshone the pedantic efforts of *Phantom* lyricist Charles Hart. With Alan Jay Lerner as lyricist, *Phantom* might have been a musical better remembered for its music than its scenery.

■

Q: **A song written for, but deleted from, the Broadway musical *My Fair Lady* appeared in a 1958 motion picture. What was the song? What was the motion picture?**

A: "Say a Prayer for Me Tonight" was written to be sung by Eliza to Mrs. Pearce and the house staff as she gets ready for the ball. It was to have been preceded by "Come to the Ball," a number in which Higgins tries to cheer the melancholy Eliza after the disaster at Ascot. Instead, the entire section was deleted and a brief linking scene took the action more or less directly from Ascot to the evening of the ball.

"Say a Prayer for Me Tonight" was incorporated by Lerner and Loewe into the film *Gigi*. In a similar dramatic moment, before she is set to debut as a courtesan on the arm of Gaston at Maxim's, the nervous Gigi sings the song…to her cat.

■

Q: **Within the first three scenes of *My Fair Lady*, fastidious linguist Henry Higgins makes two glaring grammatical errors. What are they?**

A: British critic Kenneth Tynan noted the following two gaffes, the first in Act One, Scene

One, the second in Act One, Scene Three:

> By right she should be taken out and *hung*
> For the cold-blooded murder of the English
> tongue!

Shaw would have *hanged* Higgins for that, as for—

> I'd be *equally* as willing
> For a dentist to be drilling
> *Than* to ever let a woman in my life!

—it is quite an achievement to make Higgins, the defender of pure English, commit two syntactical crimes (compounded by a split infinitive) within the space of three lines.

Courtesy of Fox Video. © CBS, Inc.

Stanley Holloway will soon sing the only song in *My Fair Lady* not written by Lerner and Loewe.

Warner Bros. Pictures presents

MY FAIR LADY

Produced by Jack L. Warner. Directed by George Cukor

Screenplay by Alan Jay Lerner

Based upon the musical play as produced on the stage by Herman Levin
Book and Lyrics by Alan Jay Lerner, Music by Frederick Loewe

From a play by Bernard Shaw

Director of Photography Harry Stradling, ASC. Camera Operator Wally Meinardus
Assistant Cameraman Roger Shearman. Color Technician Chris Schweibert

Costumes, Scenery, and Production Designed by Cecil Beaton. Art Director Gene Allen

Film Editor William Zeigler. Assistant Film Editor John Burnett
Sound by Francis J. Scheid and Murray Spivak

Lyrics by Alan Jay Lerner. Music by Frederick Loewe. Music Supervised and Conducted by Andre Previn
Additional Music by Frederick Loewe. Vocal Arrangements by Robt. Tucker. Orchestrations by Alexander
Courage, Robert Franklin, Al Woodbury. Music Cutter Hal Finley. Pianist Bobby Tucker

Choreography by Hermes Pan. Dance Assistants Frank Radcliff, Becky Vorno

Unit Manager Sergei Petschnikoff. Set Decorator George James Hopkins. Sketch Artist Ed Graves

Makeup Supervisor Gordon Bau, SMA. Makeup Artists Newt Jones, Frank McCoy
Supervising Hair Stylist Jean Burt Reilly, CHS. Hairdresser Geraldine Cole

Men's Costumer Bob Richards. Women's Costumer Anne Laune

Assistant Directors David Hall, Jack Stubbs, Mecca Graham, Dick Landry

Script Supervisor Isabelle Blodgett

Construction Coordinator Robert Irving. Assistant Construction Coordinator Eleanor Abbey

Effects Wally Honn. Boom Man Ora Hudson.

Cable Man Bernt G. Sad. Gaffer Frank Flanagan. Best Boy Everett Miller. Key Grip Charles Harris
Best Boy Glen Harris. Standby Painter Howard Teasley. Propmaster Robey Cooper
Assistant Propmaster Dick Scheerer. Craft Service Sol Litt

Unit Publicist Carl Combs. Still Camera Mel Traxel

Technical Advisor Peter Ladefoged. Production Secretary Irene Burns

Technicolor®. Super Panavision 70®. Running time 151 minutes

Released by Warner Bros. Pictures, 1964. Rights reverted to CBS, 1972
Re-released by Twentieth Century-Fox Film Corporation and CBS Video, September 1994

Cast

Audrey Hepburn	Eliza Doolittle
Rex Harrison	Henry Higgins
Stanley Holloway	Alfred P. Doolittle
Wilfrid Hyde-White	Colonel Pickering
Gladys Cooper	Mrs. Higgins
Jeremy Brett	Freddie Eynsford-Hill
Theodore Bikel	Zoltan Karpathy
Mona Washbourne	Mrs. Pearce
Isobel Elsom	Mrs. Eynsford-Hill
John Alderson	Harry
John McLiam	Jamie
John Holland	Butler
Roy Dean	Footman
Diane Rogers, Lois Battle, Jaqueline Squire	Maids
Gwen Watts	Cook

Mary Poppins

Mary Poppins is the quintessential Walt Disney fantasy. It incorporates all of Disney's strengths as a filmmaker and showman, and avoids the weaknesses and pitfalls of his other products. It is a charming and believable fantasy that avoids silliness. Effecting that credibility is a cast that is a refreshing mix of new talent and old pros. It is a melodic musical with songs that are memorable without being cloying. Importantly, it is produced with the refinement and style of a Broadway musical, and never reveals the decidedly Midwestern tastes of its creative leader. Finally, Mary Poppins has something to say. When the dancing penguins are gone and Mary Poppins has sailed away on the West Wind, the film has left a resonant statement about love, loyalty, and family that belies the fun and fancy of its whimsical presentation. Mary Poppins is the exceptional musical fantasy that is, even decades later and on repeated viewings, "practically perfect in every way."

■

Level One: The Easy Stuff
Story & Characters

Q: What is the address of the Banks' home?

A: Number 17, Cherry Tree Lane. Cherry Tree Lane is described in the book, *Mary Poppins*, as a street "where the houses run down one side and the park runs down the other and the cherry-trees go dancing right down the middle." The description was interpreted fairly literally at The Walt Disney Studio in Burbank, where the Cherry Tree Lane set occupied all of Stage 4, one of the largest sound stages in Hollywood.

Built in 1957–58, the thirty-thousand-square-foot Stage 4 had been used most prominently for the shooting of the complicated optical illusions of *Darby O'Gill and the Little People* (1958). Because its complicated lighting created a tremendous power demand, *Darby O'Gill* caused an electrical blackout in Burbank during its filming. Stage 4 was converted into two television stages (Stages 4 and 5) in 1990 for the short-lived Carol Burnett comedy anthology "Carol & Co." Later, Stage 4 became home to the long-running hit situation comedy "Home Improvement," starring Tim Allen.

In 1963–64, there were only four sound stages on the Disney lot, all of which were used during the filming of *Mary Poppins*. The Walt Disney Studio was built as a facility for making animated cartoons a full decade before Walt Disney would produce his first live-action feature.

■

Q: Bert senses Mary Poppins' arrival by the wind direction. Which direction?

A: "Wind's in the East...mist comin' in. Like somethin' is brewin', about to begin..." This eerie introspection interrupts Bert's comical poems and one-man-band performance. It establishes his near-psychic link with Mary Poppins and sets a mood of the unexpected within the first few scenes of the picture.

In the book *Mary Poppins*, as in the film, Mary stays until the wind changes. The book's first chapter is titled "East Wind"; its last chapter is "West Wind."

The refinement of the Bert character had a unique unifying effect on the story line of *Mary Poppins*. In a way it implied Mary's "past," grounding her in reality, and it also provided a mortal balance (and accomplice) to Mary's magic.

■

Mary Poppins arrives at the home of the Banks family.

Q: **What is Admiral Boom famous for?**

A: "Punc-tu-ality," Bert tells us. "The 'ole world takes its time from Greenwich. But Greenwich, they say, takes its time from Admiral Boom!"

The Admiral was played by venerable British-born character actor Reginald Owen, who had made his stage debut in 1905. He came to Hollywood in 1929, and began a film career that lasted until his death in 1972. One of his last films was Disney's *Bedknobs and Broomsticks* (1971).

The Admiral's "ship-shape" house ("the grandest house in the Lane," according to the book) was built for the film almost entirely of special effects, opticals, and matte paintings. The physical set on which Boom and Mr. Binnacle (Don Barclay) perform was pretty much just railing, a ship's wheel, and a few nautical props in front of an effects screen. If you pay close attention, you'll notice that even the cannon full of flares and rockets that Boom fires at the chimney sweeps (twice) is a painting.

Q: **Who "gets stuck with the children with no nanny in the 'ouse!"?**

A: Ellen, the maid, played by Hermione Baddeley. Born in 1906 and in pictures since 1928, Baddeley's roles include Mrs. Cratchit in the Alistair Sim version of Dickens' *A Christmas Carol* (known in Great Britain under the title *Scrooge*, 1950). She was Academy Award-nominated for her supporting role in *Room at the Top* (1959).

Baddeley is best remembered by modern audiences for her prolific work in films and television the 1960s and '70s, including roles as loyal domestics in Disney's *The Happiest Millionaire* and *The Adventures of Bullwhip Griffin* (1967), and was the voice of the wealthy Madam Bonfamille in *The Aristocats* (1970). She also played Buttercup Grogan in *The Unsinkable Molly Brown* (1964) and is probably best remembered as Mrs. Naugatuck in the Beatrice Arthur TV series "Maude." Hermione Baddeley died in 1986.

Q: What year does the action of the film take place?

A: Mr. Banks boasts "It's grand to be an Englishman in 1910, King Edward's on the throne—it's the age of men."

The original book, *Mary Poppins*, was published in 1934, and its tales were contemporary. In initially seeking the story structure for the film, the original creative team that Walt Disney had assigned to *Mary Poppins* switched the time frame of the story repeatedly. Co-composer Richard Sherman recalls: "We had to have a reason for Mary Poppins coming. I remember it was something like the father had gone off to [World War I] and there was nobody to be master of the house. We thought 1914 might be more colorful than the 1930s. Then we said, okay, it's the Boer War, the father went off in 1903. But basically we wanted the father to be removed and would come back at the end so Mary Poppins could fly away. Walt never bought that story, but he loved that

we'd come up with a story idea."

Ultimately, the Sherman Brothers discovered one of the keys to the emotional core of the film—a father doesn't have to be gone to be absent from the lives of his family. This provides one of the film's finest moments—Bert gently confronting Banks with that fact. It provides Dick Van Dyke with another level of a broad-ranging performance, and the best dramatic moment in the picture. But it's not all Van Dyke's work. It has been said that the finest actors are those who can react. Watch David Tomlinson during this scene.

■

Q: After tidying the nursery, Mary Poppins takes the children on an outing. Where do they go? Who do they meet there?

A: To the park, where they meet Bert. Bert was initially developed as three separate characters: Robertson Ay, the handyman; Bert the Match-Man and pavement artist; and a chimney sweep character from another of the "Poppins" books suggested by Don DaGradi. After the Sherman Brothers offered up "Chim Chim Cher-ee" in response to DaGradi's sketch of the sweep, Walt Disney suggested combining the three characters into a strong male counterpart for Mary Poppins. With his jack-of-all-trades characteristics and intriguing dialogue with Mary, Bert clearly became a mortal accomplice for Mary's outright magic.

Dick Van Dyke, who played Bert, was at the height of his success when *Mary Poppins* was filmed. His CBS-TV series was in its third of five seasons of huge popularity, and *Poppins* seemed to signal an easy ascent to the big screen. Van Dyke made several other films, none of which achieved the success of *Poppins*, thus eerily validating his own words at the *Poppins* premiere: "Well, it's my third motion picture [the first two were *Bye Bye Birdie* (1963) and *What a Way to Go* (1964)], but the best one I've ever been in, the best one I ever

Hermione Baddeley as Ellen, the Cockney maid.

will be in if I live to be 150 years old."

Van Dyke's most famous post-*Poppins* role is probably *Chitty Chitty Bang Bang* (1968). It is often mistaken for a Disney film, due to its fantasy subject matter, with Van Dyke starring, a Sherman Brothers score supervised and conducted by Irwin Kostal, and musical numbers staged by Marc Breaux and Dee Dee Wood.

Van Dyke has done some woefully under appreciated dramatic turns, particularly in *The Comic* (1969), *The Runner Stumbles* (1979), and a disquietingly self-effacing performance as a degenerating chronic alcoholic in the TV movie *The Morning After* (1974). His lynch-pin role as the corrupt mayor in *Dick Tracy* (1990) is also unjustly brushed aside as little more than a cameo. Van Dyke began his fourth television effort at the age of sixty-eight in 1993, a succession of "mystery movies" for CBS-TV that became the series "Diagnosis: Murder."

In a 1990 interview with the *Los Angeles Times*, Van Dyke's humility is apparent: "I never expected what happened to me. I thought I'd be lucky to be a game show host. But I met three people who changed my life: Gower Champion, Carl Reiner, and Walt Disney. And it's been terrific."

■

Q: How does the adventure in the chalk pavement picture end?

A: Rain washes away the pictures. "Oh, Bert! All your fine drawings!" Mary Poppins laments, as the backgrounds they've been standing in dissolve.

This effect bookends perfectly with the group's leap *into* the chalk picture, which produced a multi-colored cloud of dust. They continue to pat the dust from their clothes during their first moments in the chalk picture, and Mary admonishes the children, "Don't fall and smudge the drawing."

Mary Poppins is a triumph of such visual literacy, achieving as much of its mood and message from what is *seen* as from what is *spoken*. Particularly effective is the famous and oft-mentioned "Jolly Holiday" sequence, but far more subtle and just as emotionally affecting are Mr. Banks' lonely, introspective, nighttime walk to his fateful meeting with the bank board of directors, and the poetic visuals of the "Feed the Birds (Tuppence a Bag)" sequence. Both of these sequences were achieved with little more than visual suggestion—minimal sets, careful angles, matte paintings, and optical effects.

■

Q: What does Michael want to do with the tuppence intended for his savings account?

A: Michael wants to feed the birds, having been made aware of the Bird Woman the previous night by Mary Poppins.

The role of the Bird Woman, although minor, is unforgettable due to one of the great strengths of *Mary Poppins*—its casting. Co-composer Richard Sherman explains:

> Jane Darwell had been retired for twenty years by that time, and…one day in a discussion, Walt said 'I know the perfect person, and I think what we should do is, really—send her a script and treat her as…the star she should be treated as.' And they sent a script to Jane Darwell at the actors' home. She cried, she was so thrilled, and of course they sent [a car] for her and—it was just wonderful, she was on that set, and she didn't have much to do except be herself… but it seems to have encapsulated what we were trying to do in *Mary Poppins*. That is to say that it doesn't take very much to give that extra dimension, to give that extra love, and 'tuppence' signifies 'little, hardly anything,' and feeding the birds means giving to the people that *need*. And in this particular case it was the Banks children, they needed their father and mother's attention, their love. They didn't just have to be provided for, they had to be loved and paid attention to.

The haunting ballad, "Feed the Birds (Tuppence a Bag)" was one of the first songs written for *Mary Poppins*, and is well known as Walt Disney's personal favorite song. His unique and loving relationship with his songwriting team finds its voice in this lovely song, as the Sherman brothers describe:

RICHARD: The one song in *Mary Poppins* that became most near and dear to our hearts was "Feed the Birds (Tuppence a Bag)." It was one of the first songs we wrote, and it was directly inspired out of one of the stories that Mrs. Travers created…

ROBERT: Fridays, after work, [Walt would] usually invite us into his office…

RICHARD: We'd talk about things that were going on at the Studio…

ROBERT: You know, worldly matters. And then he'd look over to Dick and he'd say, "Play it."

RICHARD: Yeah. And I knew what he wanted, and sometimes he wouldn't even say anything, he'd just look out the window, and get a little misty-eyed, and we'd play it. It was just wonderful, 'cause sometimes he could say so much, just by a look, or by a silence, and we knew what he was saying. After Walt passed away, there [was] many a Friday afternoon that I'd go over to his office, while the office was still his, and there, and play it for him.

Jane Darwell had won the Academy Award for her performance as Ma Joad in *The Grapes of*

Wrath (1940). She was eighty-four when she worked on *Mary Poppins*, and had one line: "Feed the birds—tuppence a bag." She died in 1967.

■

Q: Who does the Banks family meet while kite-flying in the park?

A: The Board of Directors of the bank, including Mr. Dawes, Junior—all flying kites, too.

The finale was based on the personal childhood experiences of composers Richard and Robert Sherman, whose father (songwriter Al Sherman) was, according to the reports of his sons, a fantastic kite-maker. The portrayal of the bank's board engaged in trivialities (both in this scene and their choreography during the "Fidelity Fiduciary Bank" number) serves as an satire of and antidote to their pomposity and their perceived importance to Mr. Banks.

■

Q: What finally happens to the elder Mr. Dawes? What does this mean to George Banks?

A: "Father died laughing," Mr. Dawes, Junior tells Banks, in one of the picture's more startling jokes. Dawes continues, "He left an opening for a new partner. Congratulations," he concludes, pinning his own carnation on Banks' lapel.

Thus, as Mary departs, all has been resolved—and yet all seems naturally cyclical. A rather amazing storytelling feat, considering the anecdotal, somewhat disjointed source book.

Author's Collection. © The Walt Disney Company

Jane Darwell in her last film role, as the Bird Woman of St. Paul's Cathedral.

Level Two: Not So Easy

The Actors, Artists, & Others

Q: The credits of *Mary Poppins* contain some intriguing items. For instance, P. L. Travers is listed as "Consultant." Who is Travers? Tony Walton is listed as "Costumes and Design Consultant." What was Walton's relationship to the production?

A: P. L. Travers is Pamela Travers (b. 1906), author of the several "Poppins" books among others. The association between Disney and Travers on the *Mary Poppins* project was difficult at best. Walt's brother Roy Disney had first approached Pamela Travers about *Mary Poppins* in 1944, when she was living in New York to avoid the London Blitz. Walt later called on her in London in the 1950s, where Travers and Disney got along well. Travers was taken with Walt's charismatic personality, but another decade would pass before Travers gave serious thought to Walt's pleas for the rights to the book. One of her terms was that she be made "consultant" to any resulting film of *Poppins*. The fact that Walt agreed shows his eagerness to pursue the project.

Travers' well-reported contrary and proprietary attitude during and after the *Poppins* project makes one wonder why she ever sold her creation to Walt to begin with.

"She complained that we chose her worst chapters to use in the film," says co-composer Robert Sherman. "Then she started suggesting the chapters *she* thought we should use—and they were the ones that we thought were abominable!"

Concessions to Mrs. Travers were made during the course of development, but after the film was completed, Disney biographer Bob Thomas records that Mrs. Travers approached Walt with further complaints about the finished film. "Miss Andrews is satisfactory as Mary Poppins, but Mr. Van Dyke is all wrong, and I don't really like mixing the little cartoon figures with the live actors. When do we start cutting it?"

In 1981, Travers revised the original *Mary Poppins*, rewriting the "Around the World" sequence to eliminate racial stereotypes.

In 1988, she worked with British journalist and writer Brian Sibley on a screen treatment for a proposed sequel to *Mary Poppins*, titled *Mary Poppins Comes Back*. A revised draft script was completed in April of 1989.

Travers' most recent book is *Mary Poppins and the House Next Door* (1988).

Tony Walton created the costumes and served as an overall design consultant on the production. He had many London stage credits, and had designed the sets and costumes for the Broadway and London stage hit *A Funny Thing Happened on the Way to the Forum*. He was nominated for a Tony award for Costume Design on *The Apple Tree* (1967), and won the 1973 Tony for Scenic Design for *Pippin* (1973). Walton was again nominated for the Tony for Scenic Design for *Chicago* (1976) and *A Day in Hollywood, A Night in the*

Author's Collection. © The Walt Disney Company

Internationally-renowned children's author Pamela Travers.

Ukraine (1980). In 1995, he re-teamed with the Sherman Brothers as Production Designer on the musical *Busker Alley*.

He was also nominated for Academy Awards for his costume design on *Murder on the Orient Express* (1973), and for both Costume Design and Art Direction for *The Wiz* (1978). He won the Art Direction Oscar in 1979 for *All That Jazz*.

At the time of *Mary Poppins'* production, Walton was married to Julie Andrews.

∎

Q: What is the name of the institution where Mr. Banks is employed? What is his position? What was the occupation of Banks' father? What is Mr. Banks' middle initial?

A: Dawes, Tomes, Mousely, Grubs Fidelity Fiduciary Bank is Mr. Banks' employer. Banks tells Michael that he is "one of the junior officers." In a telephone conversation with Banks, Mr. Dawes (Junior and Senior both, actually) reminds Banks that he has "been with us a good many years, as was your father before you." When Constable Jones reports by telephone that Banks is missing, he says, "...that's right, sir. George W. Banks."

∎

Q: Karen Dotrice and Matthew Garber played Jane and Michael Banks. Name another Disney film in which they were paired (there are two).

A: Karen Dotrice played Mary MacDhui, Patrick McGoohan's daughter in *The Three Lives of Thomasina*, released in June 1964. Matthew Garber played her friend Geordie, a village lad. In 1967, the two were again paired as siblings Rodney and Elizabeth in *The Gnome-Mobile*.

Karen Dotrice continued acting, mostly in Britain; her most recognized adult role was in "Upstairs, Downstairs." Her father, Roy Dotrice, appeared in the role of Father in the television series "Beauty and the Beast."

Matthew Garber died after becoming ill on a film location in the mid-1970s.

In the book *Mary Poppins*, there were four Banks children: Jane, Michael, and infant twins John and Barbara. Since the latter two contribute little to what story there is in the book, they were excised from the film version.

∎

Q: After the adventure in the chalk pavement picture, Mary Poppins dispenses medicine to the children and herself. What flavors?

A: Michael has strawberry, Jane lime cordial, and Mary Poppins tipples rum punch ("Quite satisfactory!"), all dispensed before our eyes from the same bottle. This was one of dozens of clever visual and special effects that contribute to Mary Poppins' magic.

An interesting thing about Mary's magic is that she gives the distinct impression that she wishes others weren't watching. This backhanded approach serves to underscore the idea that everything in life is magic, including such mundane tasks as tidying the nursery. The Disney effects team relied on a variety of special effects to create Mary's offhand sorcery.

The "Spoonful of Sugar" sequence, for instance, contains stop-motion animation, camera trickery, prototype Audio-Animatronics®, and process-screen effects. The design of this sequence was supervised by Disney veterans Bill Justice and Xavier Atencio, who had overseen some of Disney's most refreshingly original work in the late fifties and early sixties. This included the stop-motion animated title sequence to *The Parent Trap* (1961) and a 1959 stop-motion short version of *Noah's Ark*.

The two later served as driving forces in the Disney theme parks. Justice was the supervising animator of most of the Audio-Animatronics figures from the mid-sixties through the early eighties. Xavier Atencio's indelible mark can be seen in the design of Pirates of the Caribbean (where he can actually be *heard* as the voice of the foreboding pirate skull—"No fear have ye o' evil curses?") and Haunted Mansion attractions. For the former, Atencio composed the song "Yo Ho (A Pirate's Life for Me)." For the latter, Atencio composed (with Buddy Baker) "Grim Grinning Ghosts."

■

Q: After the "Stay Awake" lullaby, Mary Poppins and the children embark on a series of errands. Where does Mary Poppins plan to take them? What sets those plans awry?

A: Mary and the children have a full day planned. First stop is the piano tuner—a sly reference to the previous scene where Mr. Banks winds up seated at the piano after one of Admiral Boom's house-rattling concussions.

Their second destination is Mrs. Corry's shop for some gingerbread. Mrs. Corry (Alma Lawton)

had been introduced in the opening scene with Bert ("Ah, Mrs. Corry, a story for you, your daughters were shorter than you—but they grew!). Mrs. Corry is a Travers character from one of the *Mary Poppins* chapters Disney chose not to film. In the book, Mary and the children *do* visit Mrs. Corry's shop, where they buy a baker's dozen of curious gingerbread with gilt-paper stars on them. That night, Jane and Michael see Mary, Mrs. Corry, and her daughters (Miss Annie and Miss Fannie) gluing the stars to the sky. "What I want to know," Jane asks the next day, "is this: Are the stars gold paper or is the gold paper stars?" As usual, Mary Poppins explains nothing.

The group's third stop is to be the fishmonger ("for a nice Dover sole and a pint of prawns"), also referred to in the book.

Their plans are interrupted by the dog, Andrew, introduced in the film's first scene as Miss Lark (Marjorie Bennett)'s dog, both of whom are characters from the book. Andrew tells Mary that she is needed at Uncle Albert's (although only Mary can understand what

Author's Collection. © The Walt Disney Company

Ed Wynn swings as Uncle Albert.

Andrew is saying, and, of course, does not share it with the children).

In Travers' book, Uncle Albert's full name is given as Albert Wigg. Miss Persimmon (Marjorie Eaton), who is introduced in the first scene of the film during Bert's comical poems, is Mr. Wigg's maid in the Travers book.

Ed Wynn, who played Uncle Albert, had become something of a Disney stock player in the 1960s. Born in 1886, Wynn was a vaudeville and radio star who had been the voice of The Mad Hatter in Disney's animated *Alice in Wonderland* (1950). After an initial failure in feature films, he returned to the screen in the late 1950s with strong supporting roles in *The Great Man* (1956), *Marjorie Morningstar* (1958), and *The Diary of Anne Frank* (1959). He had an in-joke appearance as the Fire Chief (his famous radio charac-

ter) in *The Absent-Minded Professor* (1961), and played the Toymaker in *Babes in Toyland* that same year. He appeared on the Disney TV series in *The Golden Horseshoe Revue* (1962), played an agricultural agent in *Son of Flubber* (1963), and appeared in Disney's *Those Calloways, That Darn Cat!* (1965), and *The Gnome-Mobile* (1967). Ed Wynn died in 1966.

Ed Wynn's son, Keenan Wynn, was also an accomplished character actor, and no stranger to Disney films. He played the corrupt Alonzo Hawk in *The Absent-Minded Professor* (1961), *Son of Flubber* (1963), and *Herbie Rides Again* (1974). Other Disney credits include *Smith!* (1969), *Snowball Express* (1974), and *The Shaggy D.A.* (1976). Keenan Wynn died in 1986.

■

Q: David Tomlinson appeared in two subsequent Disney films. Name one.

A: Tomlinson would later play the conniving Thorndyke in *The Love Bug* (1969) and charlatan magician Emelius Browne in *Bedknobs and Broomsticks* (1971).

Born in 1917, David Tomlinson's film career began in England in the forties. Generally an amiable light leading man or a pompous martinet, he appeared in British pictures like *Miranda* (1948), *Three Men in a Boat* (1955), and *Tom Jones* (1963).

■

Q: At the Bank, the children are greeted by the board, including the elder Mr. Dawes, "a giant in the world of finance." Who played the elder Mr. Dawes? Who played Mr. Dawes, Junior?

A: The credits initially list NAVCKID KEYD, which transposes into the proper credit for the role of Mr. Dawes, DICK VAN DYKE.

Legend has it that the role was originally con-

The renowned character actor Navckid Keyd as the elder Mr. Dawes, "a giant in the world of finance."

sidered for an aging character actor, but during filmed makeup and costume tests, Van Dyke began improvising comedy routines. One of them was an elderly man trying to step from the curb to the street. When Walt saw the tests in the screening room, he cast Van Dyke as Mr. Dawes, the Elder, and had a six-inch platform built outside the boardroom door set so that Van Dyke could duplicate his "old man" routine upon Dawes' entrance.

Van Dyke remembers it only slightly differently—it seems that getting his routine on film was only part of a conscious effort to convince Walt to give him the role. "The part of the old man hadn't been cast yet," Van Dyke recalled in a 1990 interview with the *Los Angeles Times*, "and I went in to Disney and asked to do it. Disney was an old horse trader. He made me give four thousand dollars to [California Institute of the Arts in Valencia]."

Mr. Dawes, Junior, is played by Arthur Malet, a fine character actor who has played old men since he was in his thirties, including an appearance on "The Dick Van Dyke Show," where his character was seventy-five. He was the hotel handyman who sawed off the bathtub faucet that Laura Petrie's toe was stuck in.

■

Q: *Mary Poppins* **was nominated for a number of Academy Awards. How many? In what categories? How many Oscars did** *Mary Poppins* **claim?**

A: *Poppins* was nominated for Academy Awards in thirteen categories in 1964, winning in five:

Best Picture, along with *Becket*, *Dr. Strangelove or: How I Learned to Stop Worrying and Love the Bomb*, *My Fair Lady* (q.v., which won), and *Zorba the Greek*.

Julie Andrews was named **Best Actress**, beating out Anne Bancroft in *The Pumpkin Eater*, Sophia Loren in *Marriage, Italian Style*, Debbie Reynolds in *The Unsinkable Molly Brown*, and

Kim Stanley in *Seance on a Wet Afternoon*.

Best Director nominees were Michael Cacoyannis for *Zorba the Greek*, George Cukor for *My Fair Lady* (the winner), Peter Glenville for *Becket*, Stanley Kubrick for *Dr. Strangelove*, and Robert Stevenson for *Mary Poppins*.

Best Screenplay (based on material from another medium) nominees were *Becket* (the winner), *Dr. Strangelove*, *Mary Poppins*, *My Fair Lady*, and *Zorba the Greek*.

Best Cinematography (color) nominees were *Becket*, *Cheyenne Autumn*, *Mary Poppins*, *My Fair Lady* (which won), and *The Unsinkable Molly Brown*.

Best Art Direction (color) nominees were *Becket*, *Mary Poppins*, *My Fair Lady* (which won), *The Unsinkable Molly Brown*, and *What a Way to Go* (which featured Dick Van Dyke).

Best Sound nominees were *Becket*, *Father Goose*, *Mary Poppins*, *My Fair Lady* (which won), and *The Unsinkable Molly Brown*.

Cotton Warburton's work on *Mary Poppins* won him the **Best Film Editing** Oscar. Other nominees were *Becket*, *Father Goose*, *Hush...Hush Sweet Charlotte*, and *My Fair Lady*.

It would be almost impossible to imagine that Richard M. Sherman and Robert B. Sherman's work would *not* win **Best Music Score** (substantially original). It won over *Becket* and *The Fall of the Roman Empire* (neither of which brings a hummable tune to my mind), as well as *Hush...Hush Sweet Charlotte* and *The Pink Panther* (both of which do).

Best Scoring of Music (adaptation or treatment) nominees were *A Hard Day's Night*, *Mary Poppins*, *My Fair Lady* (the winner), *Robin and the 7 Hoods*, and *The Unsinkable Molly Brown*.

Best Song winner was "Chim Chim Cher-ee," which was up against formidable competition from some soon-to-be standards, "Dear Heart" from *Dear Heart*, "Hush...Hush, Sweet Charlotte" from *Hush...Hush, Sweet Charlotte*, "My Kind of Town" from *Robin and the 7 Hoods*, and "Where Love Has Gone" from *Where Love Has Gone*.

Best Costume Design (color) nominees were *Becket*, *Mary Poppins*, *My Fair Lady* (the winner), *The Unsinkable Molly Brown*, and *What a Way to Go*.

Finally, *Mary Poppins* won a well-deserved Oscar for **Best Special Visual Effects** over *7 Faces of Dr. Lao*.

A sixth Oscar was won by the *Mary Poppins* team, a Scientific/Technical award to Peter Vlahos, Wadsworth Pohl, and Ub Iwerks, for "conception and perfection of techniques of color traveling matte composite cinematography."

All this makes you wonder what might have happened if *My Fair Lady* had been released in the next Academy Awards qualifying year…

■

Q: The next year's (1965) Academy Award-winning Best Picture would feature the talents of three *Mary Poppins* alumni. Who were they? What was the picture?

A: Julie Andrews would play spunky Maria Von Trapp in *The Sound of Music*, Best Picture of 1965. The music was arranged and conducted by Irwin Kostal, with choreography by Marc Breaux and Dee Dee Wood.

These were the major crossovers, although there were certainly others who worked on both of these classic pictures, including Larri Thomas, who was Julie Andrews' stand-in on both.

■

Q: Robert Stevenson was no stranger to magic-laden Disney effects films. Name two of his pre-*Poppins* Disney pictures (there are eight).

A: Robert Stevenson was a British director who had been in Hollywood since 1939. His first work

for Disney was *Johnny Tremain* (1957), which featured a pre-*West Side Story* Richard Beymer. *Old Yeller* (1957) followed, and *Darby O'Gill and the Little People* (1959) put Stevenson in close collaboration with Don DaGradi, who would feature in the development of many of Stevenson's Disney pictures. *Kidnapped* (1960), *The Absent-Minded Professor* (1961), *In Search of the Castaways* (1962), *Son of Flubber* (1963), and *The Misadventures of Merlin Jones* (1964) preceded Stevenson's Oscar-nominated work on *Mary Poppins*.

Don DaGradi was a pivotal story development man at Disney, who worked in the early stages of many projects that involved director Stevenson. His visual planning of a picture extended beyond simple sequence, into character development and even camera angles. Richard Sherman explains:

> 85 to 90 percent of the dialogue in the picture was Bill Walsh, but what you *saw* on screen, those wonderful *things* that happened—the floating through the air, the flying down the chimney—that was Don DaGradi. Everything that happened in the 'Jolly Holiday' sequence, too. This man worked literally for years developing those sequences. And he was so wonderful. My praise for him is endless, and we feel bad that no one knows who Don DaGradi is.

Oddly, *Mary Poppins'* final ingredient was the actual script. Screenwriter Bill Walsh added to an already-potent creative mix, contributing most of the dialogue and the crucial scenes involving the bank, but his work came, atypically, after the story and most of the score had been established.

Robert Stevenson worked at Disney after *Poppins* on such films as *The Monkey's Uncle*, *That Darn Cat* (1965), *The Gnome-Mobile* (1967), *Blackbeard's Ghost* (1968), *The Love Bug* (1969), *Bedknobs and Broomsticks* (1971), *Herbie Rides Again*, and *The Island at the Top of the World* (1974).

Level Three: No Easy Stuff
Minutia & Obscuria

Q: **It is often said that Walt Disney considered others for the role of Mary Poppins. Name one of those considered.**

A: Bette Davis and Mary Martin are often mentioned as having been considered by Walt for the role. It was typical of Disney in those days to assemble long "wish lists" of potential actors for a variety of roles in a given "big" project.

Julie Andrews was performing on Broadway as Guenevere in *Camelot* when she appeared on the legendary CBS Sunday night variety program, "The Ed Sullivan Show." She performed "What Do the Simple Folk Do?" with Richard Burton, which at one point contains a whistling duet (the Shermans had already written the segment of "Spoonful of Sugar" where Mary whistles with a friendly robin). Richard Sherman, Robert Sherman, Don DaGradi, and even Walt Disney's secretary, Tommie Wilck, saw the broadcast and had the same idea—Andrews would be the perfect Mary Poppins.

Coincidentally, Walt was scheduled to visit New York, and DaGradi and the Shermans suggested that Walt and his wife would want to see *Camelot*, because Julie Andrews might have potential as Mary Poppins. Walt was delighted with Andrews, and met her backstage after the performance to pitch the project to her.

Another story has it that Glynis Johns, who played Mrs. Banks, was under the false impression that Walt was meeting with *her* to discuss the title role in *Poppins*. After learning the truth, the disappointed Johns was promised by Walt that the Shermans had written a wonderful song for her—which they had not. They scurried to develop a number, and came up with an activist anthem for Mrs. Banks, "Sister Suffragette," as counterpoint to Mr. Banks' sedentary song, "The Life I Lead." They rescued the melody from a discarded Mary Poppins character anthem "Prac-

tically Perfect (In Every Way)"—try singing that title to the first line of music from "Sister Suffragette." They delivered the completed song to Walt four days after his original luncheon with Glynis Johns, and she accepted the part of Mrs. Banks.

Glynis Johns' true musical theatre immortality would arrive in February 1973, as the vulnerable middle-aged actress Désirée Armfeldt in Stephen Sondheim's *A Little Night Music*. She introduced "Send in the Clowns" to the world.

Glynis Johns is Winifred Banks, "Sister Suffragette."

Q: *Mary Poppins'* world premiere was a benefit for a renowned art institution. When and where did the picture premiere? What institution did the premiere benefit?

A: An old-fashioned red-carpet gala was held on August 27, 1964, at Grauman's (now Mann's) Chinese Theater in Hollywood to celebrate the premiere of Walt Disney's *Mary Poppins*. According to contemporary records, this was his first grand-style Hollywood premiere since that of *Snow White and the Seven Dwarfs*, twenty-seven years earlier.

For some time, yet another of Walt's many pet projects was a multi-disciplinary arts college. This interest had grown out of his ongoing relationship with the Chouinard Art Institute, whose founder and instructors had been instrumental in training so many Disney artists. In the late 1950s, both Chouinard and the venerable Los Angeles Conservatory of Music (founded in 1883)

were on the brink of demise. Walt came to the rescue with his idea of an arts institute. He donated thirty-eight acres of land in the Santa Clarita Valley (a half hour north of Hollywood), and the two institutions merged to create the California Institute of the Arts.

Walt promoted CalArts with the benefit premiere of *Mary Poppins*, and created a fifteen-minute film about the school, *The CalArts Story*, which preceded that first showing of *Poppins*.

■

Q: When negotiations with the author of *Mary Poppins* got particularly rough, Walt Disney brought another property with similar story elements to his creative team to develop should the *Poppins* project fall through. What was the book?

A: *The Magic Bed-Knob* and *Bonfires and Broomsticks*, by Mary Norton, who is best known

The world premiere of *Mary Poppins* in August, 1964.

for *The Borrowers* and its sequels. These books have been published in a combined edition, titled *Bed-Knob and Broomstick*. In an interview with Doug McClelland for *Record World* magazine, the Sherman Brothers explain:

> Actually, he [Walt] bought the Mary Norton book before *Mary Poppins*. I remember just before everything got going on *Poppins*, we were having some trouble getting okays from P. L. Travers, the author of the stories, on the songs we had written. It was very exasperating. One day Walt came to us and said, "Don't worry, boys. I've bought another story that deals with magic. If we can't work things out with Travers, we'll be able to use your stuff in the other picture."

In 1970, Walt's creative heirs proceeded with production on the Norton property, retitled *Bedknobs and Broomsticks*.

One Sherman Brothers song, "The Beautiful Briny," had been written for the discarded "Around the World" sequence of *Mary Poppins*. It was lifted intact and used in the Naboombu Lagoon sequence of *Bedknobs and Broomsticks*.

Although it bears a superficial resemblance to *Mary Poppins*, *Bedknobs and Broomsticks* was greeted with indifference upon its release in late 1971, and bears scars of heavy editing prior to its release (it was further cut for a 1979 reissue). What remains is charming, particularly the Sherman Brothers' music, strong work from Irwin Kostal, and fine performances by Angela Lansbury and David Tomlinson.

■

Q: Who provides the voice of the umbrella-handle parrot in the final sequence of the picture?

A: Although the Walt Disney Archives is unable to verify it, it's fairly obvious on a close listen that it is David Tomlinson. If you compare the pace and inflection of Banks' dialogue in the bank board room (after he finds Michael's tuppence in his pocket) with the parrot dialogue, the parallel becomes pretty sharp. And really, it's appropriate, considering the lines the parrot delivers:

PARROT-HEAD: Look at them! You know, they think more of their father than they do of you?
MARY: That's as it should be.
PARROT-HEAD: Don't you care?
MARY: Practically perfect people never permit sentiment to muddle their thinking.

■

Q: Another, less famous soprano has various links to *Mary Poppins*. Who is she?

A: This one is a tangled web, so hang on. Marni Nixon is the soprano.

She dubbed the vocals for Audrey Hepburn in the film version of *My Fair Lady* (q.v., 1964).

Julie Andrews had originated the *My Fair Lady* role on Broadway, but was replaced by Hepburn in the film.

So, Julie Andrews was available to film *Mary Poppins* (the two pictures were shooting at pretty much the same time, *My Fair Lady* at Warner Bros., *Poppins* a mile away at the Disney Studio).

Andrews beat out Audrey Hepburn (with Marni Nixon's voice) for the 1964 Best Actress Oscar—Hepburn wasn't even nominated.

Marni Nixon performed Julie Andrews' *Poppins* material on a popular "low-price" record of songs from *Mary Poppins* for Disneyland Records.

In *The Sound of Music*, Marni Nixon worked with Julie Andrews, playing Sister Sophia.

Whew!

As mentioned before, Marni Nixon had also vocalized for Deborah Kerr in *The King and I* (1956) and *An Affair to Remember* (1957), and Natalie Wood in *West Side Story* (1961).

■

Q: Richard M. Sherman and Robert B. Sherman wrote more than thirty-five songs for *Mary Poppins* over the course of five years. Several songs landed in other Disney projects. Can you name any?

A: "The Land of Sand," a hypnotic desert theme for the deleted "Around the World" segment of *Poppins* showed up, appropriately, as Kaa the snake's hypnotic "Trust in Me" in *The Jungle Book.*

A haunting melody composed as "West Wind" for *Poppins* was retooled as "Mon Amour Perdu" for Disney's *Big Red* in 1962.

And of course, if you were paying attention to the previous answers, there was "Practically Perfect (in Every Way)," reconfigured as "Sister Suffragette," and "The Beautiful Briny," which was used intact in *Bedknobs and Broomsticks.*

There may be more, but Dick and Bob Sherman won't tell. "People will think that all we've done since *Poppins* is put new words on old songs," Dick laughs.

The Shermans also wrote a keynote ballad as the character theme for Mary, called "Through the Eyes of Love," which Julie Andrews dismissed, asking for "something more snappy and crisp, more Mary Poppins-ish," say the Shermans.

■

Q: As Jane and Michael flee from the bank, an aged crone accosts them. This "crone" had played a much more prominent and menacing Disney villain. Which one?

A: A call sheet for Mary Poppins reveals that the crone was played by none other than Betty Lou Gerson, the voice of the villianous Cruella De Vil from *101 Dalmatians* (1961). Her stay on the *Poppins* set? One day.

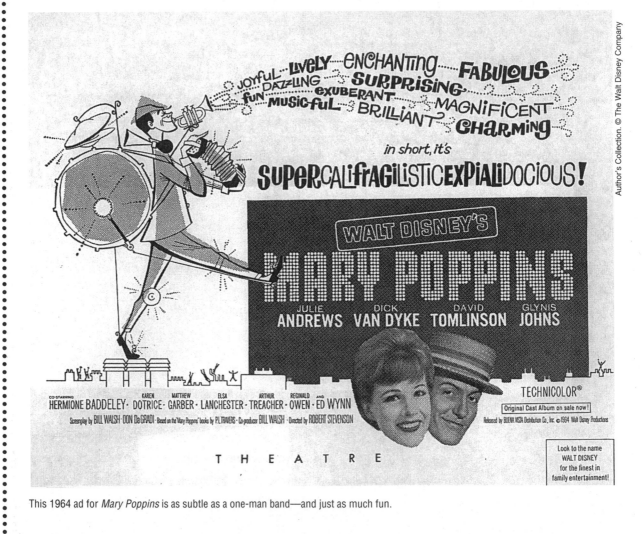

This 1964 ad for *Mary Poppins* is as subtle as a one-man band—and just as much fun.

MARY POPPINS

Released by Buena Vista Distribution Company, October 1964

Technicolor®

Coproducer: Bill Walsh

Director: Robert Stevenson

Screenplay: Bill Walsh, Don DaGradi,
based on the *Mary Poppins* books by P.L. Travers

Songs by Richard M. Sherman and Robert B. Sherman

Photography: Edward Coleman

Editor: Cotton Warburton

Art directors: Carrol Clark, William T. Tuntke

Set decorations: Emile Kuri, Hal Gausman

Costume and design consultant: Tony Walton

Costume designer: Bill Thomas

Costumers: Chuck Keehne, Gertrude Casey

Consultant: P. L. Travers

Music supervisor, arranger, conductor: Irwin Kostal

Choreography: Marc Breaux, Dee Dee Wood

Assistant directors: Joseph L. McEveety, Paul Feiner

Makeup: Pat McNalley

Hairstyling: LaRue Matheron

Sound supervision: Robert O. Cook

Sound mixer: Dean Thomas

Music editor: Evelyn Kennedy

Dance accompanist: Nat Farber

Assistant to the conductor: James MacDonald

Live-action second unit director: Arthur J. Vitarelli

Animation director: Hamilton Luske

Animation art director: McLaren Stewart

Nursery sequence design: Bill Justice, Xavier Atencio

Animators: Milt Kahl, Oliver Johnston, Jr., John Lounsbery, Hal Ambro,
Franklin Thomas, Ward Kimball, Eric Larson, Cliff Nordberg, Jack Boyd

Backgrounds: Albert Dempster, Don Griffith, Art Riley, Bill Layne

Special effects: Peter Ellenshaw, Eustace Lycett, Robert A. Mattey

Running time: 140 minutes

Cast

Julie Andrews	Mary Poppins
Dick Van Dyke	Bert
David Tomlinson	Mr. Banks
Glynis Johns	Mrs. Banks
Ed Wynn	Uncle Albert
Hermione Baddeley	Ellen, the maid
Karen Dotrice	Jane
Matthew Garber	Michael
Elsa Lanchester	Katie Nanna
Arthur Treacher	Constable Jones
Reginald Owen	Admiral Boom
Reta Shaw	Mrs. Brill, the cook
Arthur Malet	Mr. Dawes, Junior
Jane Darwell	The Bird Woman
Cyril Delevanti	Mr. Grubbs
Lester Matthews	Mr. Tomes
Clive L. Halliday	Mr. Mousely
Don Barclay	Mr. Binnacle
Marjorie Bennett	Miss Lark
Alma Lawton	Mrs. Corry
Marjorie Eaton	Miss Persimmon
Betty Lou Gerson	Old Crone

Willy Wonka and the Chocolate Factory *made its debut during a strange and unsettled period in the history of the movie musical and of movies in general. For this reason, it has a hybrid style that contributes to its fantastic, satirical, otherworldly appeal. Willy Wonka and the Chocolate Factory is really as much a comedy as it is a musical, as much a satire as it is a family film. Structurally,* Willy Wonka and the Chocolate Factory *is actually two films. The first half is a frantically-paced, internationally-set, TV-based Richard Lester-esque comedy-drama. The second half is more of a standard musical fantasy, all taking place within the confines of Wonka's magical candy plant. Taken all together,* Willy Wonka and the Chocolate Factory *is an engaging, stylish, and endearing whatever-it-is, and those of us who saw the film as children tend to hold an especially fond place in our hearts for this offbeat movie musical mutt.*

Level One: The Easy Stuff

Story & Characters

Q: **Although Willy Wonka gets his name in the title of the film, *Willy Wonka* is really about whom?**

A: Charlie Bucket. Poverty-stricken young Charlie is the fulcrum of the picture, and he is skillfully portrayed by the then thirteen-year-old unknown Peter Ostrum. The August 10, 1970, issue of *The Hollywood Reporter* carried the first announcement of his casting: "Title role for Roald Dahl's 'Charlie and the Chocolate Factory' has been won by 12-year-old Peter Ostrum of Cleveland, Ohio. He leaves today for the David L. Wolper Production Munich location."

Ostrum was born in Dallas, Texas, on November 1, 1957, the youngest of four children. His family moved to Ohio, where young Peter was taken to a children's theatre performance at the Cleveland Playhouse. When the same group later performed at Ostrum's school, he learned that the Playhouse gave Saturday theatre classes to children. Ostrum appeared in several children's theatre productions, and three main stage plays at the Cleveland Playhouse. It was in one of these productions that Ostrum was seen by casting agent Marian Dougherty, who recommended him for the role of Charlie Bucket.

Ostrum's performance is a fine one, and one of the strong points of *Willy Wonka and the Chocolate Factory*. Dialogue Coach Frawley Becker points out that "Peter was a child who acted—he wasn't a child actor. He had none of the obvious technique, tricks, or affectations of the kind that TV kid actors had, and continue to have. He was genuine, and his sincerity as a person shines through in his performance. He was an extremely intelligent kid, who was both self-aware and skilled at what he was doing."

■

Q: **How many people live in the Bucket home?**

A: Six. Charlie, Mrs. Bucket, Grandpa Joe, Grandma Josephine, Grandpa George, and Grandma Georgina. The four grandparents share one big bed, and haven't set foot on the floor in twenty years, for reasons never explained. Part of the mean-spirited absurdity that runs through *Willy Wonka and the Chocolate Factory* is the offhanded treatment given the grandparents, who appear to be bedridden for no other reason than having lived too long.

Apart from the key role of Grandpa Joe, Charlie's confidante/mentor/surrogate (but crippled) father, only one of the other grandparents has what can be called "lines." When Charlie is presented with the birthday gift of a hand-knitted muffler, Grandma Josephine beams, "I did the end pieces with the little tassels." Frawley Becker remembers, "We worked on the word 'tassels' for the longest time. She was a German actress, and she had such a hard time with that word."

When the Golden Ticket contest is broadcast on television, she exclaims, "They're all crazy!" As the phony fifth ticket is found, she grouses, "A lot of rubbish, the whole thing." And when Charlie hands Grandpa Joe the Golden Ticket he has discovered, Grandma Josephine urges, "Read it, Joe, for Heaven's sake!"

Grandma Georgina does get *one* line, as the phony ticket finder is announced: "Who's going to tell him?"

■

Q: What does Charlie's father do for a living? What does his mother do?

A: A trick question, since Charlie doesn't have a father in the film. In the source book, Charlie's father worked in a toothpaste factory, screwing the caps on toothpaste tubes. The idea of a small town with a gigantic candy plant *and* a toothpaste factory seems perfectly logical.

The elimination of the ineffectual father streamlines the storytelling of the film, and creates the obvious character connection between orphan child Charlie and surrogate father Willy Wonka.

Charlie's mother, played with world-weary, poignant sympathy by Diana Sowle, is a washerwoman. Her song, "Cheer Up, Charlie," is one of the loveliest moments of the film.

■

Q: Charlie Bucket lives in a small town with a prominent chocolate manufacturing plant. Who makes candy under the hungry Charlie's very nose?

A: Willy Wonka, of course, the chocolate maker of the film tile. In the source book, Wonka is described as a sprightly little man with a goatee, dressed in a plum-colored velvet coat and a black top hat. His demeanor is compared to that of "a quick clever old squirrel in the park."

"Squirrely" could certainly be used to describe Gene Wilder's performance as Willy Wonka. His controlled schizoid manner perfectly suits the mysterious, mad, mercurial candy man.

Wilder was born Jerry Silberman in Milwaukee, Wisconsin, in 1935. He attended the University of Iowa, and furthered his acting studies at Bristol Old Vic and Actors Studio. His first screen role was in *Bonnie and Clyde* (1967), followed by an hysterical turn as the frenetic accountant Leo

easy

Author's Collection. © Wolper Pictures Ltd. and The Quaker Oats Company

Gene Wilder in the deft but uneven characterization of Willy Wonka.

Bloom in Mel Brooks' *The Producers* (1968). This led to the further Wilder/Brooks collaborations *Blazing Saddles* (1973) and *Young Frankenstein* (1974). Other early Wilder films include *Quackster Fortune Has A Cousin in the Bronx*, *Start the Revolution Without Me* (1970), and *Everything You Always Wanted to Know About Sex (But Were Afraid to Ask)* (1972).

Wilder made his directorial debut with *The Adventure of Sherlock Holmes' Smarter Brother* (1975). His subsequent films, both before and behind the camera, have been mostly disappointments.

He teamed with Richard Pryor in *Silver Streak* (1976). This collaboration was repeated in *Stir Crazy* (1980) and *See No Evil, Hear No Evil* (1989).

Wilder met Gilda Radner while filming *Hanky Panky* (1982). They were married in 1984 and appeared together that year in *The Woman in Red* and *Haunted Honeymoon* (1986). Radner died of cancer in 1989.

Gene Wilder debuted an NBC television series, "Something Wilder," in 1993. After a rocky start the series had a complete retooling, but never established itself as an audience favorite.

■

Q: During the film, the hometown of each child is seen. Where are all the children from?

A: Augustus Gloop is said by the newscaster to be from "the small town of Duzelheim, Germany." He is the son of the town's most prominent pork butcher.

Although it's unspecified, it seems that Veruca Salt comes from England. Her mother, father, and she all speak with English accents, and her father offers a "one-pound bonus" to his assembled work force for the discovery of a Golden Ticket. Later in the film, on a ticket-finder toteboard map of the world behind a TV anchorman, the tag for lucky finder number two is smack on top of the British Isles.

Violet Beauregarde is from Miles City, Montana. Her father, Sam Beauregarde, is "a prominent local politician, a great civic leader, a philosopher." In other words, a used car salesman ("Square-deal Sam to you...").

Mike Teevee is from Marble Falls, Arizona. Among the hometown pals that he greets on the air are Billy, Maggie, and Fish-face.

Charlie's picturesque home town, although decidedly European, is never identified.

■

Q: Wonka's factory is staffed by a unique work force. Who are they? Where do they come from? What are their distinguishing characteristics?

A: Wonka's employees are Oompa-Loompas, from Loompaland. They are dwarfs, with orange faces and green hair.

Wonka has rescued the Oompa-Loompas from Loompaland, which he describes as "a terrible place," and transported the entire population to his factory. The Oompa-Loompas had been prey to the Whangdoodles, Hornswogglers, Snozzwangers, and Rotten Vermicious Knids of their native country. In the Wonka factory, the Oompa-Loompas find peace and safety. Wonka gets a resident work force, without the threat of encroachment from his competitors and the theft of his candy-making secrets.

In the first several editions of the original book, the Oompa-Loompas were described as tiny men no bigger than dolls, with brown skin so dark it is almost black. Charlie exclaims that Mr. Wonka must have made them from chocolate. An accompanying illustration shows little black men dressed in loincloths. In subsequent editions of the book, the description has been changed to eliminate racial implications. Although the Oompa-Loompas remain dwarfs, their distinguishing feature has been changed to "funny long hair."

Q: Each child is offered a bribe to steal something from the Wonka factory. Who offers the bribe? What must they steal?

A: A man identifying himself as Oskar Slugworth, president of Slugworth Chocolates Incorporated, approaches each of the children directly after they discover their Golden Tickets. Slugworth has been established by Grandpa Joe as being Wonka's key competitor, and one who engaged in the confectionery espionage that caused Wonka to fire his work force and shutter his factory for three years.

In the source story, Wonka's other competitors are identified as Ficklegruber (a play on Shicklgruber, often rumored to be the "real" name of Adolf Hitler—it was actually his mother's maiden name) and Prodnose. They send spies into Wonka's factory disguised as workers and steal Wonka's great inventions, like non-melting ice cream, twenty-four-hour gum, and edible balloons. In Bill's candy shop set in the film, you can see the Slugworth and Ficklegruber labels quite clearly.

What Slugworth wants the children to steal is Wonka's latest candy invention—the Everlasting Gobstopper. This is a candy, Wonka says, for children with very little pocket money—you can suck them forever, and they'll never get any smaller. Slugworth will be ruined, he tells Charlie, if this invention succeeds.

An entire line of Willy Wonka candy brands made their debut at the time of the first release of *Willy Wonka and the Chocolate Factory*. Among them were a foot-long chocolate-covered caramel twist called a Scrumdidlyumptious Bar, a peanut butter chocolate bar called Willy Wonka's Super Skrunch, peanut butter drops in candy shells called Willy Wonka's Oompas, and a jawbreaker called…the Everlasting Gobstopper. To this day, "Willy Wonka" still exists as a candy brand, on a license from the original trademark holder. Their most prominent candies are still the Gobstopper and another hard candy called Runts.

As part of a Cap'n Crunch cereal premium in 1971, a Willy Wonka chocolate factory kit was offered. It contained two Wonka chocolate molds and several beautifully designed Wonka Bar

Author's Collection. © Wolper Pictures Ltd. and The Quaker Oats Company

The Oompa-Loompas from Loompaland. With Wonka, they find peace and safety. In them, Wonka finds a captive labor force.

wrappers, so juvenile confectioners could create their own authentic Wonka Bars. All this came packed in a box designed to look like a Wonka factory building.

"Gob," by the way, is an English colloquialism dating back to the eighteenth century. It means "to spit" or "spittle," derived from street jargon for "mouth." It is left to the reader to further define the name of Wonka's marvelous candy.

■

Q: Wonka has three vehicles that are seen in the film. What are they? What are their names?

A: All of the Wonka vehicles seen in the film are fantastic theme park ride-like contraptions of questionable efficiency and safety.

The first is the Oompa-Loompa Powered paddle boat *Wonkatania*, which takes the tour group down the Chocolate River to The Inventing Room.

The second is the "gas-powered" Wonkamobile, powered by the gas of "ginger pop, ginger beer, beer bubbles, bubble-ade, bubble cola, double-cola, double-bubble burp-a-cola, and all that crazy carbonated stuff that tickles your nose." After the Wonkamobile has run its hundred-foot course, thoroughly dousing its passengers with

The *Wonkatania*, one of Willy Wonka's several fantastic conveyances. It will come as no surprise that the designer of the factory and its vehicles was a key designer of Disneyland.

foam, it is cleaned in the Wonkawash.

The final fantasy conveyance is The Great Glass Wonkavator, which can travel in all directions and get to any room in the factory at the push of a button.

That these contraptions, and, indeed, the entire factory, should have a theme park feel is no surprise, due to the background of production designer Harper Goff.

Goff attended Chouinard Art Institute in Los Angeles, and began his art career as an illustrator for *Colliers*, *Esquire*, and *National Geographic*.

He began his film career at Warner Bros., designing sets for films such as *Captain Blood* (1935), *Sergeant York* (1941), and *Casablanca* (1942).

An accidental meeting with Walt Disney in a London hobby shop (both Goff and Disney were model train enthusiasts) brought Goff to the Disney Studio, where he was a key visual designer of *20,000 Leagues Under the Sea* (1954). Shortly thereafter, Goff contributed to the initial development of Disneyland, with designs for Main Street, U.S.A. and the Jungle Cruise. Goff's other production design work included *Pete Kelly's Blues* (1955), *The Vikings* (1957), and *Fantastic Voyage* (1966).

Goff designed the Unisphere, the gigantic steel globe that was the icon of the 1964–65 New York World's Fair and which still stands in Flushing Meadows State Park in Queens, New York. Later he designed several of the World Showcase pavilions at EPCOT Center in Walt Disney World. Goff died in 1993.

The Wonka factory designs certainly make use of Goff's skill at environmental design, born in film and honed in the theme park. The Chocolate Room is a good example. Note that there are several layers of "development" in the room. A base of industrial revolution-era factory is visible: brick walls, paned windows, and wrought-iron structural supports are overlaid with the fantasy of a chocolate waterfall and a candy landscape. The fantasy is thus grounded in reality; the viewer is never allowed to visually forget the basic factory building, no matter how fantastic the surroundings become.

■

Q: What business is Veruca's father in?

A: "Nuts." Part of the frenetic "Richard Lester" quality of *Willy Wonka and the Chocolate Factory* is due to the casting of Lester "talisman" Roy Kinnear in the central comic role of nut magnate Henry Salt. The greedy factory boss offers a one-pound bonus to his sweat shop employees for the discovery of the priceless Golden Ticket. They labor, shelling peanuts (and, temporarily, shucking Wonka Bars), under two great banners. One reads "Willing Hands Make Happy Hearts," the other, "Busy Hands Make Profits."

Roy Kinnear was born in 1932, was educated in Scotland, served in the Royal Artillery Regiment, and graduated from the Royal Academy of Dramatic Art. He gained experience in British repertory companies, eventually moving to a West End debut in *Sparrows Can't Sing*. This was followed by appearances with the Royal Shakespeare Company in Stratford, at the Aldwych, and in the United States. Kinnear then performed a short stint at the National Theatre. He became one of the original members of the influential British satire "That Was the Week That Was." This led to three other British series: "A World of His Own," "A Slight Case of…," and "Inside George Webly."

Kinnear appeared in Richard Lester's *The Knack, Help!* (1965), *A Funny Thing Happened on the Way to the Forum* (1966), *How I Won the War* (1967), *The Bed-Sitting Room* (1969), *Juggernaut, The Three Musketeers* (1974), *The Four Musketeers*, and *Royal Flash* (1975). Kinnear died of internal bleeding due to injuries sustained in a riding accident while filming Lester's *The Return of the Musketeers* in 1988. Kinnear's widow won a negligence claim against the film company in 1994 in the amount of £650,000.

Q: What is the final fate of the four "naughty, nasty little children"?

A: Augustus Gloop falls in the Chocolate River and shoots up a pipe to the Fudge Room. Violet Beauregarde chews a piece of experimental gum, blows up like a blueberry, and is rolled to the Juicing Room for squeezing. Veruca Salt falls down the garbage chute after being judged a "bad egg" by Wonka's eggdicator. Mike Teevee is reduced to action figure size after being transmitted by Wonkavision. Charlie is assured that the four brats will be restored to their normal, terrible old selves, but that maybe they'll be a little bit wiser for the wear.

In the original book, Veruca's fate is a little different. Apropos to her father's job, she meets her demise in the Nut Room. Wonka has trained a hundred squirrels to skillfully shell walnuts. They judge a bad nut by the sound it makes when tapped. When Veruca demands one of the squirrels for a pet, Wonka refuses, sending greedy Veruca running towards the squirrels. They pick up the girl, tap her head, and, discovering that she's a bad nut, throw her down the garbage chute.

Author's Collection. © Wolper Pictures Ltd. and The Quaker Oats Company

Oops. Augustus Gloop (Michael Bollner) meets his confectionery fate in the Chocolate River.

Q: Who wrote the book on which *Willy Wonka* is based? Who wrote the screenplay?

A: Two questions, one answer. Famed short story and children's writer Roald Dahl adapted his own best-selling book *Charlie and the Chocolate Factory* in a deal made by Irving "Swifty" Lazar. David L. Wolper reportedly paid $500,000 plus a percentage for the film rights.

Dahl is probably best known as a writer of juvenile fiction, his most famous books being *James and the Giant Peach* (1962), *Charlie and the Chocolate Factory* (1964), *Fantastic Mr. Fox* (1970), *Danny, the Champion of the World* (1975), and *The Witches* (1984).

Born in South Wales to Norwegian parents, Dahl was educated at Repton and joined the Royal Air Force at the beginning of World War II. After training as a fighter pilot, he fought in Greece, Syria, and Libya. It was in Libya that the injuries sustained in a crash landing ended his R.A.F. career.

Dahl turned to writing at the suggestion of writer C. S. Forester, penning his first short story about his Libyan plane crash. It sold to *The Saturday Evening Post*, beginning his long writing career. His first short story collection, *Over to You*, was published in 1946. In the ensuing years, Dahl wrote dozens of short stories, collected in such books as *Someone Like You* (1953), *Kiss Kiss* (1960), and *Switch Bitch* (1974). Several of his macabre stories were produced as an anthology TV series from Anglia Television, "Roald Dahl's Tales of the Unexpected," in 1979.

Dahl dabbled in screenwriting, penning the scripts to *Willy Wonka and the Chocolate Factory* and *You Only Live Twice* (1967). With Ken Hughes, Dahl wrote the lamentably bloated and slightly nasty screenplay for *Chitty Chitty Bang Bang* (1968).

Oddly, although the screenplay for *Willy Wonka and the Chocolate Factory* makes several decided improvements to its source book, and has come to be regarded as something of a classic, Dahl considered it "a rotten movie."

It has been noted that the key to his success was that Dahl conspired with children, *against* adults. Indeed, for his juvenile audience, one of the primary enjoyments of Dahl's work was its essential rudeness. It is apparent that as he got older, Dahl's writing became more and more what his critics had accused it of being for many years: ugly, cynical, antisocial, and subtly (and not-so-subtly) racist and anti-feminist. His later books for children are appallingly petty and mean-spirited, without the redeeming moral qualities of his earlier works. An astute and unsettling biography by Jeremy Treglown was published in 1994, which revealed Dahl as a self-serving, dominating, bullying anti-Semite.

Roald Dahl died in 1990 at the age of seventy-four.

In addition to the motion picture, *Charlie and the Chocolate Factory* inspired a 1972 sequel, *Charlie and the Great Glass Elevator*, which contained a lot of fairly adult political satire. In 1976, a play for schoolchildren, *Roald Dahl's Charlie and the Chocolate Factory: A Play* (adapted by Richard George) was published. This was followed in 1978 by a board game, *Charlie and the Chocolate Factory: A Game*. All were published by Alfred A. Knopf.

■

Q: One of the *Willy Wonka* cast won an Emmy Award for his guest appearance on the "Cher" TV show. Who?

A: Jack Albertson. No kidding. The seasoned veteran of stage, screen and television played the warm and kindly Grandpa Joe in *Willy Wonka*. Albertson was one of only three actors (along

Grandpa Joe (Jack Albertson) is best friend, surrogate father, and co-conspirator to Charlie (Peter Ostrum). Joe shares his grandson's case of "Wonka-mania."

with Melvyn Douglas and Paul Scofield) to win the Oscar, Emmy, and Tony awards.

Albertson's roots reached back to vaudeville, burlesque, and the Broadway stage. In fact, one of Albertson's first significant motion pictures, *Top Banana* (1954), was filmed at Broadway's Winter Garden Theater. Albertson's first vaudeville partner was Phil Silvers, and he also played straight man to Milton Berle and Bert Lahr.

Albertson's other notable films include *Miracle on 34th Street* (1947, Albertson is the postal worker who cooks up the idea of delivering all Santa Claus letters to Kris Kringle in court), *Man of a Thousand Faces* (1957), *Teacher's Pet* (1958), and *Days of Wine and Roses* (1962).

Albertson appeared in *two* Elvis pictures, *Kissin' Cousins* and *Roustabout* (1964), as well as *The Flim Flam Man* (1967), *The Subject Was Roses* (for which he won the Oscar, 1968), and *The Poseidon Adventure* (1972).

Albertson also made his mark as a TV star,

appearing in dozens of shows beginning in television's "golden age" and continuing all the way up to his death. He won his first Emmy for "Chico and the Man," which aired from 1974 to 1978. This was followed by a one-season series called "Grandpa Goes to Washington" in 1978.

Albertson died in 1981. His last film role was the voice of Amos Slade in Disney's *The Fox and the Hound*.

By the way, Albertson beat out both Tim Conway (on the venerable "Carol Burnett Show") and John Denver (on "Doris Day Today") for that "Cher" Emmy. The category was Supporting Actor—Continuing or Single Performance—Variety or Music.

■

Q: What city was *Willy Wonka and the Chocolate Factory* filmed in?

A: Exteriors were filmed in the capital city of Bavaria, Munich. Interiors were filmed in the sound stages of the Bavaria Studios there. Located in in a forest clearing named Geiselgasteig, the studios had been built in the 1930s, and had been occupied by the U.S. Army immediately after World War II.

Though the production notes attempt to explain the location as a "storybook setting" suitable to the tale being told, there is little doubt that cost was also an issue. At the time of shooting, *Willy Wonka and the Chocolate Factory* became the center of the Hollywood "runaway" controversy. Labor unions decried the fact that more and more productions, like *Willy Wonka*, were shooting away from the union control and union costs of Los Angeles.

Danny Peary, in his book *Cult Movies 2*, makes note of the "foreign" feel of *Willy Wonka* to an American audience: "The locations have an inhospitably foreign look. And the film seems to take place in several centuries simultaneously. Adding to the otherworldly nature, American and British actors mingle freely in the foreground, while those in the background have a Teutonic appearance."

Although this statement, on the face of it, seems just a bit xenophobic, it is not without its accuracy. Whether this "foreign look" impairs or augments the overall success of the film is a completely subjective matter. Some might argue that this "otherworldliness" is perfectly appropriate to the decidedly bizarre subject matter.

■

Q: Only one of the kids has a song to sing. Which one? What is the song?

A: Greedy Veruca Salt bursts into the song "I Want It Now" over her desire to possess one of Willy Wonka's golden–chocolate–egg–laying geese. Young Julie Dawn Cole as the covetous brat Veruca is the only one of the children with a

character song. Structurally, this makes the second half of the film a bit lopsided, since it is the inhabitants of the factory, Wonka and his employees, who sing the rest of the songs (only two, really, with three reprises of one number). It also seems that, if any one child might logically burst into song, the emotional weight would lie with our hero, Charlie. But *Willy Wonka and the Chocolate Factory* is an oddity among musical films—a musical that does not rely on its score at all, but still manages to succeed as a film, as well as having some lovely songs.

Cole's vocal was dubbed by adult singer Diana Lee. Lee had dubbed the singing voice of Samantha Eggar in *Doctor Dolittle* (1967) and would later dub the singing for Liv Ullman in her American film debut, the disastrous musical version of *Lost Horizon* (1973).

■

Q: Name the popular composing team who wrote the song score to *Willy Wonka and the Chocolate Factory*.

A: Leslie Bricusse and Anthony Newley. This multi-talented composing team had collaborated on the 1964 stage hit *Stop the World—I Want to Get Off* (as well as the subsequent film versions in 1966 and 1978) and *The Roar of the Greasepaint—The Smell of the Crowd* (1965). They had also written the theme song for *Goldfinger* (1964).

Born in 1931, Anthony Newley made his film debut at the age of sixteen, in something called *The Guinea Pig* (1948). He made a terrific impression as The Artful Dodger in David Lean's *Oliver Twist* the same year, and also appeared in *Vice Versa*. After serving in the military, Newley returned to a contract with Warwick Films. He acted in *The Cockleshell Heroes*, *The Last Man to Hang*, *Port Afrique* (1956), *The Good Companions*, *Fire Down Below* (1957), *The Man Inside*, *High Flight*, and *Tank Force* (1958).

In the 1959 picture *Idol on Parade*, Newley played a rock singer drafted into the Army. He sang four of his own songs in the film. They jumped to the top of the pop charts and established him as a singer.

Newley returned to the stage that same year, and then entered the fledgling British television industry hosting his own show, "Saturday Spectaculars."

Other films in which he appeared solely as a performer include *The Lady is a Square, Johnny Ten Percent, The Bandit of Zhobe, Killers of Kilimanjaro* (1959), *Jazz Boat* (1960), *Doctor Dolittle* (1967), *Sweet November* (1968), *It Seemed Like a Good Idea at the Time* (1975), and the ignominious *The Garbage Pail Kids Movie* (1987).

Newley had the unwieldy title of director, screenwriter, composer, lyricist, and performer in the equally cumbersome *Can Hieronymus Merkin Ever Forget Mercy Humppe and Find True Happiness?* (1969), was director of *Summertree* (1971), was songwriter for the embarrassing *Old Dracula* (1974, U.K. title *Vampira*), and served as performer, composer, and lyricist for the underrated *Mr. Quilp* (a.k.a. *The Old Curiosity Shop*, 1975).

Leslie Bricusse was also born in 1931. He attended Cambridge University, and during his final year there he wrote, produced, directed, and appeared in the revue *Out of the Blue*. He segued from this West End success to writing his own material for and appearing in *An Evening with Beatrice Lillie*. After writing scripts and music for films and television, and spending one season hosting the BBC-TV series "Line Up for Tonight," he wrote a stage musical titled *Lady at the Wheel*.

Between his collaborations with Newley, Bricusse wrote the lyrics for the London and Broadway stage musical *Pickwick*, and in collaboration with John Barry wrote songs for films like *Thunderball, The Knack, The Ipcress File* (for which he wrote the theme, 1965), and *You Only Live Twice* (1967). Other Bricusse compositions include "My Kind of Girl" and "If I Ruled the World." With Newley, his song list contains standards like "What Kind of Fool Am I?," "Who Can I Turn To?," "Once In a Lifetime," "A Wonderful Day Like Today," and "Gonna Build a Mountain."

In 1967, Bricusse replaced Alan Jay Lerner on the ill-fated *Doctor Dolittle*, contributing both screenplay and songs. His "Talk to the Animals" won the Oscar for Best Song that year. He wrote the music and lyrics for the underrated *Goodbye, Mr. Chips* (1969), which was adapted for the stage in a 1982 Chichester Festival Theatre production. He penned screenplay, music, and songs for the likewise underrated *Scrooge* (1970). This film, too, was adapted for the stage (with Anthony Newley in the title role!) at the Alexandra Theatre in Birmingham in 1992.

Bricusse has written songs for *Revenge of the Pink Panther, Superman* (1978), *The Sea Wolves* (1980), *Santa Claus: The Movie* (1985), and *Hook* (1991).

He has written lyrics for projects such as *That's Life!* (1986), *Home Alone* (1990), *Home Alone 2: Lost in New York*, and the animated feature *Tom and Jerry: The Movie* (1992).

Bricusse collaborated with Henry Mancini on the popular *Victor/Victoria* (1982), as well as a complete revision of the song score for the stage musical version, which debuted in 1995.

■

Q: Name the *Willy Wonka* creative whose Oscar-nominated work includes *Hans Christian Andersen* (1952) and *Funny Girl* (1968).

A: Conductor/arranger Walter Scharf. Scharf has created music in all performance media, and for all genres—drama, comedy, westerns, musicals, operas, and documentaries; in idioms ranging from rock and pop to classical.

A New York native, Scharf attended NYU and the Walter Damrosch Institute (now known as the Juilliard School of Music) as well as several

medium

European conservatories. He first came to Hollywood under contract to Warner Bros., later worked under contract to Twentieth Century-Fox and Paramount, and was head of the music department at Republic Studios. After Republic, he relocated to Universal-International.

The versatile Scharf's motion picture work over the years has ranged from drama to comedy to musicals to documentaries. Some of his best-known works include *Alexander's Ragtime Band* (1938), *Holiday Inn* (1942, for which he arranged "White Christmas"), nine Dean Martin-Jerry Lewis films and seven of Jerry's solo efforts, *Pocketful of Miracles* (1961), *The Cheyenne Social Club* (1970), and *Ben* (1972; the famous title song was composed by Scharf with lyrics by Don Black).

On television, Scharf composed, arranged, and conducted for diverse series such as "Mission: Impossible," "Ben Casey," and "Slattery's People." Scharf's TV special work includes *Mr. Magoo's Christmas Carol* and *The Dangerous Christmas of Red Riding Hood*. Scharf composed, arranged, and conducted for several Jaques Cousteau specials, and for two seasons served in the same capacities for the Cousteau series "The Undersea World of Jaques Cousteau."

Scharf has received ten Oscar nominations and seven Emmy nominations.

■

Q: Name the pop pal of Bricusse and Newley who made "The Candy Man" a number one hit.

A: Sammy Davis, Jr. made a hit of the silly "The Candy Man," even ad-libbing lyrics to "hip" them up (changing the inane line "soak it in the sun and make a strawb'ry lemon pie" to the equally fatuous "soak it in the sun and make a groovy lemon pie").

Davis had made smash hit recordings of Bricusse and Newley's "What Kind of Fool Am I?" and "Who Can I Turn To?" and starred in the abysmal 1978 remake of their *Stop the World—I Want to Get Off*, titled *Sammy Stops the World*.

■

Q: The fraud winner of the fifth Golden Ticket is "lucky Alberto Miñoleta." Whose photograph is shown as Alberto?

Bill, the sweet shop owner, sings the praises of "The Candy Man."

A: Nazi war criminal Martin Bormann. Bormann had been head of the Nazi Party Chancery, and had inherited Rudolf Hess's position as Hitler's Deputy for Nazi Party Affairs. He later served additionally as Secretary to the Fuehrer.

Bormann was last reported in the bunker at the time of Adolf Hitler's death, but escaped and, like many other Nazis, was rumored to be living in hiding in South America. He was tried and convicted of his war crimes in absentia at the Nuremberg Trials.

This sort of zany visual joke is typical of *Willy Wonka and the Chocolate Factory*, which has a certain arch spirit akin to contemporary comedies like *Monty Python's Flying Circus* and the films of Richard Lester. Indeed, apart from the action involving Charlie and his family, the first half of the film is told in the anecdotal vernacular of television.

■

Q: Many of the behind-the-camera talents of *Willy Wonka and the Chocolate Factory* had collaborated on a popular 1969 comedy. Which one?

A: *If It's Tuesday, This Must Be Belgium*. Produced by David L. Wolper and directed by Mel Stuart, this comedy is said to be the first cartoon caption ever made into a full-length movie. *If It's Tuesday, This Must Be Belgium* was remade as a

TV movie, titled *If It's Tuesday, It Still Must Be Belgium*, in 1987.

Other *Belgium* alumni to work on *Wonka* included Production Manager Pia Arnold (the first woman to hold the post on a major feature), Conductor/Arranger Walter Scharf, and Dialogue Coach Frawley Becker.

■

Q: How many Academy Awards did *Willy Wonka* win?

A: None. *Willy Wonka* was only nominated for one Academy Award:

Music Scoring Awards (Best Scoring: Adaptation and Original Song Score): *Willy Wonka and the Chocolate Factory* (Leslie Bricusse & Anthony Newley—Song Score, Walter Scharf), *Bedknobs and Broomsticks* (Richard M. Sherman & Robert B. Sherman—Song Score, Irwin Kostal), *The Boy Friend* (Peter Maxwell Davies, Peter Greenwell), *Fiddler on the Roof* (the winner, John Williams), and *Tchaikovsky* (Dimitri Tiomkin).

This question inspired the following from Robert Tieman of the Walt Disney Archives:

If awards did *Willy Wonka* win
When awards were won, I wonder
Why *Willy* won not even one
And Williams won asunder.

Inspiration lurks in the mundane.

hard

Q: **Another famous film musical shot on the same sound stages as *Willy Wonka*. Which one?**

A: *Cabaret*, Bob Fosse's sophisticated film version of the Broadway musical and the play *I Am a Camera*, starring Liza Minnelli, Michael York, and Joel Grey.

Willy Wonka and the Chocolate Factory was filmed on location in Munich, and in the sound stages of the Bavaria Studios there.

According to Frawley Becker, "As the sets for *Wonka* were struck in the Fall of 1970, they were being quickly replaced by the Kit Kat Club and other sets for *Cabaret*."

■

Q: **Name two of Peter Ostrum's other films.**

A: A trick question. *Willy Wonka and the Chocolate Factory* was Ostrum's one and only film. When he contracted for the part of Charlie, he was offered a three-picture contract with

David L. Wolper, which he refused. Ostrum later recalled that he wanted to play Charlie Bucket because he liked the source story so much.

Frawley Becker became a close and enduring friend of Ostrum's during the several months of shooting in Germany. "Peter was extremely bright for his age, and we would talk about just everything. He worried that he might be making a mistake in turning down the Wolper contract, and we discussed it at length. In the end, he just didn't want to lose the freedom to choose what he played, and in what picture. That's the kind of intelligence he had, even at thirteen." Becker and Ostrum remain close friends to this day.

After the film, Peter's life went back to normal. Acting still interested young Ostrum, but not as a career. His only subsequent brush with professional acting came in 1977, when he auditioned for the role of the stable boy that Peter Firth had originated in the Broadway production of *Equus*. He didn't get the part.

Ostrum returned to school, continuing his majors in animal husbandry and veterinary

The fanciful *Wonka* sets, like the Inventing Room, were struck to make way for the filming of another atypical movie musical.

Author's Collection. © Wolper Pictures Ltd. and The Quaker Oats Company

Peter Ostrum's portrayal of Charlie Bucket is one of the most skillful child performances in film history.

medicine. In 1985, Ostrum opened his veterinary practice in upstate New York. Peter Ostrum, D.V.M., is married and has one child.

■

Q: A unique new technology is displayed during a *Willy Wonka* musical number. What?

A: During the Augustus Gloop and Veruca Salt renditions of the song "Oompa-Loompa Doompadee-Doo" there is a very early type of computer animation used. In both cases, the film scene is compressed into a small area of the frame, while computer-animated words twist, swirl, and bounce in synch with the music through the rest of the frame area.

This was the era of "Sesame Street," whose gatling-gun pace and hyperactive graphics and animation were a portent of the quick-cutting, short-attention-span type of television that would soon become the norm.

■

Q: Who provided the financial backing for *Willy Wonka*?

A: In a unique arrangement, The Quaker Oats Company provided the three million dollar budget for *Willy Wonka and the Chocolate Factory*.

At the time, the major studios were foundering—Twentieth Century-Fox and MGM had both sold off their costumes, props, and most of their real estate; cut production; and laid off most of their permanent staffs. Independent producers, unencumbered by real property, flourished.

At the same time, in a reaction to the increasingly "adult" tone of Hollywood product, many independents structured multi-picture deals for "family" films. Robert Radnitz, who had produced *A Dog of Flanders* (1959) and *My Side of the Mountain* (1969) signed such a deal with Mattel. General Electric announced the formation of a subsidiary to back film production.

And David L. Wolper joined them with this announcement in *Variety* on November 12, 1969: "Producer David L. Wolper has set a summer start for 'Charlie and the Chocolate Factory,' first Wolper project in his new arrangement for financing through Quaker Oats." Although Quaker Oats was able to gear their existing product (like breakfast cereals) to cross-promote with Willy Wonka, and launched a Willy Wonka candy line to correspond with the film's release, Robert N. Thurston, the company's then-vice president for corporate affairs, insisted that direct exploitation and commercial tie-ins were simply ancillary synergy to the company's key goal. "Our primary objective…is to use our resources to help create programming of exceptionally high quality for all family viewing," Thurston explained. "As a marketer of consumer products, we believe that the public will respond favorably to those companies which show a genuine concern for quality in the entertainment media with which the company and its products are associated."

Sure, Bob. And selling a little extra Cap'n Crunch® won't hurt business, either.

Q: Who does Mr. Slugworth turn out to be? What is his real name?

A: Slugworth is actually an employee of Willy Wonka, hired to enact his rather brutal test of loyalty. Wonka introduces him to Charlie and Grandpa Joe as "Mr. Wilkinson."

Slugworth/Wilkinson was played by the multi-talented, multilingual German character actor Gunter Meisner. Meisner appeared in more than a hundred feature films and television shows, but he actually began as a sculptor and painter, and went on to study drama at the State Conservatory in Dusseldorf.

In theatre, Meisner specialized in comedies, theatre of the absurd, and classical drama. He played the lead in the 1984 U.S. tour of Franz Kafka's *Report to the Academy*, and appeared off-Broadway in *Fairwell* the same year.

His films include *Babette Goes to War* (1959, with Brigitte Bardot), *Is Paris Burning?* (1966), *The Odessa File* (1974), *Voyage of the Damned* (1976), *The Boys From Brazil* (1978), *Avalanche Express* (1979), *Night Crossing* (1981), *Under the Volcano* (1984), and the 1982 French comedy *L'as des As* (*Ace of Aces*) as both Adolf Hitler...and his sister Angela.

Meisner had played Hitler in the TV mini-series *The Winds of War*, and he also appeared on television in *Blood and Honor* as well as the daytime dramas "One Life to Live" and "The Edge of Night."

He directed a 1970 film on racial problems in Africa, *Don't Look for Me at Places Where I Can't Be Found*, and *Bega Dwa Bega* (*One for All*) in Swahili for the Tanzanian Film Unit.

Gunter Meisner died in late 1994.

■

Q: Willy Wonka has been said to have been inspired by a real person. Who?

A: During World War II, Roald Dahl achieved some fame by chronicling the legendary Royal Air Force pookas, the Gremlins (he later claimed to have named them—he didn't). His telling of the legend came to the attention of Walt Disney, who began developing an animated feature around them. Although the project was eventually shelved, Random House published a storybook of *The Gremlins*, illustrated by the artists of the Walt Disney Studio.

During the initial development of *The Gremlins*, Dahl came to Burbank as Disney's guest, and spent several weeks in the Disney cartoon factory. It has been surmised that his memories of the benevolent master of the mouse factory, combined with a self-confessed chocolate mania, led to the inspiration for the novel *Charlie and the Chocolate Factory*.

■

Q: Why was the name of the film changed from *Charlie and the Chocolate Factory* to *Willy Wonka and the Chocolate Factory*?

Author's Collection. © The Walt Disney Company

The benevolent master of the Mouse Factory may have been the original inspiration for the daft chairman of the Chocolate Factory.

A: A December 10, 1969, trade announcement in *Weekly Variety* trumpeted:

JULY 13
(filming begins)
**"CHARLIE AND THE
CHOCOLATE FACTORY"**
Screenplay by ROALD DAHL
based on his book
PRODUCED BY WOLPER PICTURES, LTD.

Trade coverage of the film referred to it by the title *Charlie and the Chocolate Factory* until August 17, 1970, when the announcement of the title change to *Willy Wonka and the Chocolate Factory* was made in the trade press.

Why the title change? The reasons are unclear, and although the revised title is somewhat unwieldy, the alliterative exoticism evoked by the name "Willy Wonka" does cause a double take. And there might have been some advantage in giving the title role to the film's only "star," Gene Wilder.

But according to syndicated entertainment columnist James Bacon, the title change was made due to "pressure from black groups." In a September 1, 1970, *Los Angeles Herald Examiner* column, Bacon reported that, "It seems 'Charlie' is a black label used for white men. Its association with chocolate touched off the protests."

■

Q: Charlie Bucket has a job. Doing what? What is his product? What is his boss's name?

A: Charlie delivers newspapers, specifically the nondescript English-language *Daily Chronicle*, for Mr. Jopek, the news vendor.

Q: One of the *Willy Wonka* cast of characters made an odd appearance on the music scene in 1994. Which one?

A: A Chicago quartet comprised of Nina Gordon, Jim Shapiro, Louise Post, and Steve Lack skyrocketed to fame in a popular new band called…Veruca Salt.

■

Q: What are Willy Wonka's corporate titles? What are his distinctive office furnishings?

A: According to what can be seen on his office door, Willy Wonka is Chairman of the Board, President, Vice President, Director, and Superintendent of Invention.

His office is half-furnished. Half-pictures and a half-clock hang on half-wallpapered walls. Wonka sits at a half-desk, with a half-lamp and half-phone, with his cigar in a half-ashtray. He reaches into a half-safe, and reads from a half-copy of a contract with a half-magnifying glass. I guess the inference that Wonka is only half a man would be a facile observation at this point.

As has been stated, the orphan child/surrogate father angle is emphasized in the film version of this story, never more so than in these final scenes.

hard

David L. Wolper presents

WILLY WONKA
AND THE
CHOCOLATE FACTORY

Produced by Stan Margulies and David L. Wolper

Directed by Mel Stuart

Screenplay by Roald Dahl, based on his book, *Charlie and the Chocolate Factory*

Director of Photography Arthur Ibbetson, BSC; Film Editor David Saxon
Art Director Harper Goff

Music Arranged and Conducted by Walter Scharf; Lyrics and Music by Leslie Bricusse and Anthony Newley
Musical Numbers Staged by Howard Jeffrey; Music Editor Jack Tillar

Dance Arrangements Betty Walberg; Production Manager Pia Arnold

Assistant Directors Jack Roe and Wolfgang Glattes

Unit Manager Renate Neuchl

Casting by Marion Dougherty Associates, New York

Associate Editor Mel Shapiro; Script Supervisor Trudi von Trotha

Camera Operator Paul Wilson

Sound Karsten Ullrich; Re-recording Dick Portman

Special Effects Logan R. Frazee; Sound Editor Charles L. Campbell

Construction Manager Hendrick G. Wynands

Dialogue Coach Frawley Becker; Wardrobe Head Ille Sievers

Costume Designer Helen Colvig; Make-up Raimund Stangl; Hairdresser Susi Krause

Optical Effects Jim Danforth, Richard Kuhn/Opticals West, Al Whitlock, Pacific Titles

Color by Technicolor®

A Wolper Pictures, Ltd. Presentation

Originally released by Paramount Pictures Corporation, May 1971

Distribution rights currently held by Warner Bros

MPAA Rated G. Running time: 97 minutes

Cast

Gene Wilder	Willy Wonka
Jack Albertson	Grandpa Joe
Peter Ostrum	Charlie Bucket
Roy Kinnear	Mr. Salt
Julie Dawn Cole	Veruca Salt
Leonard Stone	Mr. Sam Beauregarde
Denise Nickerson	Violet Beauregarde
Dodo Denney	Mrs. Teevee
Paris Themmen	Mike Teevee
Ursula Reitt	Mrs. Gloop
Michael Bollner	Augustus Gloop
Diana Sowle	Mrs. Bucket
Aubrey Woods	Bill, the Candy Shop Man
David Battley	Mr. Turkentine, the Teacher
Günter Meisner	Oskar Slugworth
Peter Capell	The Tinker
Werner Heyking	Mr. Jopek, the News Vendor
Peter Stuart	Winkleman, Charlie's Classmate

Chapter Seven

The Music Man

The musical, as a quintessentially American art form, is particularly charming when portraying Americana. There seems to be something quite natural about a musical when it depicts barbershop quartettes, summer picnics, and small town folks on the village green. And there is no probably no better musical portrait of Americana than The Music Man. A Broadway hit, skillfully and lovingly translated to film, The Music Man effervesces with the visceral energy of the source material and a galvanic lead performance. The songs are either clever, catchy, sweet, romantic, or some combination of these attributes. A talented and lovable cast immediately create an amiable, comical, and endearing portrait of rural America that is as fun as an ice cream social, as sweet as fresh watermelon, as reassuring as a rest on the front porch swing, and as fondly remembered as a happy childhood in a small town.

■

Level One: The Easy Stuff
Story & Characters

Previous page:
Shirley Jones
and Robert
Preston in the
spectacular finale
of *The Music Man*.

Q: When Harold Hill is introduced on screen, where does he say he is going?

A: "Wherever the people are as green as the money…friend." The role of Harold Hill, a "bang beat bell-ringin' big haul, great-go, neck-or-nothin' rip-roarin' ever' time-a-bull's-eye salesman" was played to perfection by (as rarely happens in film adaptations of stage musicals) the creator of the role, Robert Preston.

Preston was born Robert Preston Meservey in 1918 in Newton Highlands, Massachusetts (also the birthplace of Jack Lemmon and Robert Morse, just outside Boston). His family relocated to Los Angeles when Preston was two years old. Although not from a "show business" family, Preston began appearing locally with a family friend, described by Preston as "a canny Scots actor who needed a boy to play him as a child in one-night stands." His high school drama teacher introduced Preston to the canon of Shakespeare, and he joined the repertory company of Patia Power (Tyrone Power's mother). "I was only sixteen," Preston recollected, "and there I was, playing Julius Caesar." When the company folded, Preston became a supernumerary at the Pasadena Playhouse, eventually appearing in forty-two plays there.

In 1962 Preston remembered, "I was a husky, beetle-browed type, and my hairline was considerably lower than it is now." Through Bing Crosby's brother, Everett (who was a friend of Preston's mother), he was taken to a casting director at Paramount, who said, "Kid, if I want to see wrestlers, I'll go to the stadium on Monday night." A Paramount producer interceded the next day, giving Preston a screen test. At nineteen years of age, Preston was signed to a contract with Paramount Pictures.

He starred in a couple of B pictures like *King of Alcatraz* (1938), but quickly rose to secondary roles in A pictures like *Beau Geste*, *Union Pacific* (1939), *Moon Over Burma*, and *Northwest Mounted Police* (1940). His first co-star billing was in *Typhoon* (1940).

Preston made a series of "battle" pictures during World War II, including *Parachute Battalion* (1941), *Pacific Blackout*, *Wake Island* (1942), and *Night Plane From Chungking* (1943).

He was featured in *The Macomber Affair* (1947) and had memorable supporting parts in the Westerns *Blood on the Moon* and *Whispering Smith* (1948).

He continued to work in films until the mid-1950s, including Westerns such as *The Sundowners* (1950), *Best of the Badmen*, and *My Outlaw*

Brother (1951), as well as his last "snowshoe epic," *The Last Frontier* (1957, a.k.a. *Savage Wilderness*).

Preston also appeared on television, in the early series "Man Against Crime" (1951) and "Anywhere, USA" (1952).

Naturally, Preston's prestige ascended with his acclaimed musical debut in *The Music Man* at New York's Majestic Theater on December 19, 1957. Preston played Harold Hill in 882 of the show's 1,375 performances, and won the Tony award for Best Actor in a Musical.

He returned to Hollywood for a well-regarded lead performance in Delbert Mann's version of William Inge's *The Dark at the Top of the Stairs* (1960), after which he starred in the Warner Bros. film version of his Broadway triumph, *The Music Man*.

After *The Music Man*, Preston appeared infrequently in films, considering his star status. He had roles in *How the West Was Won* (1962), *All the Way Home*, and *Island of Love* (1963), but afterward returned to the theatre, winning another Tony Award in 1966. His next film role was in *Child's Play* (1972), followed by *Junior Bonner* the same year. He next played Beauregarde Jackson Pickett Burnside in the disastrous 1974 maiming of *Mame*. (The role had been played in the film *Auntie Mame* by Forrest Tucker, who had assumed the role of Harold Hill in the national touring company of *The Music Man*.)

His remaining big-screen appearances were in *Semi-Tough* (1977), *S.O.B.* (1981), *Victor/Victoria* (1982, for which he received a Best Supporting Actor Oscar nomination), and *The Last Starfighter* (1984, in which he played sort of an alien Harold Hill). Preston spent a little more time on the small screen late in his career, in the mini-series *The Chisolms* (1979), and in TV movies like *My Father's House* (1975), *September Gun* (1983), and the delightful May–December romance *Finnegan Begin Again* (1985). His last film was the TV movie *Outrage!* in 1986.

It cannot be overstated how bizarre the casting of Robert Preston as Harold Hill in *The Music Man* appeared to the world at large in 1957. His B movie and character parts had strait-jacketed his opportunities to even be *considered* for roles outside of rugged outdoorsman or hero's best friend. When Preston was suggested for Hill by one of the creative team on the original Broadway show, even the composer responded with, "You're talking about Robert Snowshoes Preston, half-brother of Chingachgook, and inventor of the igloo and the aluminum dogsled?"

Later, the same nay-sayer recanted. "How this leprechaun of a volatile-witted seventh son of Thespis' most lighthearted and most happily gifted seventh son could have been chained for so long in the ambling black-bear masquerade that not only obscured his true abilities but showed him, alas, all too convincingly, in complete—and unfortunately highly successful—juxtaposition to everything his great gifts clamored to really reveal, remains one of the fascinating mysteries of the theatre."

And Brenda Davis, in a 1962 issue of *Sight & Sound*, succinctly stated that, although Preston was "not a natural singer or dancer, he has mastered the art of appearing to be both."

Preston's performance, both on stage and as immortalized on film, is the signature role of his career. It established his star for the rest of his life. But, sadly, in the words of Leslie Halliwell, "He [spent] years on Broadway before Hollywood realized the star it had lost."

Preston died on March 21, 1987, in Santa Barbara, California. His Harold Hill is as fascinating, visceral, and buoyant today as ever—it's difficult to count the number of times Preston's feet touch the ground during the film.

■

Q: In what city does Harold Hill leave the train? What is the city's population?

A: Harold decides to "give Iowa a try," and debarks in River City Iowa, population 2212.

River City is a wry but loving tribute to Mason City, Iowa, the boyhood home of the creator of *The Music Man*. (His mother had led a campaign to get Mason City's Willow Creek renamed Willow River. "Mason City is a River City," she reportedly said, "not a Creek City." Mason City, she maintained, had been settled as an Indian village, and Indians *always* located their settlements at the confluence of two rivers—not creeks, rivers.)

The town of River City was realized on the back lot of the Warner Bros. Burbank studio. Harold Hill leaves the train at the River City station, a railroad depot located on the south berm of the back lot (the south side of which overlooks the concrete bed of the Los Angeles River). He walks north through an undeveloped portion of the lot toward the southwest side of the Western Street (which at that time had recently been used in the TV series "Maverick"). Hill enters River City from the south side, heading toward City Hall.

The small town business district was a standing set built in 1943 for *Saratoga Trunk*, an adaptation of Edna Ferber's novel starring Gary Cooper and Ingrid Bergman, which wasn't released until 1945.

The residential street to its west side was part of a standing set built for the 1941 melodrama *King's Row*—the *Peyton Place* of its time, the picture was called "half masterpiece and half junk" by James Agate. Both of these sets were used contiguously, and were completely redressed for the 1912 period of *The Music Man* to include a billiard parlor, a candy kitchen, a public library, and a stern-visaged statue of the town founder in the village square.

Much of River City, including the picnic park featured in the second act, was created indoors on the Warner sound stages.

The River City set still exists today on the Warner lot, and is rarely idle. Now called "Midwest Street," it has served hundreds of films and television shows since it was River City. Its identities have included Hazzard County in the TV series "The Dukes of Hazzard" (1979–1986), Bedford Falls in the distaff remake of *It's a Wonderful Life*, *It Happened One Christmas* (1977), and Clark Kent's boyhood home, Smallville, in "Lois & Clark: The New Adventures of Superman." Both the town and residential streets were used often in the long-running series "The Waltons" (1972–1981). The residential street was even extensively redressed and used as Fall River, Massachusetts in the cult favorite TV movie *The Legend of Lizzie Borden* (1975).

■

Q: Hill runs into an old friend who calls him by another name. What is the name? What is Hill's friend's name?

A: "Gregory!" Marcellus Washburn exclaims. "Of all the people t'run inta in Iowa—Gregory!"

A rather inspired bit of movie casting has

Four views of "River City" on the Warner Bros. back lot. From left, the Madison Public Library facade, the Billiard Parlor, Center Street, and

Buddy Hackett playing Harold Hill's former con shill Marcellus. In a film that has recast virtually every role but the lead from the Broadway original, *The Music Man* actually avoids any clinkers.

Brooklyn-born comic and actor Buddy Hackett (born Leonard Hacker) began working as an apprentice to his father, an upholsterer. He broke into show business in the "borscht belt" of the Catskills, as a waiter-comic. Hackett became the idol of his contemporaries for his wacky and inventive stand-up routines, and shot to success in nightclubs and on television. His first film role was as Donald O'Connor's Army buddy in the musical *Walking My Baby Back Home* (1953), which he followed with *Fireman Save My Child* (1954, originally begun with Abbott and Costello, recast with Hackett and Spike Jones!), *God's Little Acre* (1958), *All Hands on Deck*, and *Everything's Ducky* (1961).

After *The Music Man*, Hackett starred in *The Wonderful World of the Brothers Grimm* (1962), *It's a Mad Mad Mad Mad World* (1963), *Muscle Beach Party* (1964), and Disney's *The Love Bug* (1969), among others. In 1988, Hackett did a hysterical turn as Ebeneezer Scrooge in the TV-event-within-a-film in *Scrooged*. He was also the voice of Scuttle, the befuddled seagull, in Disney's *The Little Mermaid* (1989).

Marcellus Washburn has definitely left the confidence business in which he and Harold Hill were once colleagues. He epitomizes the small town interconnections of River City—he lives there, and he likes it there. His girl is Ethel Tof-flemeyer (the Pianola girl, played by Peggy Mondo), whose uncle (Vernon Reed as Jacey Squires) owns the stable where Marcellus works. Jacey Squires is a solid "River City-zien," serving on the school board (and is, naturally, one of the barbershop quartette). His wife is Mrs. Squires, a member of the inner circle of the Mayor's wife, as well as the River City Ladies Eurhythmic Dance Group. Mrs. Squires is played by the indefatigable Mary Wickes.

■

Q: Marcellus reveals some of Hill's previous confidence games. What are they?

A: In Joplin (Missouri), Harold "Gregory" Hill had apparently imitated a famous Italian "band leader" in the park. He had been a salesman of steam-powered automobiles as well, until somebody actually invented one. But, according to all available information, the Boy's Band scam is his "old stand."

■

Q: Marcellus tells Harold that they have music in town. What are the two sources of music?

A: A Gramophone at the barber shop, and a stuck-up librarian who "gives piano." The stuck-up librarian is Marian Paroo, played by Shirley Jones.

Jones was born in 1934, in the tiny town of

The City Hall of River City (the library facade is barely visible on the left).

Photographs by the Author

Smithton, Pennsylvania (population 800). She studied music, voice, acting, and movement at the Pittsburgh Playhouse. On a vacation trip to New York with her parents, Jones caught the eye of an agent who rushed to sign the talented young singer. Although she felt she needed more training and wanted to stay in Smithton, Jones returned to New York and was sent by her agent to an open audition at the Broadway Theater for Rodgers and Hammerstein, who were replacing chorus members in *South Pacific*. Rodgers was so taken with Jones that he went across the street to the St. James Theater to fetch his partner, who was rehearsing an orchestra. She sang three songs from the *Oklahoma!* score and was immediately placed in the Broadway company of *South Pacific*. What Jones didn't know at the time was that she was already being considered for the film role of Laurey in *Oklahoma!*

After six months with *South Pacific*, Jones understudied the Broadway lead and then went on the road with the touring company of *Me and Juliet*. While in Chicago with that show, she was summoned to Hollywood to screen test with Gordon MacRae for *Oklahoma!* "I didn't even know what a camera looked like," Jones recalls, "but I found it much easier to act before a camera than on stage. I took to it like a duck to water." After the test, Jones resumed the tour of *Me and*

Marcellus Washburne (Buddy Hackett) delivers a warning to Harold Hill (Robert Preston).

Juliet. A month later, Jones's agent telephoned, and greeted her with, "Hello, Laurey." It had been almost exactly one year since her first audition for Rodgers and Hammerstein.

Following *Oklahoma!* (1955), Jones was cast as Julie Jordan in the Twentieth Century-Fox film version of Rodgers and Hammerstein's *Carousel* (1956). Initially, Frank Sinatra had been cast as Billy Bigelow, but after finding that the film was to be shot twice, for two different presentation formats (just as *Oklahoma!* had been), he quit. Jones was again joined in *Carousel* by Gordon MacRae.

Several films followed, including *April Love* (1957), *Never Steal Anything Small* (1959), *Elmer Gantry*, *Pepe* (1960), and *Two Rode Together* (1961).

In late 1960, Jones's agent called to ask if she'd be interested in the role of Marian in the Warner Bros. film version of *The Music Man*. "One of the reasons I loved Marian was because she was sort of a seasoned lady, compared to the ingenues I had played in the other musicals," Jones recalls. "She knew where she was going, what she was doing, and would have the upper hand at all times." Jones' casting was announced on January 3, 1961.

Jones plays Marian with remarkable finesse, considering that not only is she playing opposite Robert Preston, who had played his role on stage for two years, but also amidst the biggest and best-known of Hollywood's character actors. Jones finds in Marian an assurance that highlights the character as the moral center of the film, but with the depth of a sometimes-confused romantic who may, in fact, do the wrong thing (but for the right reason). "I never felt like an outsider, or a 'new kid,' even among Bob, Pert, the Buffalo Bills, and all those people who had been in the stage productions. They actually helped and guided me in finding Marian."

It was during the production of *The Music Man* that Shirley Jones won the Oscar for Best Supporting Actress for her role in *Elmer Gantry*.

Jones continued making films, including *The Courtship of Eddie's Father*, *A Ticklish Affair*

Author's Collection. © Warner Bros. Inc.

(1963), *Bedtime Story, Dark Purpose* (a.k.a. *L'Intrigo*, 1964), *Fluffy*, and *The Secret of My Success* (1965).

In 1968, Jones appeared in her only Broadway lead, with then-husband Jack Cassidy, in the musical *Maggie Flynn*, which did not fare well, running only eighty-three performances.

Jones returned to film, appearing in *The Happy Ending* (1969), and *The Cheyenne Social Club* (1970).

Shirley Jones achieved television fame starring opposite stepson David Cassidy in the hit situation comedy "The Partridge Family" (1970–74). The show made a teen idol of Cassidy, and made Shirley Jones a household name again.

Jones has only made two more films, *Beyond the Poseidon Adventure* (1979) and *Tank* (1984). But she has returned to her real love, music, performing concerts with symphony orchestras several times a month all over the United States. She also recently toured in a production of *The King and I*.

Most recently, Jones has appeared in a series of "Burke's Law" TV movies opposite Gene Barry.

■

Q: According to the town ladies, Marian has a suspicious past. What is she supposed to have done?

A: She is supposed to have had a brazen affair with wealthy River City philanthropist Henry Madison, referred to by the ladies as "Old Miser Madison." Marian has been suspected by many in the town of being a gold digger, since "she was seen going and coming from his place." Naturally, the suspicions of the small-town gossips were confirmed when Madison died, leaving the library building to the city, but all the books to Marian Paroo!

As it turns out, Madison is, unknown to the ladies, Marian's "god-uncle," her father's best friend. He has left the library books to Marian to ensure her job in the face of malicious small-town rumor.

Miser Madison's only other apparent or implied sin is generosity to the little town. Marian works in the Madison Public Library. Harold stands in the shadow of a statue of Madison in the town square. The Fourth of July assembly is held in the Madison Gymnasium, and the Fourth of July picnic is in Madison Park.

■

Q: How does Harold Hill win over the skeptical school board of River City?

A: He performs his first "miracle," transforming the squabbling school board into a harmonious barbershop quartette. The creator of *The Music Man* maintained that this was the first authentic barbershop quartette ever to appear in any Broadway show or motion picture. "Those familiar handlebar-mustache beer-barrel guys in the sleeve garters…bear no relationship to any barbershop quartette," he declared, for the following reasons: First, no real barbershopper would have any musical accompaniment. Second, the stereotyped "barbershop" numbers contain little in the way of challenging harmony, and tend to have an unyielding tempo. Finally, and most importantly (and as portrayed in *The Music Man*), the joy of barbershop, for a barbershopper, is not performing, it is "practicing"—seeking harmonies and experimenting with modulations, for the pleasure they themselves derive from the experience.

The Buffalo Bills (Vernon Reed as Jacey Squires, William Spangenberg as Olin Britt, Al Shea as Ewart Dunlop, and Wayne Ward as Oliver Hix) were the original quartette in the Broadway cast of *The Music Man*, as well as in the film. The national touring company of the show featured The Frisco Four (Jay F. Smith as Jacey Squires, Allan Louw as Olin Britt, Byron Mellberg as Ewart Dunlop, and James Ingram as Oliver Hix).

As follow-up to his barbershop quartette miracle, Harold Hill also organizes the town ladies (incorporating the quartette's wives and the

Mayor's wife) into something called the Ladies Auxiliary for the Classic Dance, later referred to by Mayor Shinn as the River City Ladies' Eurhythmic Dance Group. The part that's missing from the film is that Marian Paroo is established by Harold as the group *leader*, and the ladies end up adoring her. Hill even convinces the ladies to read the "dirty books" that Marian keeps in the library…and they love them!

■

Q: The entire town finds excitement in the arrival of the band instruments. By what means are the instruments being delivered?

A: The Wells Fargo Wagon, the much anticipated-carrier of goodies from all over the country.

The Wells Fargo & Company Express Carrier, "Over Railroad, Stage and Steamboat Routes," was a primary carrier of goods across the United States, Canada, and Mexico from the days of the California Gold Rush to the 1960s.

Founded in 1852 by Henry Wells and William G. Fargo (co-founders of American Express Company in 1850), Wells Fargo & Company was an enterprise of high reputation and greatly varied services. According to an express receipt of a vintage close to the time of *The Music Man* story, the Company maintained lines covering some forty thousand miles, reaching "nearly every Hamlet, Town and City in the UNITED STATES and CANADA."

Services included the carriage and delivery of money, valuable parcels, packages, merchandise, and letters; recording of deeds; payment of taxes for non-residents; service of legal papers; reclamation of baggage at depots and hotels; redemption of goods in pawn; issuing of money orders (domestic and international); and collection of drafts, notes, bills, coupons, dividends, and other paper.

The celebratory arrival of the Wells Fargo Wagon is by no means exaggerated in *The Music Man*. A Wells Fargo agent described entering a western town in 1863: "I heard a shout, 'Wells

Shirley Jones and Robert Preston in a classic studio publicity portrait for *The Music Man*.

Fargo have come.' In less than three minutes I was surrounded by an excited crowd of three hundred men."

Today, Wells Fargo & Company is the fifteenth largest bank holding company in the United States. Wells Fargo Bank, N.A. is the principle subsidiary of Wells Fargo & Company, with assets of fifty-two billion dollars as of December 31, 1994. The bank subsidiary was the seventh largest bank in the United States based on assets at June 30, 1994. Wells Fargo & Company stock is traded on the New York, Pacific, London, and Frankfurt stock exchanges.

And the song about their delivery wagon is pretty catchy, too.

■

Q: There's a unexpected hitch in Harold's plan to demonize the game of pool in the eyes of River City's populace. What is the unexpected complication?

A: The Mayor owns the Pleez-All Billiard Parlor (located at Avon and Center Streets, River City, Iowa) and the new pool table. As if Mayor

Shinn wasn't suspicious enough ("Get that spell-binder's credentials!"), Harold also plays cupid between the Mayor's oldest daughter, Zaneeta, and the town roughneck, Tommy Djilas.

Paul Ford played the Mayor of River City in his trademark fashion, as a sort of a pompous-but-befuddled basset hound. Ford had been born Paul Ford Weaver in 1901, but didn't step onstage until nearly middle age. He was an unemployed father of five when, during the Depression, he began performing a WPA-sponsored puppet show. He soon moved on to acting, first in radio, and then to Broadway, where he debuted in 1944.

His first film appearance, in *The House on 92nd Street*, came in 1945. Other films followed, including *The Naked City* (1948) and *All the King's Men* (1949).

His performance as a put-upon colonel in the Broadway hit *The Teahouse of the August Moon* (1953) sealed his public identity, and he was often cast as self-inflated comic authority figures. He recreated his *Teahouse of the August Moon* role for film in 1956, and played a similar role in "The Phil Silvers Show," a.k.a. "You'll Never Get Rich," a.k.a. "Sergeant Bilko" (1955–1959), and again later in the short-lived "Baileys of Balboa" (1964).

Ford jumped back to films, appearing as Horace Vandergelder to Shirley Booth's Dolly Gallegher Levi in *The Matchmaker* (1958), *Advise and Consent* (1962), and, of course, *The Music Man*.

After *The Music Man*, Ford returned to Broadway and another acclaimed performance as a middle-aged man whose wife becomes pregnant in *Never Too Late* (1962). In 1963, he appeared in *It's a Mad Mad Mad Mad World*, which he followed with a reprise of his Broadway role in the film version of *Never Too Late* (1965).

His last films were *A Big Hand for the Little Lady*; *The Russians Are Coming! The Russians Are Coming!* (1966); *The Comedians* (1967); *Lola* (1969, a.k.a *Twinky*, a.k.a. *Statutory Affair*); and a character voice in the 1974 animated feature *Journey Back to Oz*.

Paul Ford died in 1976.

Q: How many trombones led the big parade? How many cornets were right behind?

A: According to the lyric, 76 trombones led the big parade, with 110 cornets right behind. According to Warner Bros. music department documentation, for the film's finale parade there were 72 trombones, 24 clarinets, 30 cornets, 6 piccolos, 6 French horns, 6 baritones, 6 euphoniums, 6 bassoons, 12 snare drums (military), 6 bass drums, 6 bass drum carriers, 6 glockenspiels, 6 sousaphones, and 6 cymbals.

An April 10, 1961, Warner Bros property department memo explained:

> We have received this date, April 10, 1961, shipped from Elkhart, Indiana:
> 185 assorted New BAND INSTRUMENTS AND CASES on a loan basis from Richards Music Corporation, to be used for our production of "Music Man" No. 10864; with an approximate valuation of $35,000.00 (thirty-five thousand dollars).
> These musical instruments will be in our possession for the entire duration of this picture and after that time we will receive shipping instructions for the return of same.

The finale scene was shot in just two days, Tuesday, May 9 and Wednesday, May 10, 1961.

The creator of *The Music Man* was actually the honorary leader of the marching band at the opening of Walt Disney World in 1971—he led a band fronted by 76 trombones.

River City Mayor George Shinn (Paul Ford) addresses his fellow "River City-ziens."

easy

medium

Q: Who was the creator of *The Music Man*?

A: Meredith Willson was the real-life music man behind *The Music Man*. Born in Mason City, Iowa, in 1902, Willson went to New York after graduating high school, where he studied at Damrosch's Institute of Musical Art (now known as the Juilliard School of Music).

His virtuosity on flute and piccolo led to his first professional post, first flutist with John Philip Sousa's Band, at the age of nineteen. He joined the New York Philharmonic, under the direction of the legendary Arturo Toscanini, before turning to conducting and composing in 1929. For the next twelve years he was musical director of San Francisco radio station KFRC and of NBC's western division. He then moved south to Hollywood, where he became musical director for several radio programs. After serving in the Army in World War II, emerging with the rank of major, he returned to radio, starring in several network programs. Among them were "Meredith Willson's Sparkle Time" (sponsored by Canada Dry), "Meredith Willson's Show Room" (sponsored by Ford), and "The Meredith Willson Show" (sponsored by General Foods).

In 1950, he was musical director and co-star of the Tallulah Bankhead radio program "The Big Show." It was at about this time that he began work on what would become *The Music Man*.

Willson met his wife, the former Ralina Zarova, a concert, opera, and radio singer of Russian-French extraction, in San Francisco in 1949. Willson called her "Rini." Typical of Willson's sly comic nature, Rini "appears" in *The Music Man*. As the school board corners him, Harold Hill produces a bogus testimonial (actually his overdue hotel bill) from "the only female bassoon player on the Red Path Circuit"...Madame Rini.

"I don't think people realize how hysterically funny Meredith's writing is," Shirley Jones says.

"Even being with him in person was funny, because he was such a straight-laced Hawkeye gentleman, and yet he would say these hysterical things with such a straight face."

Willson composed popular song hits like "May the Good Lord Bless and Keep You" (inspired by his mother's weekly farewell to her Sunday school class) and "I See the Moon." He also wrote the novel *Who Did What to Fedilia*, and the autobiographical volumes *And There I Stood With My Piccolo* and *Eggs I Have Laid*.

Upon his death in 1984, Willson was, not surprisingly, eulogized chiefly as the creator of *The Music Man*.

"I think it's the quintessential American musical," says Shirley Jones. "Meredith's work so completely depicts America."

■

Q: What was the source material for *The Music Man*?

A: The real answer lies in the childhood of Meredith Willson. In the words of Gilbert Millstein of The New York Times in 1958, "*The Music Man* is largely a recapitulation, tenderly altered in recollection and shaped to the exigencies of musical comedy, of things that happened to Willson and about him in Mason City (which he calls 'River City') when he was ten years old."

In 1959, Willson wrote a detailed, rambling, and above all, funny account of how *The Music Man* came to be, *But He Doesn't Know the Territory*. In it, he recalls being nudged by his wife (and a certain amount of "Iowa stubbornness") to combine his writing and composing. He typed "Act One, Scene One" on a piece of paper, and that's pretty much where it stayed. Over the desk in his music room, Willson had a framed picture of Mason City's first High School Band, circa 1912. A piccolo (Willson), two clarinets, two cornets, one euphonium, one tuba, one snare drum, one bass drum, and an alto. Willson contemplated this photo, and a rush of childhood memories led to the development of a story concept—a boy's band with a phony leader/instrument salesman named Harold Hill.

Outline in hand, Willson approached Cy Feuer, who with partner Ernest Martin had produced *Guys and Dolls* (1950), *Can Can* (1953), *The Boy Friend* (1954), and *Silk Stockings* (1955). Feuer, Martin, and Willson worked together for several years to develop the outline into a workable libretto, tentatively titled *The Silver Triangle*. After many coast-to-coast trips and Herculean effort, Willson and Feuer and Martin parted company. They had, however, given Willson a new title for his embryonic musical: *The Music Man*.

Willson continued his efforts on *The Music Man*. In August 1956, he and Rini traveled to San Diego, where Willson was to write and conduct the music for a dramatic and musical pageant called *The California Story*. There the Willsons met Franklin Lacey, who became Willson's collaborator on the script of *The Music Man*. Later that month, Willson approached the producer of Frank Loesser's Broadway hit *The Most Happy Fella*, Kermit Bloomgarden, with a new draft of *The Music Man* ("draft #32," Willson claimed). Bloomgarden and his producing partner Herb Greene were wowed, and offered to produce the show.

The Music Man premiered on Broadway at the Majestic Theater on December 19, 1957, and was an immediate smash.

■

Q: Who was the gifted director of *The Music Man*?

A: Morton Da Costa. Born Morton Tecosky in Philadelphia in 1914, his real name inspired the nickname by which his intimates called him: "Tec," pronounced "Teak." Meredith Willson appreciated this peculiar nickname because it helped identify sycophants and phonies: "So when somebody says 'Mort asked me to speak to you about an audition,' or 'Morty said you ought to hear my voice,' you know they're making it up."

Da Costa attended Temple University, and made his Broadway debut as an actor in 1942, then as a director in 1950. He directed the hits *Plain and Fancy* (1955) and *No Time for Sergeants* (1955) on Broadway, as well as both the stage (1956) and film (1958) versions of *Auntie Mame*, and the stage version of *The Music Man*. He both produced and directed the film version of *The Music Man*.

Da Costa made only one more film, the flop comedy *Island of Love* (1963), which starred Robert Preston as a con artist (hmmm). Da Costa returned to the stage, where he was involved in several interesting projects, including a 1967 musical version of Kaufman and Hart's *The Man Who Came to Dinner*, titled *Sherry!* (no kidding). Da Costa bowed out and was replaced by Joe Layton, and the finished production limped on to Broadway for sixty-five performances. In the mid-1980s, Da Costa supervised a production of *Welcome to the Club* (under the title *Let 'em Rot!*) at the White Barn in Westport, but was not involved in the Broadway (flop) staging in 1989. In 1968, Da Costa reunited with Shirley Jones for her Broadway lead debut, *Maggie Flynn*, which did not fare well either.

Jones remembers that Da Costa was never comfortable in California. "He was a real New Yorker, and he had a little needlepoint shop, I believe in Connecticut. He did fantastic needlepoint himself. To me that somehow ties directly to the focus and meticulousness of his stage and film work." It's not surprising to note, then, that 1975 saw the publication of *Morton Da Costa's Book of Needlepoint*.

Da Costa never duplicated the glory, either on stage or screen, that he attained with *Auntie Mame* and *The Music Man*, and he has unjustly become a footnote in theatre history. Morton Da Costa died in 1987.

medium

Q: Susan Luckey, who plays Zaneeta Shinn, had appeared in another musical with Shirley Jones. Which one? Who did she play?

A: Susan Luckey had played Julie Jordan and Billy Bigelow's daughter, Louise, in the 1956 film version of *Carousel*. Luckey had played Zaneeta in the national touring company of *The Music Man*, which debuted in Los Angeles at the Philharmonic Auditorium on August 18, 1958.

After the film was made, Luckey continued to dance, and in 1964 married Larry Douglas, who had played Lun Tha in the Broadway company of *The King and I*. The couple toured together in *Promises, Promises* for three years, and Luckey later taught stagecraft, playwriting, and producing in the gifted children's program of the Los Angeles Unified School District. Luckey and Douglas have a daughter, Shayna, and mother and daughter toured Scotland and England in 1990 with a vocal group from the San Fernando Valley.

Although Luckey was essentially a dancer, the role of Zaneeta offered a character part full of childish fun and the memorable exclamation, "Ye Gods!"

In fact, among the dozens of letters, notes, and telegrams of praise contained in Jack L. Warner's files, from senators, editors, producers, and "just-plain-folk," there is one exception. A letter from Montgomery, Alabama, complains about the use of "Ye Gods!" by Zaneeta and "By God" by Mayor Shinn, saying that "The Bible very plainly teaches that it is wrong to take the name of the Lord our God in vain."

■

Q: The Broadway choreographer of *The Music Man* also directed the dancing in the film. Who was the choreographer?

A: Onna White. White's career as a choreographer began as assistant to renowned choreographer Michael Kidd, with whom she worked on the Broadway and London productions of *Finian's Rainbow* and *Guys and Dolls*.

Author's Collection. © Warner Bros. Inc.

Confrontation in the Candy Kitchen. Susan Luckey, Hermione Gingold, Paul Ford, and Timmy Everett mix it up as Robert Preston and Shirley Jones look on.

White was born in the small mining town of Inverness, Cape Breton Island, Nova Scotia. She began ballet lessons while attending school at Powell River, British Columbia. White struck out on her own at an early age, and joined the San Francisco Opera Ballet Company, touring as one of the sixteen dancers in their corps de ballet. She stayed with the company for seven years, attaining the status of prima ballerina.

White's first show as a choreographer was *The Music Man*, which she also choreographed for film. She choreographed the stage and film versions of *Bye Bye Birdie* (stage 1960, film 1963), *Mame* (stage 1966, film 1974), and *1776* (stage 1969, film 1972).

Other Broadway shows included *Take Me Along* (1959), *Irma La Douce* (1960), and *Half a Sixpence* (1965); other films include *Oliver!* (1968) and *Pete's Dragon* (1977).

White's inventive and highly athletic choreography inspired this story (which may or may not be true): Two male dancers meet and shake hands. "Ouch!" says one, cringing. "Oh," the other responds knowingly, "working for Onna, huh?"

■

Q: One of the supporting players in *The Music Man* had also been in a major movie musical that had been nominated for the Best Picture Oscar. Who?

A: Hermione Gingold had appeared in *Gigi* as Madame Alvarez, Gigi's Grandmama. *Gigi* won the Academy Award for Best Picture in 1958.

Gingold was born in London in 1897, and began her theatre career on stage at age eleven. She established herself as a favorite revue comedienne in London and New York. Gingold appeared infrequently in films, beginning in 1936 with *Someone at the Door*.

Other films prior to her performance in *The Music Man* include *The Butler's Dilemma* (1943), *Pickwick Papers* (1954), *Around the*

World in 80 Days (1956), *Bell, Book and Candle* (1958), the previously-mentioned *Gigi*, and *The Naked Edge* (1961).

Her performance as the pompous, judgmental, and small-minded Eulalie MacKecknie Shinn is one of the many delights of *The Music Man*.

Gingold continued to appear in occasional films, on stage, and on television. Movies included *I'd Rather Be Rich* (1964), *Harvey Middleman, Fireman* (1965), *Munster, Go Home* (no kidding), *Promise Her Anything* (1966), and *Those Fantastic Flying Fools* (a.k.a. *Blast-Off*, 1967).

She originated the role of Madame Armfeldt in *A Little Night Music* on Broadway in 1973, a role she reprised (her last film performance) in the lamentable film version of 1978.

Hermione Gingold died in 1987.

■

Q: Besides Robert Preston and the Buffalo Bills, name one of the key roles in *The Music Man* to be played by its Broadway original.

A: Pert Kelton created the role of ever-lovin' Widda Paroo on Broadway.

"Dear Pert Kelton," recalls Shirley Jones, "she was a real pro. Of course, she had done the role on stage, and the fact that she got to play it in the film was sensational—I can't think of anyone who could have played it like Pert, with her Irish lilt and the hint of haughty pride that really define her character."

Kelton was born into a vaudeville family in 1907, and, in stereotypical fashion, she joined the act in 1910 and began a solo act in 1919. She debuted on Broadway in 1925 in the musical *Sunny*, and made her first movie in 1929. She appeared in several films over the next decade, including *The Bowery* (1933), *Annie Oakley* (1935), *Cain and Mabel* (1936), and *You Can't Take It With You* (1938).

She left films in the late 1930s, and appeared on stage and television until *The Music Man* brought her back to the screen, after which she appeared in *Love and Kisses* (1965) and her final film, *The Comic* (1969). Kelton died in 1968.

Kelton was the original Alice Kramden in "The Honeymooners" sketches on Jackie Gleason's "Cavalcade of Stars" on the Dumont Network, from 1950 to 1952. Kelton was felled by a coronary thrombosis just as Gleason was moving his show to CBS. "Pert, who was damn good as Alice Kramden, never played her again after that setback," Gleason recalled in 1985. Alice Kramden was played by Audrey Meadows (1952–1957), Sue Ann Langdon (1962–63), and finally Sheila MacRae (1966–1971). Kelton did reappear on "The Honeymooners"; on

the 1966–67 season of "The Jackie Gleason Show," she played Mrs. Gibson, Alice's mother!

■

Q: **Who played Marian the Librarian's little brother?**

A: Ronny Howard (now Ron Howard) was all of seven years old and already a pro when he played Winthrop Paroo in *The Music Man*. He was appearing at the time as Opie Taylor on "The Andy Griffith Show" (1960–68). Howard had made his professional debut at eighteen months of age, and his feature film debut in *The Journey* (1959). Howard's father, actor Rance Howard, appears in *The Music Man* as Oscar Jackson, one of River City's Iowa-stubborn townsfolk.

Howard appeared with his *Music Man* sister Jones in *The Courtship of Eddie's Father* (1963), and appeared sporadically in features such as *Village of the Giants* (1965), *Smoke* (1970), *The Wild Country* (1971), and *American Graffiti* (1973).

Howard spent the next decade as squeaky-clean Richie Cunningham in the hit TV series "Happy Days" (1974–84). During this long TV haul, Howard starred in several feature films, including the low-budget—and surprisingly successful—*Eat My Dust!* (1976) and *Grand Theft Auto* (1977, which he also produced, directed, and co-wrote with his father). He also delivered a thoughtful performance in *The Shootist* (1976).

Night Shift (1982) established Howard's reputation as a director. He followed it with many popular films with short titles, including *Splash* (1984), *Cocoon* (1985), *Gung Ho* (1986, also executive producer), *Willow* (1988), *Parenthood* (1989), *Backdraft* (1991), *Far and Away* (1992, also story and producer), *The Paper* (1994), and *Apollo 13* (1995).

Howard served as executive producer of *No Man's Land* (1987), *Vibes* (1988), *Clean and Sober* (1989), and *Closet Land* (1991) and as producer of *The 'burbs* (1989).

Author's Collection. © Warner Bros. Inc.

Robert Preston presents Ronny Howard with "the motht thcrumthuous tholid gold thing you ever thaw" as Shirley Jones looks on.

Q: How was the Broadway score of *The Music Man* changed in its translation to the screen?

A: Two numbers appear in slightly truncated form: the opening number with the salesmen has been shortened, and "It's You," a barbershop quartette song in the second act, is relegated to the background of the Fourth of July Picnic scene.

Two numbers are missing completely. A second-act reprise of "Pick-a-Little, Talk-a-Little," in which the town ladies express their affection for Marian (and the "smutty books" she keeps in the library) has been cut, and, perhaps the unkindest cut of all, Marian's expression of longing, "My White Knight," has been replaced with "Being in Love."

"One of the many reasons I was excited to play Marian was because of the song 'My White Night,' which for any soprano is the ultimate," says Shirley Jones. "I was sick when they didn't let me sing it. But they wanted what they felt might be a 'hit' song for the movie, and that's why Meredith wrote 'Being in Love' to replace it."

■

Q: How many Academy Awards did *The Music Man* win?

A: At the 1962 Academy Awards, *The Music Man* was nominated in six categories, but only won one:

Best Picture: *Lawrence of Arabia* (the winner), *The Longest Day*, *Mutiny on the Bounty*, *To Kill a Mockingbird*, and *The Music Man*.

Art Direction/Set Decoration (Color): *The Music Man* (Paul Groesse, Art Direction; George James Hopkins, Set Decoration), *Lawrence of Arabia* (the winner; John Box and John Stoll, Art Direction; Dario Simoni, Set Decoration), *Mutiny on the Bounty* (George W. Davis, Joseph McMillan Johnson, Art Direction; Henry Grace, Hugh Hunt, Set Decoration), *That Touch of Mink* (Alexander Golitzen, Robert Clatworthy, Art Direction; George Milo, Set Decoration), and *The Wonderful World of the Brothers Grimm* (George W. Davis, Edward C. Carfagno, Art Direction; Henry Grace, Richard Pefferle, Set Decoration).

Costume Design (Color): *The Music Man* (Dorothy Jeakins), *Bon Voyage!* (Bill Thomas), *Gypsy* (Orry-Kelly), *My Geisha* (Edith Head), and *The Wonderful World of the Brothers Grimm* (the winner, Mary Wills).

Film Editing: *The Music Man* (William Ziegler), *Lawrence of Arabia* (the winner, Anne V. Coates), *The Longest Day* (Samuel E. Beetley), *The Manchurian Candidate* (Ferris Webster), *Mutiny on the Bounty* (John McSweeney, Jr.), and *The Cardinal* (Louis R. Loeffler).

Music Scoring Awards (Scoring of Music Adaptation or Treatment): *The Music Man* (the winner, Ray Heindorf), *Billy Rose's Jumbo* (George Stoll), *Gigot* (Michel Magne), *Gypsy* (Frank Perkins), and *The Wonderful World of the Brothers Grimm* (Leigh Harline).

Sound: *The Music Man* (George R. Groves, Warner Bros. Studio Sound Department), *Bon Voyage!* (Robert O. Cook, Walt Disney Studio Sound Department), *Lawrence of Arabia* (the winner; John Cox, Shepperton Studio Sound Department), *That Touch of Mink* (Walden O. Watson, Universal City Studio Sound Department), and *What Ever Happened to Baby Jane?* (Joseph Kelly, Glen Glen Sound Department).

hard

Q: **Name two of Meredith Willson's other Broadway musicals.**

A: There are only two. *The Unsinkable Molly Brown*, the story of the rags-to-riches Denver socialite who survived the sinking of the *Titanic*, opened at the Winter Garden Theater on November 3, 1960, and ran 533 performances. The original cast included Tammy Grimes in the title role, Harve Presnell, and Christopher Hewitt.

A film version, with a much-altered book and score, was released by MGM in 1964. It starred Debbie Reynolds as the buoyant heroine, with Harve Presnell repeating his stage role as Leadville Johnny Brown.

Here's Love, a musical version of *Miracle on 34th Street*, opened October 3, 1963, at the Shubert Theater, and closed on July 25, 1964, after 338 performances. The cast included Janis Paige and Craig Stevens, with Laurence Naismith as Kris Kringle.

A third Willson musical never made it to Broadway. It was *1491*, which was about the events leading to Columbus's voyage of discovery. The seasoned cast included John Cullum as Columbus, Jean Fenn as Queen Isabella, and Chita Rivera as Columbus's true love, Beatriz. *1491* opened in Los Angeles on September 2, 1969, and played for four months there and in San Francisco before closing.

■

Q: **Name two of Robert Preston's other musicals.**

A: Preston's second musical was an adaptation of Ben Hecht's screenplay, *Viva Villa!*, called *We Take the Town*, in which Preston played Pancho Villa. *We Take the Town* opened in New Haven in February 1962, and closed on the road.

In 1964, Preston starred in *Ben Franklin in Paris*, the story of Franklin's visit to France to gain French recognition of American independence. The show had some pleasant songs and a formulaic book, but the presence of Preston and its general inoffensiveness led to a seven-month, 215-performance run at the Lunt-Fontanne Theater.

In December 1966, Preston starred opposite Mary Martin in the hit musical *I Do, I Do*, which was a critical and popular hit, and for which Preston received his second Tony Award.

One of Preston's most vexing musical failures, *Mack & Mabel*, was one of those shows that simply refused to work. *Mack & Mabel* opened promisingly in San Diego, then toured to Los Angeles, St. Louis, and Washington, D.C., with degenerating reviews along the way. It was panned when it opened on Broadway at the Majestic Theater (the site of Preston's triumph as Harold Hill) and ran only sixty-six performances. Preston and his leading lady, Bernadette Peters, were both Tony-nominated for *Mack & Mabel*, as was the show itself, director Gower Champion, Michael Stewart's book, the scenic design, the costume design, and the choreography. None of them won awards, and, inexplicably, the engaging Jerry Herman score (which continues to be a popular cast album to this day) was ignored at Tony time.

Preston's final musical was the ill-fated *The Prince of Grand Street* (1978), loosely based on the life of Jewish actor Boris Thomashefsky (renamed Nathan Rashumsky). Scheduled to open at the Palace Theater in May 1978, *The Prince of Grand Street* closed on the road in April.

In musical films, Preston played a charming Beau to Lucille Ball's dreadful *Mame* (1974), and created the role of the engaging, lovable "Toddy" in Blake Edwards' *Victor/Victoria* (1982), for which he was nominated for the Best Supporting Actor Oscar.

Q: According to Harold Hill, one of the tell-tale signs of corruption is young men memorizing jokes from a certain publication. Which magazine is degrading the youth of River City?

A: During "Trouble," a flabbergasted mother pulls a copy of *Cap'n Billy's Whiz-Bang* out of her boy's pocket.

Cap'n Billy's Whiz-Bang was actually created during World War I, several years *after* the 1912 of *The Music Man*. The magazine was founded as a mimeographed joke-and-cartoon paper by Captain Wilford H. Fawcett. After his return from the service, he managed to continue the magazine, a digest-sized, saddle-stitched volume (much as depicted in *The Music Man*). This was the founding publication of what became the Fawcett Publishing empire, the second-largest comic book enterprise of its time, and publisher of Captain Midnight, Spy Smasher, Bulletman, and the original Captain Marvel comic book lines. Fawcett also published women's magazines, movie magazines, and the original, scandalous *True Confessions*.

A lengthy lawsuit against Fawcett by National Comics (accusing Fawcett's Captain Marvel of plagiarizing National's Superman) spurred Fawcett's decision to quit the comics publishing business in 1953. Fawcett continued publishing how-to books and paperback books for the mass market, and later published the durable *Dennis the Menace* comic books.

■

Q: Jack L. Warner wanted to recast *The Music Man* for the screen. Who was he considering, instead of Robert Preston, for the role of Harold Hill?

A: Warner was well-known for his desire to recast "movie people" in his film versions of Broadway shows. Doris Day replaced Janis Paige in Warner's *Pajama Game* (1957), Tab Hunter replaced Stephen Douglass in Warner's *Damn Yankees* (1958), and Rosalind Russell replaced Ethel Merman in Warner's *Gypsy* (1962).

In casting the *stage* musical, the creators had a wide variety of leading men they considered suitable for Harold Hill: Gene Kelly, Danny Kaye, Dan Dailey, Ray Bolger, and Bing Crosby were among those who were either considered for or offered the part before the unlikely casting of Robert Preston. At one point in the casting of the stage *Music Man*, co-producer Herb Greene announced to his colleagues, "Fellas, I got it. The only one to play this Harold Hill part is Ethel Merman."

Forrest Tucker played Hill in the national touring company, and Van Johnson in the London company.

Cary Grant was apparently a publicly-discussed contender for the role (!), as a May 25, 1960 petition, mailed to Jack Warner, contains hundreds of signatures of protest against Grant (or anyone other than Robert Preston) being cast. When Shirley Jones was offered the role of Marian, she was told that her co-star would be Frank Sinatra. (Jones had been down this road before, with *Carousel*.)

Finally, Meredith Willson and Morton Da Costa went directly to Warner (some say with the threat of pulling the film rights) and demanded

The cast of *The Music Man:* Robert Preston, Shirley Jones, Buddy Hackett, Hermione Gingold, Paul Ford, and Ronny Howard.

that Preston be cast. Warner hedged his bets by surrounding Preston with well-known "movie people," but worries about Preston's cinematic star quality proved ill-founded.

Oddly, Jack L. Warner's final film, the vastly underrated *1776*, was translated to the screen with actors (dozens of 'em) who had played their roles on Broadway or in touring companies of the stage musical.

■

Q: **The director employed a unique "trademark" transitional technique that emulated stage lighting. What was it? How did it work?**

A: It's usually called the Da Costa Iris, sometimes the Da Costa fade. Morton Da Costa introduced it on *Auntie Mame* (1958), and used it again in *The Music Man*.

The Da Costa Iris represents an effort to bring the dramatic lighting focus and transitional impact of the stage to the mundane fade-to-black or dissolve of the motion picture. In essence, the background lighting in a transitional scene fades to black, leaving the principal(s) in key light,

which subsequently fades to blackout. The next scene then begins with a fade up from the black.

This simple, somewhat self-conscious, and seldom-used technique still draws the desired appreciative response from modern audiences.

■

Q: **What is the title of the opening number of** *The Music Man*?

A: The rhythmic, expository patter of the salesmen is titled "Rock Island," created in a style that Meredith Willson called a "speak-song." The piece is rhythmic speech imitating the sounds of a train—there is no melody and no rhyme scheme. The title of the speak-song refers to the Rock Island Railroad Line.

Willson reportedly used this speak-song style extensively in *1491*, the flop musical about Columbus discussed previously.

The process photography of the "Rock Island" sequence seems pretty shoddy, even by 1961 production standards. The process work in question is the separately-photographed scenes of rolling countryside that appear in the windows of the

"Don't believe I caught your name, friend." Professor Harold Hill and the traveling fraternity cross the state line into Iowa.

railroad car. This effect is accomplished by photographing the scenes in front of a cyclorama screen (usually bright blue or green in recent films), and adding the background shots to the blue areas later, by optical means. Files in the Warner Bros. Archives at the USC Library of Cinema and Television may reveal why the process scenes in *The Music Man* look so rubbery and fake. An internal Warner Bros. memo dated September 13, 1961, claims:

> The separations made by Technicolor on all blue background scenes were not made for our conditions and in conformance with the tests that Technicolor had previously made for us. As a result, the blue area is extremely vivid, and we will try to eliminate this with a high density matte.

Even so, the process work is quite obvious in this opening sequence.

The background photographic effects plates of fields and countryside for "Rock Island" were shot near Bakersfield, California. Foreground miniatures were shot on Warner Bros. Stage 5.

Train exteriors (rolling wheels and smokestack) for "Rock Island" were shot on July 17, 1961, at Travel Town, a railroad museum in Los Angeles' Griffith Park. The shot required a payment of $62.50 to "get up steam," a $125.00 Parks Department photography use fee, and the payment of the train engineer and foreman.

■

Q: When Harold and Marian are at the footbridge, Marcellus interrupts. Harold excuses himself by telling Marian that he's expecting a telegram. From whom?

A: "I'm expecting a telegram from…Rudy Friml, and this could be it."

Charles Rudolf Friml was born in Prague, Czechoslovakia, in 1879. Between 1912 and 1934, he was a renowned creator of Broadway operettas, including *The Firefly*, *Rose-Marie*, and *The Vagabond King*, all of which were eventually made into motion pictures (*The Firefly* in 1937,

Rose-Marie in 1936 and 1954, *The Vagabond King* in 1920, 1930, 1938, and 1956).

Other film work for Friml included *The Lottery Bride* (1930), *Cain and Mabel* (1936, which contains one Friml song—and Pert Kelton!), *Music for Madame*, and *Northwest Outpost* (1937).

Harold's telegram seems just a throw-away (albeit funny) joke, another attempt to infer musical legitimacy by associating himself with contemporary musical greats. But it's actually a little more than that. According to a Warner Bros. Staff and Cast listing for *The Music Man*, dated March 30, 1961, the Music Coordinator for *The Music Man* was…the eighty-two-year-old Rudy Friml! (In the stage musical, Harold is expecting a cable, and it's from Hector Berlioz.)

Rudolf Friml died in 1972.

■

Q: Another famous composer was influential in getting the original stage production of *The Music Man* off the ground. Who?

A: Frank Loesser. A friend and contemporary of Meredith Willson, Loesser had, of course, written *Guys and Dolls* (q.v.). He encouraged Willson to continue working on *The Music Man* when things looked bleak.

Frank, Inc., Loesser's production entity, was a co-producer of *The Music Man* on Broadway, along with Kermit Bloomgarden and Herbert Greene, who had produced Loesser's *The Most Happy Fella*. Frank, Inc. also published the sheet music for *The Music Man*.

■

Q: In the library, Zaneeta says she can't meet Tommy. Why?

A: "Epworth League tonight." What the heck is that? According to Meredith Willson, it's the Methodist version of Christian Endeavor, a

Christian education and fellowship group.

There is another scene in the final script with Tommy and Zaneeta, where they actually get a little privacy. After Marian tells off Harold ("I am not impressed by your credentials, which I have not seen, nor your manners, which I have!"), there was a short scene of "cute" romance on the Madison Park playground, culminating in a kiss between the two teenagers. This scene was apparently deleted prior to being shot.

In the final cut, after Marian's explosion there is a Da Costa fade to the scene with Feril Hawkes (Lucille Ball crony Barbara Pepper) and her tone-deaf twins.

hard

■

A 1962 newspaper ad for *The Music Man* reveals its sprightly sense of fun.

Q: **Shirley Jones and Morton Da Costa shared a big secret during the first several months of filming. What was their secret?**

A: Shirley Jones was pregnant during the filming. *The Music Man* spent six weeks rehearsing prior to going before the cameras, and then spent six months doing the actual filming. In the first few months of shooting, Jones discovered she was pregnant. "I took Tec to lunch and told him," Jones reveals, "and after he picked himself up off the floor, he told me not to worry about it—'we'll do what we can.'"

"What we can" involved carefully selected camera angles, corseting Jones as she began to "show," and adding panels, bows, and other drapery to her midriff. "Fortunately, it was a period picture," Jones laughs. "Da Costa only asked one thing of me: 'Don't tell anyone.' And we kept it under wraps until it was obvious. The costumers kept pulling me in—it's a wonder Patrick doesn't have a squashed nose from all the corseting."

Shortly after *The Music Man* wrapped production, Jones's second son, Patrick Cassidy, was born.

■

Q: **Here's a silly, obscure, who-cares, tie-buster question. Where did Timmy Everett (Tommy Djilas) live during the filming of *The Music Man*?**

A: Timmy Everett lived at the Montecito Apartments, 6650 Franklin Avenue, Hollywood. A grand 1920s apartment house, the Montecito was the home to many of the Hollywood film community. Ronald Reagan had lived there during the late 1930s, and later residents included Mickey Rooney, George C. Scott, Julie Harris, and Gene Hackman.

The Montecito still stands in threadbare grandeur. It is now a retirement home.

Warner Bros. Pictures presents Meredith Willson's

THE MUSIC MAN

Technirama® Technicolor®

Produced and Directed by: Morton Da Costa; Screenplay: Marion Hargrove

Based on Meredith Willson's "The Music Man" with his music and lyrics

Book written in collaboration with Franklin Lacey

Produced by Kermit Bloomgarden with Herman Greene in association with Frank Productions, Inc.

Director of Photography: Robert Burks, ASC; Art Director: Paul Groesse

Film Editor: William Ziegler; Sound by M.A. Merrick and Dolph Thomas

Set Decorator: George James Hopkins; Production Supervisor: Joel Freeman

Music Supervised and Conducted by Ray Heindorf; Vocal Arrangements: Charles Henderson
Orchestrations: Ray Heindorf, Frank Comstock & Gus Levene

Costume Design: Dorothy Jeakins; Choreography by Onna White
Assistant Choreographer: Tom Panko

Makeup Supervisor Gordon Bau SMA; Supervising Hair Stylist Jean Burt Reilly, C.H.S;
Miss Jones' Hairstyles: Myrl Stoltz

Assistant Director: Russ Llewellyn

Running time: 151 minutes

Cast

Robert Preston	Harold Hill
Shirley Jones	Marian Paroo
Buddy Hackett	Marcellus Washburn
Hermione Gingold	Eulailie McKecknie Shinn
Paul Ford	Mayor Shinn
Pert Kelton	Mrs. Paroo
The Buffalo Bills	
Vernon Reed	Jacey Squires
William Spangenberg	Olin Britt
Al Shea	Ewart Dunlop
Wayne Ward	Oliver Hix

With

Timmy Everett	Tommy Djilas
Susan Luckey	Zaneeta Shinn
Ronny Howard	Winthrop Paroo
Harry Hickox	Charley Cowles
Charles Lane	Constable Locke
Mary Wickes	Mrs. Squires
Jesslyn Fax	Avis Grubb
Peggy Mondo	Ethel Tofflemeyer
Sarah Seegar	Maud Dunlop
Patty Lee Hilka	Gracie Shinn
Ronnie Dapo	Norbert Smith
Garry Alan Potter	Dewey
J. Delos Jewkes	Harley McCauley
Ray Kellogg	Harry Joseph
William Fawcett	Lester Lonnergan
Rance Howard	Oscar Jackson
Roy Dean	Gilbert Hawthorne
David Swain	Chet Glanville
Arthur Mills	Herbert Malthouse
Rand Barker	Duncan Shyball
Jeannine Burnier	Jessie Shyball
Shirley Claire	Amy Dakin
Natalie Core	Truthful Smith
Therese Lyon	Dolly Higgins
Penelope Martin	Lila O'Brink
Barbara Pepper	Feril Hawkes
Ann Loos	Stella Jackson
Peggy Wynne	Ada Nutting
Mary Adams	Saleslady
Pat Colby	Soda Jerk
Vicki Lee, Robin MacGregor	Little Girls
Natalie Masters	Farmer's Wife
Milton Parsons	Farmer
Alma Platt	Elderly Lady
Adam Richards	Teenager
Ruth Robinson	Little Old Lady
George Spicer	Teenage Boy
Anna Capri	Teenage Girl
Raymond Van Holten, Frederick Van Holten	Twins
Hank Worden	Undertaker

Hugo Stanger . . . . Elderly Man

Harold Kennedy . . . . Wells Fargo Man

Madge Irwin . . . . Spinster

Casey Adams, Peter Walker,
   Lee Goodman, Robert Van Hooten,
   Chuck Karel . . . . Salesmen

James Milhollin . . . . Desk Clerk

Charles A. Bell . . . . Prologue Constable

Percy Helton . . . . Conductor

Stephen Coit . . . . First Newspaper

Tom Rose . . . . Second Newspaper

Richard Gardner . . . . Third Newspaper

Dancers

Michele Abele, Ed Balin, Michele Barton, Lysa Baugher, Sandra Bonner, George Bornyek, Owen Brannen, Buddy Bryan, Anna Cheselka, Bradford Craig, Fred Curt, Meurisse Du Ree, Pat Ellis, Bonnie Evans, Jeannine Fetterolf, Kathy Gale, Alex Goudovitch, Glenda Guilfoyle, Bruce Hoy, Elaine Joyce, Bob Karl, Sally Lee, Jack Leigh, Kitty Malone, Paula Martin, Gary Menteer, Dick Monahan, Jack Moore, Marilyn Morris, Judy Niklos, Valentina Oumansky, Diane Parenti, Noel Parenti, Currie Pederson, Ralph Phraner, Diane Robb, Bruce E. Stowell, David Sutherland, Larri Thomas, James White

An original lobby card from the first release of *The Music Man*.

Hello, Dolly! *may well be the symbol of "the end of an era," the era of the roadshow movie musical. In fact,* Hello, Dolly! *has become the symbol of so many things—purported miscasting, the "epic mentality," the bad adaptation from Broadway—that many people have lost sight of the charming movie at the heart of it all. The truth is, people with no preconceptions about* Hello, Dolly! *tend to fall in love with it. The farcical story, the engaging characters, the lush and memorable music, and the opulent production design all contribute to what might be called "the last 'MGM musical.'"*

Author and historian Tony Thomas probably summed up this much-maligned and misunderstood musical best: "It is a genial, handsome, old-fashioned musical dogged by bad luck in its timing and in the decision to spend so much money making it."

■

Level One: The Easy Stuff
Story & Characters

Previous page:
The original Amsel
key art from the
1969 road show
release of
Hello, Dolly!

Q: **In the opening number, Dolly Levi enters a great public building. What is it?**

A: Dolly enters a railway station meant to evoke New York's old Grand Central Station. According to the 1882 classic *New York by Sunlight and Gaslight*:

> The Grand Central Depot, at the corner of Fourth avenue and 42nd street, and extending from Fourth to Vanderbilt avenues, and from 42nd to 45th streets is one of the most imposing edifices in New York, and the most superb and complete railway terminus in America. With the exception of the old Hudson River Railroad Depot, at Ninth avenue and 30th street, now used for suburban trains only, it is the only railway station in the city.

It is here that Dolly boards the New York Central and Hudson River Railroad for her trip to Yonkers to finish her business with Horace Vandergelder.

The real old Grand Central was replaced in 1913 by the practically world-famous Grand Central Station at 42nd Street and Park Avenue.

The interior set of the old Grand Central was on a sound stage at Twentieth Century-Fox's West Los Angeles lot. Aged two thousand years and redressed, it can be seen as the mutant's council chamber in *Beneath the Planet of the Apes* (1970), in the scene during which Brent

(James Franciscus) is first interrogated.

The outside of the railroad station was part of the gigantic Manhattan exterior set built on the Fox lot. It was located at the southwest corner of the principal "14th Street" set, nearest the Pico Boulevard entrance of the studio lot. The marquee for the train station set, reading "Central & Hudson RR" can be seen out of the front windows of Miss Molloy's hat shop.

The loading platform where Dolly boards the train immediately prior to the credit sequence was shot in the turn-of-the-century glass-roofed terminal of the Poughkeepsie, New York, train station.

■

Q: **The Grand Central ticket agent asks, "Where to, Dolly?" Her answer?**

A: "Yonkers, New York, to handle a highly personal matter for Mr. Horace Vandergelder..." The hamlet of Garrison, New York (near West Point), sixty miles north of Manhattan, doubled for the 1890 Yonkers. The buildings of Garrison had been erected in the 1840s, and so actually required "modernizing" with period architectural detailing to fit the epoch of *Hello, Dolly!*

Garrison was on a railroad, the main line of the

Penn-Central, which was essential in its selection for the Yonkers set, since the "Put on Your Sunday Clothes" number ends with the departure of Dolly and her charges by rail for New York City. The railroad station itself was architecturally admirable, and once the pride of the New York Central Railway. J. P. Morgan, Hamilton Fish, and other financial giants had once owned great estates in this area of New York State.

Despite its illustrious past, Garrison had fallen into disrepair, and local residents had formed two preservation organizations to protect and restore the little town. These groups had purchased the railroad station, park, and marina from the New York Central Railroad. The train station had been converted into a little theater and exhibit space (members of the *Hello, Dolly!* company were initially confused by signs in the station's restrooms that read "Do Not Flush During Performance"). Permission from and agreement with these two

groups was reached for the film company to transform the town into a movie set. At the time of filming, seven families lived in the town, which consisted of sixteen buildings—a small former hotel, a ferry house, and a store among them. Two of the families relocated during the month of shooting, in order to provide production offices and dressing rooms to the staff and cast. In addition to the principal cast, there were two hundred crew and sixty dancers on location.

The new construction for the Yonkers set included a thirty thousand-dollar period barn, erected to conceal the automobiles of eighty commuters who regularly used the railroad station. The helicopter shot at the end of "Put on Your Sunday Clothes" would have revealed this parking lot to the camera.

The steam engine and three cars used on the Garrison shoot came from a railroad built in and in continuous operation since 1832. Its normal

From the Collection of Tony Baxter

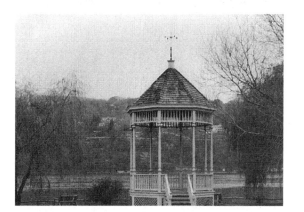

Four views of Garrison, New York, the village that played Yonkers in *Hello, Dolly!* Upper left: The Railroad Station as viewed from the bridge. Upper right: The Golden Eagle is an inn used as Vandergelder's Hay & Feed (the water tank remains from the film production). Lower left: The "eloping window" where Ambrose and Dolly climb up the ladder. Lower right: The bandstand in the park, one of Garrison's few reminders of the filming of *Hello, Dolly!*

route was on "The Road to Paradise" (Paradise, Pennsylvania), a nine-mile circuit through Amish country near East Strasburg, PA. That route, and the train itself, had been saved from extinction in the late 1950s by the Strasburg Railway Museum.

A gymnasium was converted to a "standby set," where interiors could be filmed in the case of bad weather. It was on this stand-by set that Dolly's solo of "Love Is Only Love" was shot. Near Garrison, the location for the finale number was found, a picturesque river valley where the church set was built.

Shooting in Garrison took twenty-seven days. The cast and crew returned to the studio on July 5, 1968. Two further weeks of second-unit shooting (most probably including the picturesque main title sequence), with a crew of thirty-eight, were supervised by production designer John De Cuir and production manager Chico Day.

The residents of Garrison were divided over whether to keep the set elements of *Hello, Dolly!* intact after production. Ultimately the producer decided that everything would go, except for a

Cornelius Hackl (Michael Crawford) and an amused Irene Molloy (Marianne McAndrew).

bandstand in the park and the park itself, which the film company had re-landscaped and improved for shooting. Also remaining is the Victorian graphics and signage on the water tower of The Golden Eagle, the inn that was used as Vandergelder's Hay and Feed. The Golden Eagle still sports signs that advertise "Best Quality Grains" and "Feed, Wholesale—Retail."

■

Q: Who was the twenty-eight-and-three-quarters-year-old chief clerk? Who played him?

A: Cornelius Hackl is the twenty-eight-and-three-quarters-year-old chief clerk, as played by Michael Crawford. Crawford might seem an odd choice to play the All-American role of Cornelius Hackl, having been born Michael Dumble-Smith in England in 1942. Crawford had been a boy soprano—Benjamin Britten had cast him in the world premiere of *Noah's Flood* and *Let's Make an Opera*. He broke into acting on the BBC School Broadcasts and participated in more than five hundred radio dramas and dozens of BBC television plays. He began his film career at the age of sixteen in a 1958 film called *Soap Box Derby*, and had become an international favorite in *The Knack* (1965) and *The Jokers* (1967). *Hello, Dolly!* associate producer Roger Edens saw Crawford's agile physical comic performance in *Black Comedy* (1967) on Broadway, and recommended Crawford to producer Ernest Lehman. According to the *Hello, Dolly!* program book, Crawford picked up his American accent listening to recordings of drunk stories by American comic Woody Woodbury.

Crawford later appeared in *Billy* (1969), which ran for two years at the Drury Lane Theatre; a musical version of *Flowers for Algernon*; and *Barnum* (1980), another role that highlighted his physical agility and expression. He was a regular presence in Britain through his portrayal of Frank Spencer in the hit TV comedy "Some

Author's Collection. © Twentieth Century-Fox Film Corporation.

Mothers Do 'Ave 'Em." He has made few films since *Hello, Dolly!*, among them the expensive British misfire *Alice's Adventures in Wonderland* (1972; why do people keep trying to make a film out of this?) and the spectacular Disney flop *Condorman* (1981).

Crawford's greatest renown would come from his creation of the title character in Andrew Lloyd Webber's musical adaptation of *The Phantom of the Opera* in 1986. In 1995, he became a Las Vegas landmark, headlining at the MGM Grand in a multimedia musical stage show called *EFX*.

The role of Cornelius Hackl had been played on Broadway by character actor/director/*Match Game* panelist Charles Nelson Reilly.

■

Q: Horace Vandergelder vents his spleen at a "so-called artist." Who is the artist? Who plays him?

A: Ambrose Kemper, "so-called artist," is played by musical theatre legend Tommy Tune. It's his real name, all right, and *Hello, Dolly!* marked the film debut of the 6' 6" dancer (at

that time he had yet to become choreographer/director/producer). Ernest Lehman had spotted Tune in the Broadway cast of *How Now Dow Jones* (1967) and offered him the role. He had appeared in the 1960s road company of *Irma La Douce* and spent a year as a featured dancer in the musical *Baker Street* (1965) on Broadway.

After *Hello, Dolly!*, Tune was assistant choreographer for "The Dean Martin Show" on television and appeared in Ken Russell's *The Boy Friend* (1972), but has not appeared in a film since. He truly found his niche on the musical stage, where he has won eight Drama Desk and two Obie Awards, as well as nine Tony Awards. Tune is the only person in theatrical history to win in four different Tony categories, and to win the same two Tony categories two years in a row. He appeared in Michael Bennett's *Seesaw* (Best Featured Actor in a Musical), *The Best Little Whorehouse in Texas* (1978), *A Day in Hollywood/A Night in the Ukraine* (1980, Best Choreography), *Nine* (1982, Best Direction of a Musical), *My One and Only* (1983, Best Choreography, Best Actor in a Musical, and in which he was again paired with his *The Boy Friend* co-star, Twiggy), *Grand Hotel* (1989, Best Choreography,

Joyce Ames, Tommy Tune (he's the tall one in the middle), and Barbra Streisand in one of only two motion pictures in which Tune has appeared.

Author's Collection. © Twentieth Century-Fox Film Corporation

Best Direction of a Musical), and *The Will Rogers Follies* (1991, Best Choreography, Best Direction of a Musical). He also directed *The Club* and *Cloud 9* off-Broadway. He appeared in a national tour of *Bye Bye Birdie* (as Albert Peterson) and a song and dance revue *Tommy Tune Tonite*, and produced the 1994 revival of *Grease* and the 1994 flop *The Best Little Whorehouse Goes Public.*

Tune starred in the 1995 musical *Busker Alley* (by veteran *Mary Poppins* composers Richard M. Sherman and Robert B. Sherman).

■

Q: As Dolly arrives, Horace Vandergelder is leaving. Where is Horace going?

A: "To march in the 14th Street parade," formally identified as "The 14th Street Merchants' Association Parade." It's never explained exactly what the parade is celebrating; nonetheless, Horace dutifully marches with his brothers from the Knights of the Hudson Lodge 26. The legendary parade scene is the opulent centerpiece of *Hello, Dolly!* and takes place on a set meant to evoke the Union Square area of old New York. According to the 1882 *New York by Sunlight and Gaslight*:

> Twenty-third and 14th streets are broad, handsome thoroughfares, extending across the island from river to river. Twenty years ago [c. 1860s] they were chosen seats of wealth and fashion, and from Broadway westward were lined with superb mansions. Now they are busy, bustling marts of trade. The old mansions have disappeared, and in their places stand huge iron, marble and stone structures, devoted to the various branches of the retail trade. Dry goods, furniture, millinery, sewing-machines, and musical instruments, are the trades chiefly to be found on 14th street. Scarcely a vestige of the old street remains, and those who, twenty years ago, thought it the perfection of a residence street, would fail to recognize it, so thoroughly has it gone over to trade.

14th Street is just one of the many New York locales evoked by the enormous complex of sets created for the Manhattan exteriors of *Hello, Dolly!*

Q: Dolly instructs Ambrose and Ermingarde to deliver a message for her. What is the message?

A: "Tell Rudolph that Dolly's coming back." Dolly instructs the young lovebirds to ask for Rudolph Reisenweber, the headwaiter of the Harmonia Gardens restaurant, and tell him of her planned return to "the lights of 14th Street." Where had she been? And for how long? Just how old is Dolly supposed to be?

The issue of Dolly Levi's age, in the person of Barbra Streisand, proved to be a controversial point in casting. Streisand's youth relative to those who had played the role before her is an excuse used to this day (by people who should know better) to dismiss Streisand's performance and the film version of *Hello, Dolly!* out of hand.

This age-related ruckus began as soon as Streisand was announced for the role over the Broadway original, Carol Channing. In May 1967, shortly after the casting announcement, Richard Coe in *The Washington Post* fueled the fires of a baseless "controversy" that is still

Streisand's casting as Dolly Levi caused an unfounded conflict that, inexplicably, continues to this day.

parroted today. "Would you believe Barbra Streisand for the screen's 'Hello, Dolly!'?" Coe lamented. "Well, that's the knuckle-headed fact…with all due respect to Miss Streisand, the mournful Nefertiti is clearly not the outgoing, zestful Irish woman whose vitality brightens Thornton Wilder's mature, life-loving Dolly Gallegher Levi."

Later that month, John L. Scott leapt to Streisand's defense in the pages of the *Los Angeles Times*, pointing out the fact that there had been nary a rumble when Julie Andrews was cast in the place of Mary Martin for the film version of *The Sound of Music*. The screenwriter of *Hello, Dolly!* is quoted in the same article as saying that "nothing in my screenplay will indicate that Dolly had been married for X years and widowed for Y years. As a matter of fact, in Thornton Wilder's original play, 'The Matchmaker,' from which 'Dolly!' was adapted as a stage musical, he noted all the characters' ages except that of Dolly, which he set down as 'uncertain age.' She could well be a widow in her thirties."

In his 1981 book *The Hollywood Musical*, musical expert Ethan Mordden concurred: "In her big number she *returns* to the night life after an absence…Actually, [the director] is at pains, in a dandy opening, to establish that Streisand is not an unknown in town…She may be young, but a station porter and ticket man know her well—so she *has* been around."

Why the almost embarassing focus on the subject of age, which (as the screenwriter and Mordden point out) is essentially immaterial to the *character* of Dolly? Some of it seems like late 1960s generationalism. Some of it smacks of anti-Semitism. Some of it feels like an orchestrated campaign, either to the defense of Carol Channing or to gain "controversy" for a project completely lacking in the stuff of controversy.

All her talent aside, the reason for Streisand's casting seems pretty clear: she was the only musical-comedy star who could be depended upon to attract a certain crossover audience to a decidedly old-fashioned motion picture, in a film market that was growing increasingly youth-oriented.

■

Q: **What restaurant does everyone wind up in?**

A: "The Harmonia Gardens on 14th Street." All of the film's principle characters "accidentally" convene in this ornate evocation of a Gay Nineties bar/restaurant/nightclub. This elaborate confection of a set is the film's centerpiece interior, a dazzling tribute to the artistry of production designer John De Cuir.

The decorative style of the fictitious Harmonia Gardens is based on elements of the New York Castle Gardens, Maxim's in Paris, and London's Crystal Palace. The set was constructed on four different levels, and filled with fountains, candelabra, chandeliers, statuary, and greenery. According to production notes for the film, the walls were constructed of translucent plastic, and different colored lights were bounced from off-white muslin-lined stage walls and back into the set to fully light the interior. Upon first seeing the completed set, the producer is reported to have commented to De Cuir, "I'd say you built one hell of a saloon."

About 25 percent of the action in *Hello, Dolly!* takes place in the Harmonia Gardens, including, of course, the title number. During this famous number, Miss Steisand makes her spectacular diva entrance at the top of a monumental staircase and then leads a 360-degree tour around this amazing set. "The Waiter's Galop," Michael Kidd's complex musical slapstick, used the intricacies of this set to great advantage. As described by Jack Hirshberg in the program for *Hello, Dolly!*, it's "a precision drill in the serving of food, a psuedo-military compendium of rapid-fire manuevers attendant upon the delivery of delectables from kitchen to patron's table. The corps de ballet here consists of several dozen scarlet-

easy

Courtesy of Edward Sotto

Elevations of the John De Cuir-designed Harmonia Gardens Restaurant set.

coated waiters juggling stacks of plates, dueling with flaming shish-kebob swords, swooshing tablecloths off tables, popping corks of champagne bottles, and performing the ceremonial lighting of Cherries Jubilee."

According to the production notes, more food was consumed in the Harmonia Gardens than on any other film set. The catering was supervised by Bruno Moeckli, the Swiss maitre d' at the VIP room of the Hollywood Playboy Club. As many as four hundred extras (so say the production notes) dined on shish-kabob, crepes suzettes, and other suitably photogenic foodstuffs. The director was particular that those extras near the camera be seen actually enjoying a meal. One extra claimed to have gained eight pounds in ten days' shooting.

The Harmonia Gardens set makes another appearance in a Twentieth Century-Fox film. For *Beneath the Planet of the Apes*, the lavish restaurant set was converted to a house of worship (represented as the ruins St. Patrick's Cathedral) of the radiation-scarred mutants. At the top of the redressed Harmonia Gardens stairs, where

Dolly had made her grand entrance, is an altar for an A bomb! When the ape army penetrates this mutant sanctum sanctorum, they ascend ropes to the top of the bomb, and the elaborate glass ceiling of the Harmonia Gardens entry portico is visible above them. The re-use of this set was probably appealing for both its cost-effectiveness and the visually fascinating possibilities of its multiple levels.

■

Q: Mr. Hackl doesn't want to go where Dolly suggests. "It isn't the money or anything," he explains. What is it?

A: "It's the dancing!" But naturally, Dolly Levi can teach him to dance—after all, she's been tutored by the great chorographer Michael Kidd.

Born in 1919, Kidd was once a *New York Daily News* copy boy and was studying engineering (which he found a bore) when he began ushering at performances of modern dance. He was hooked, and eventually won a scholarship to the

School of American Ballet, a fact which embarrassed his parents. Later, he won a contract to dance with the Ballet Theatre, where he attained stardom.

Ballet Theatre director Antal Dorati asked him to submit his own ballet, and Kidd delivered "On Stage." The success of "On Stage" pursuaded Kidd to concentrate on choreography. His first Broadway show was *Finian's Rainbow* (1947). He came to Hollywood and embarked on a distinguished career in musical film, with movies such as *Where's Charley?* (1952), *The Band Wagon* (1953), and the 1954 Danny Kaye vehicle, *Knock on Wood*.

One of Kidd's breakthrough achievements, and the film for which he is perhaps best known, is the graceful, athletic, knockabout dancing featured in *Seven Brides for Seven Brothers* (1954). He brought the Johns and Janes of Times Square to life in Samuel Goldwyn's production of *Guys and Dolls* (q.v., 1955), and teamed with Gene Kelly and Dan Dailey for the psuedo-sequel to *On the Town*, *It's Always Fair Weather* (1955). In 1958, he choreographed and directed the Danny Kaye vehicle *Merry Andrew* for MGM.

Kidd spent a big chunk of 1967 and 1968 at Twentieth Century-Fox. He went directly from the Julie Andrews musical *Star!* (1968) to *Hello, Dolly!* with scarcely a breath in between assignments.

He appeared as a performer in *Smile* (1975) and the pastiche film *Movie Movie* (1978).

As stated, Kidd was a friend and associate of Gene Kelly, and *Hello, Dolly!* is infused with their dancers' sensibilities. The rhythmic, choreographed opening sets the tone for the choreography of *Dolly!* It springs forth from elemental story points, and builds to exuberant and encompassing physical expression.

■

Q: When she makes her grand entrance at the restaurant, Dolly shares the film's title tune with a gregarious orchestra leader. Who is he?

A: Louis Armstrong played the orchestra leader, conveniently named "Louis." Of course, Louis Armstrong was a world-renowned jazz performer, and had already made a sensation with his recording of the title song from *Hello, Dolly!* The casting of Armstrong in the minor but spotlighted role was both for promotion, since Armstrong was so associated with the song in the public mind, and for cachet: Armstrong's name had marquee value.

Born in 1900, Armstrong's more than half-century career included live performances, recordings, radio broadcasts, and appearances in movies and on television. He appeared in more than twenty motion pictures, the most memorable being *Cabin in the Sky* (1943), *A Song is Born* (1948), *The Glenn Miller Story* (1954), and *High Society* (1956).

His trademarks were virtuoso trumpet playing, mopping his face with a white handkerchief, and a voice that sounded like warm gravel over wet sandpaper. He was often referred to by his nickname, "Satchmo," short for "Satchelmouth."

Hello, Dolly! was Armstrong's final film appearance. He died in 1971.

Ol' Satchelmouth and Barbra Streisand in a gregarious duet of the film's title number.

medium

Q: The film version of *Hello, Dolly!* is adapted from what source?

A: The answer is the popular Tony Award-winning stage musical, *Hello, Dolly!*, and that's correct, as far as it goes.

The book of the stage musical was written by Michael Stewart, with music and lyrics by Jerry Herman. They had based their work on Thornton Wilder's 1955 play, *The Matchmaker*, which was produced by *Dolly!* producer David Merrick and starred Ruth Gordon. The film version was produced by Paramount Pictures in 1958, with Shirley Booth in the title role (supported by Paul Ford as Vandergelder, Shirley MacLaine as Irene Molloy, Anthony Perkins as Cornelius, and Robert Morse as Barnaby!).

There was as much controversy surrounding Booth's casting in the role created by Ruth Gordon in *The Matchmaker* as there was a decade later when Barbra Streisand was cast in the role created by Carol Channing in *Hello, Dolly!* Interestingly, the March 5, 1956, *Hollywood Reporter* announced that "Katharine Hepburn is about set to co-star with Spencer Tracy in *The Matchmaker*, which Don Hartman will produce from the New York play now starring Ruth Gordon." Hepburn and Tracy as Dolly Levi and Horace Vandergelder? The mind reels...

Wilder's *The Matchmaker* was itself a rewritten version of his own second play, *The Merchant of Yonkers*, which premiered in New York in 1938, produced by Herman Shumlin and directed by Max Reinhardt ("under the inept direction of Max Reinhardt," according to legendary Broadway observer Brooks Atkinson).

The Merchant of Yonkers was based on a comedy by Johann Nestroy titled *Einen Jux will es Machen*, produced in Vienna in 1842.

And finally, *Einen Jux will es Machen* was based on John Oxenford's play, *A Day Well Spent*, which ran in London in 1835.

However, there may be cave paintings that tell the story of a couple of clerks who pull a fast one on the boss and have a day of adventure in the big city...

■

Q: *Hello, Dolly!* owes much of its visceral style to a talented song and dance man. Who is the former hoofer who directed *Dolly!*?

A: At the time *Hello, Dolly!* was in pre-production, Twentieth Century-Fox had three other major "roadshow" productions in preparation: *Doctor Dolittle*, *Star!*, and *Tom Swift*. Song and dance great Gene Kelly had been named as director of *Tom Swift*, a spectacular along the lines of *The Great Race* and *Those Magnificent Men in Their Flying Machines* (1965), based on the boy's adventure tales by Victor Appleton. When *Tom Swift* was put on hold by the studio, Kelly was offered the plum assignment of *Hello, Dolly!*

Born in 1912, Kelly was, by the time of *Hello, Dolly!*, not only a legendary screen performer, but also a respected choreographer and director. He was famous for his breezy charm in such classic MGM musicals as *For Me and My Gal* (1942, his screen debut), *Thousands Cheer* (1943, which also featured his choreography), *Anchors Aweigh* (1945, again as both performer and choreographer—this is the film in which he danced with the animated mouse, Jerry), and *The Pirate* (1948).

With *On the Town* (1949), Kelly first sat in the director's chair; a two-man chair, actually—he shared the chore with Stanley Donen. This team reunited for the classic *Singin' in the Rain* (q.v., 1952) and *It's Always Fair Weather* (1955).

Kelly's first solo directing assignment was *The Happy Road* (1956), in which he also starred. He wrote, choreographed, directed, and starred in the noble 1957 MGM flop *Invitation to the Dance*. In 1958 he directed the first film in which he did not star, *The Tunnel of Love*. He next directed the Jackie Gleason vehicle, *Gigot* (1962) and the widely-praised comedy *A Guide for the Married Man* (1967), while still appearing often as a performer in films and on television.

His final director credit was *The Cheyenne Social Club* (1970, which he also produced). His last screen appearance was in *That's Entertainment III* (1994).

Kelly brought many things to *Hello, Dolly!* Certainly there was prestige—his name had publicity and marquee value. His directorial style was reportedly easygoing, artist-friendly, and highly respected. And the end result, from the very first scene, reveals the sensibility, vision, and assured rhythm of a man fully versed in the musical-comedy genre.

Kelly asserted, "It's all too easy to ridicule Fox for spending all that money making *Dolly* but they took a brave stand—they had spent so much getting hold of the property that they wanted to turn it into a whale of a good show. It takes guts to make that kind of decision, and as the director I was excited by the challenge of blowing it up into a big and exciting picture. I'm not sorry I did it."

Gene Kelly died in February 1996.

■

Q: *Hello, Dolly!* is a categorically "old-fashioned" musical, and in many ways is a reflection of the production values of the golden age of MGM musicals. Part of the reason might be the associate producer. Who was he?

A: Roger Edens was a musician, composer, arranger, music supervisor, and, finally, a producer.

Edens was Arthur Freed's longtime associate producer at MGM, where this musical jack-of-all-trades—musical supervisor, composer, and arranger—brought much of the renowned "style and taste" to the Freed Unit. This style and taste is much in evidence in *Hello, Dolly!*

Disney Archivist Robert Tieman made a cogent observation about the result of Edens' influence over the films that bear his name: "I always feel that, through Edens' work, Paramount was able to make an MGM musical—*Funny Face* (1957). Then Edens went to Fox, and made the last great MGM musical there—*Hello, Dolly!*"

Hello, Dolly! was Edens' last film. He died in 1970.

■

Q: Another part of the opulent visual world of *Hello, Dolly!* is the rich costuming, particularly of Barbra Streisand. Who was responsible for putting "Sunday Clothes" on the cast?

A: Irene Sharaff. Born in Boston in 1910, Sharaff began her career in the theatre, and it should be no surprise, given what she did on *Hello, Dolly!*, that her first film credit was the rich Victorian wardrobe of *Meet Me in St. Louis* (1944). There is even an homage to the finale of that film in *Hello, Dolly!* During the "Put On Your Sunday Clothes" number, a white-wardrobed family descends the steps of a gingerbread Victorian house, all very reminiscent of the Smith family departing for the World's Fair.

Sharaff made something of a trademark of elaborate costume productions, including *A Star is Born*, *Brigadoon* (1954), *Guys and Dolls* (1955), *Can-Can* (1960), and *The Taming of the Shrew* (1967).

Sharaff won Academy Awards for Costume Design for *An American in Paris* (1951), *The King and I* (1956, which she had costumed on Broadway), *West Side Story* (1961, which she had also costumed on Broadway), *Cleopatra* (1963), and *Who's Afraid of Virginia Woolf?* (1966).

In his enthralling record of Twentieth Century-Fox in 1968, *The Studio*, John Gregory Dunne sheds some light on the "creative collaboration" of two people in the top echelons of their fields: Sharaff and choreographer Michael Kidd.

At a rehearsal of the film's title number,

Streisand was wearing a muslin "rehearsal" copy of the heavy beaded topaz dress she would wear for filming. Both the ensemble dancers and the star kept tripping over the train of the dress, and Kidd was worried that the heavier, finished gown would disable the kicks he had choreographed for the number's finish. A standoff ensued. Kidd, although never directly, questioned the practicality of the dress for the big musical number. Irene Sharaff asked the choreographer, "Is the kick necessary?" Kidd replied, "I think it is, yeah." "The [final] dress will be finished next week, Michael," Sharaff replied. "Why don't we wait until we see it on Barbra before we talk about changes?" "Sure, Irene," Kidd said cheerfully. "And if the dress doesn't work, there'll be some changes made."

Author's Collection. © Twentieth Century-Fox Film Corporation

Barbra Streisand, Michael Crawford, and Marianne McAndrew in the "Dancing" production number. McAndrew gives a performance of gentle grace and good humor.

Q: One performer's singing voice is dubbed. Which actor?

A: Marianne McAndrew uses a voice double for "Ribbons Down My Back" and her lyric in "It Only Takes a Moment." The fact is unabashedly stated in some contemporary press material for *Hello, Dolly!* and completely skirted or ignored in other statements. According to Fox archivist Alan Adler, "Ribbons Down My Back" was recorded twice. On November 8, 1968, Gilda Maiken recorded the song. It was re-recorded on March 3, 1969, by Melissa Stafford. Reportedly, sections of both vocalists' tracks were edited together for use in the finished film.

Marianne McAndrew had appeared in the 1968 Universal picture *A Lovely Way to Die*, and was working on a television pilot in New York when she auditioned for the director of *Hello, Dolly!* Although she had no formal training in dance, lessons were arranged for her after signing her to the role of the lady milliner.

After *Hello, Dolly!*, McAndrew appeared in *The Seven Minutes* (1971), *The Bat People* (1974), *She's Dressed to Kill* (1979, TV), and *Drop-out Father* (1982, TV) as well as on series television. She married character actor Stewart Moss at the time of *Dolly!*

In retrospect, McAndrew appears to be a victim of the times. The year after *Hello, Dolly!* she resignedly told the *Los Angeles Herald-Examiner* "'I've talked with other young actors, and we feel the same. There's something heartbreaking about waiting for your big chance, getting it in such a big, splashy picture as *Hello, Dolly!* and then finding the studios shut down in your face. It's'—she hesitated for the right word—'disheartening.'" It seems that, at the time of McAndrew's ascent, the studios had neither the need for, or interest in, developing a burgeoning leading lady.

The fact that her singing voice is dubbed is no slight to Miss McAndrew's performance. Both her physical beauty and her skillful acting create a character for Irene Molloy that is at once sophisticated, poised, yearning, vulnerable, and not above a little playful mischief. The life and spirit that she brings to this role is a real credit to her sadly underutilized talent.

■

Q: Minnie Fay is played by a giggly sprite named E. J. Peaker. What does E. J. stand for?

A: Edra Jean Peaker was born in Tulsa, Oklahoma, in 1942, but considers Pueblo, Colorado, her home town. She was chosen from more than two hundred contenders to play Minnie Fay, her first film role.

During production, she was cast opposite Robert Morse in the musical ABC-TV series "That's Life," which presented the young actress with a problem: "That's Life" was scheduled to begin production at ABC Studios in Hollywood on August 12, 1968. *Hello, Dolly!* was not scheduled to wrap until August 30, 1968, at the Fox studio lot in West Los Angeles. The producers all worked out an ingenious—but exhausting—schedule for Peaker. She spent her days with the *Hello, Dolly!* company, and immediately at day's wrap traveled to Hollywood to rehearse "That's Life" at night. Shoot days for "That's Life" were rescheduled to Saturday and Sunday for the duration of shooting on *Hello, Dolly!*

Peaker continued with a prolific acting career after *Hello, Dolly!* She did *eight* episodes of "Love, American Style" in the early 1970s, as well as episodes of "Quincy," "Charlie's Angels," "The Rockford Files," "Hunter," "Houston Knights," and dozens of other television series.

Her films have included *All-American Boy* (1973), *Four Deuces* (1975), and *Graduation Day* (1981).

Peaker currently lives in Encino, California, and continues to keep busy in film, television, and on the musical and concert/cabaret stage.

■

Q: Who was the only member of the principal cast to have appeared in the stage version of *Hello, Dolly!?*

A: Danny Lockin played the part of Barnaby Tucker for two years in road companies of *Hello, Dolly!* He was born in Hawaii in 1943 and was raised in Omaha, Nebraska, where he started dancing professionally in county fairs at the age of eight. He had appeared in New York in *West Side Story*, and in touring and regional companies of *The Sound of Music*, *The Music Man*, and *Take Me Along*.

Marianne McAndrew had played the role of Irene Molloy on stage, but in a staging of *The Matchmaker* in Pennsylvania. E. J. Peaker had played Dolly Levi, but again in a production of *The Matchmaker*, this one in Colorado.

Author's Collection. © Twentieth Century-Fox Film Corporation

Cornelius Hackl (Michael Crawford) and Barnaby Tucker (Danny Lockin) dream of a world outside Yonkers.

Sadly, Danny Lockin died in 1977. The August 26, 1977, issue of *The Hollywood Reporter* carried this information about Lockin's death: "Danny Lockin, 34, died August 21 in an auto accident." Two days later, *Variety* reported: "Danny Lockin, 34, actor, was stabbed to death Aug. 21 in Anaheim, Calif., where police have charged [a suspect] with homicide."

Further information has, so far, not been made available to the author by the Anaheim Police Department.

■

Q: John De Cuir's magnificent Manhattan exterior sets for *Hello, Dolly!* are replicas of what famous New York neighborhood?

A: A trick question, really, since De Cuir's designs duplicate no single specific street. Instead the sets, in several bits and pieces, evoke the gaslit charm of "little old New York," including intersections of Manhattan's Fifth Avenue, Broadway, and Mulberry Street, with subsections for Madison Square Park, 14th Street, and the Bowery.

The New York Street set was originally planned as a fifteen-acre complex to be built from the ground up at the Twentieth Century-Fox movie ranch in Malibu Canyon, about thirty-five miles from the Fox lot in West Los Angeles. A little production accounting revealed that transportation charges for construction crews, materials, equipment, and talent, including the thousands who would be needed for the parade sequence, would prove an absolute fiscal impossibility.

Production designer John De Cuir developed an ingenious plan to use the basic layout of the existing studio lot as the footprint for his set design, enclosing eleven existing studio structures (including the Administration Building) in his ornate evocations of 1890s New York, without interfering with their function. The set, when

Collection of Tony Baxter

Four views of John De Cuir's magnificent Manhattan set for *Hello, Dolly!* These shots were taken the day before the parade scene started shooting in July 1968.

completed, was the largest and most expensive—costing more than two million dollars—ever attempted in the history of its studio.

De Cuir's sophisticated visual designs for *Hello, Dolly!* are different from any large scale musical set to that time. His fantasy Manhattan has a solid base in reality. The architecture and design of the buildings and their facades looks organic, there is nothing pristine or pre-planned about them. Surfaces are aged and distressed, and there are layers of time, use, and dirt everywhere (note the handrails in the park during the "Dancing" number). There is also prominent period advertising everywhere, just as there was in any large city at the time represented.

Several soundstages in the background had architectural detail or storefronts simply painted on their flat exteriors. But, in keeping with the visual style at hand, the trompe l'oeil painted window frames and ledges were so realistic that it was reported that pigeons tried to land on them and slid down the plain concrete walls!

Ultimately what De Cuir produced was a breathtaking visual marvel, which portrayed both parade-sized spectacle and romantic charm, while evoking a fond and loving nostalgia of New York that may not have existed in the truth, but is present in the heart.

Perhaps producer Ernest Lehman best summed up the feel that De Cuir was able to attain with his artistry: "I found myself strangely moved, suddenly filled with nostalgia for a New York I never knew; a world of time and place that perhaps had never existed, but seemed to exist in *Hello, Dolly!*—a kind of gay and charming world in which even the wicked were innocent."

■

Q: How many men does Horace say he'll march with in the 14th Street Parade?

A: After finding that Miss Molloy has hidden two men in her shop, Horace storms out, "to march in the 14th Street Parade with the kind of people I can trust—seven hundred men!"

The staging of the parade sequence is itself worthy of a *chapter* of trivia. The production notes called the parade sequence "statistically the most stupendous effort ever attempted by a motion picture company in America."

Parking spaces for thirty-seven hundred cars were leased at Century City and Rancho Park, adjoining the Twentieth Century-Fox studio lot. The schedule of all Fox TV series had been adjusted so they would be on hiatus during the week of July 15–19, 1968, and Fox employees were encouraged to take vacation during this week to minimize congestion on and around the studio lot.

Rehearsal began on Monday, July 15, 1968, with a rehearsal of parade personnel (that is, those people who comprised the parade, as opposed to the parade observers).

On Tuesday, July 16, the parade, comprised of 675 persons in 16 units, passed through a crowd of just over 3000 extras. Seven Todd-AO® cameras, including one mounted on a 80-foot boom, took in the action. In addition to the human numbers, the spectacle contained 28 horse-drawn vehicles including a double-decker bus, a Bekins van, the Anheuser-Busch Clydesdale horse team, 4 streetcars, and 3 fire engines. Two soundstages and 3 large tents were dedicated to wardrobe and make-up for the extras, and these facilities were staffed by 122 make-up artists and costumers. Fifteen radio-equipped special assistant directors were costumed to blend in with the crowd and keep the parade moving while in full view of the camera, as were 15 policemen and 5 detectives. Forty-two hundred boxed lunches were prepared (the overage was insurance against having to pay union meal penalties), and 2 additional tents were erected to house meal seating areas. Five catering trucks, 60 watering stations, 5 first aid stations, and 17 toilet facilities were also positioned around the gigantic set. The large establishing and overall long shots were completed in one day, July 16, 1968.

The number of spectators was reduced to about 1200 for shooting on Wednesday and Thursday, July 17 and 18. It was on these two days that the medium shots and close-ups involving the principals were filmed.

The cost of the parade sequence was estimated at $200,000, including services and control, and not including any of the expenses of the regular *Hello, Dolly!* company, sets, or equipment, or any of the preparation for the sequence.

By the way, Horace is wrong about the number and gender of the parade participants. According to Twentieth Century-Fox publicity, the parade consisted of: The UCLA Marching Band (160 pieces); the "10th Cavalry Troop" (40 mounted men recreating the famed Black U.S. Army organization of the period); "The Academy of Music Float" (7 women portraying characters from *Tannhäuser*); High Wheeler Bicycles (15); the "Coronettes" from Santa Monica City College (56); Highland Society Bagpipers (40); the "Tony Pastor Float" (10 girls from various countries); Civil War Veterans (48); the "Wagon with Maypole Streamers" (8 clowns, 5 midgets); the "Meat Packer's Float" (4 girls); Prohibitionists (20 men, 20 women); the San Fernando Valley Youth Band (100); "Vandergelder's Lodge Marchers" (42); California High Girls of Whittier, California (75 gymnasts); Fire Engines (3); Suffragettes (12); and the Anheuser-Busch Clydesdales (2 men, 6 horses).

■

Q: Two of the stars of *Hello, Dolly!* were rumored to have had a catty conflict during the filming of the picture. Who were they?

A: The two leads, Barbra Streisand and Walter Matthau, were alleged to have been on resolutely ungracious terms during the filming of *Hello, Dolly!* According to critic and historian Tony Thomas, Matthau called Streisand "Miss Ptomaine," and she referred to him as "Old Sewer-Mouth."

In her 1978 book, *Flesh and Fantasy*, Penny Stallings reports it this way:

> After Walter Matthau had completed filming *Hello, Dolly!* with Barbra Streisand, the best he could say of his co-star for publication was, "I have no disagreements with Barbra Streisand. I was merely exasperated by her tendency toward megalomania." But a crew member tells of [Matthau's] off-the-record *bon mot* to Barbra after a particularly noisy altercation: "I have more talent in my smallest fart than you do in your entire body."

To all public appearances, their conflicts of the past must be long forgotten. Matthau and his wife Carol were prominent guests at Streisand's September, 1986, *One Voice* concert, as well as her 1994 concert at the Arrowhead Pond in Anaheim, California.

The *Hello, Dolly!* parade scene became a facile symbol of the film's reputed epic excess.

Author's Collection. © Twentieth Century-Fox Film Corporation

Level Three: No Easy Stuff
Minutia & Obscuria

Q: Who was originally scheduled to direct *Hello, Dolly!?*

A: According to John Gregory Dunne in *The Studio*, Fox had initially intended *Hello, Dolly!* producer Ernest Lehman to be the film's director as well.

Born in 1920, Lehman had studied chemical engineering, but switched to literature after two years. He first made his mark as a freelance writer, selling to many major national magazines. This exposure brought him to the attention of Hollywood, where he provided the screen story for *The Inside Story* (1948), and the screenplays for *Executive Suite* and *Sabrina* (1954).

He became something of a musical screenwriting specialist, transferring *The King and I* (1956), *West Side Story* (1961), *The Sound of Music* (1965), and *Hello, Dolly!* from the Broadway stage to the screen—and improving each one in the process.

Lehman's other credits include the screenplays for *Somebody Up There Likes Me, Trapeze* (1956, uncredited), *The Sweet Smell of Success* (1957, screenplay adapted from his novella), *North by Northwest* (1959), *From the Terrace* (1960), *The Prize* (1963), *Who's Afraid of Virginia Woolf?* (1966), *Family Plot* (1976), and *Black Sunday* (1977).

Lehman adapted, produced, and directed *Portnoy's Complaint* (1972). His Chenault Productions was the production entity for *Hello, Dolly!* (Lehman lived on Chenault Drive in Beverly Hills.)

A charming compilation of Lehman's satirical musings on life in the movie industry, *Screening Sickness and Other Tales of Tinsel Town*, was published in 1982.

■

Q: How much did Twentieth Century-Fox pay for the film rights to *Hello, Dolly!?*

A: On February 9, 1965, the Hollywood trade papers trumpeted the sale of the screen rights for

Author's Collection. © Twentieth Century-Fox Film Corporation

Hello, Dolly! spent more than a year in post-production—and then storage—before it saw its world premier in December of 1969.

Hello, Dolly! to Twentieth Century-Fox for two million dollars, plus an undisclosed percentage of the film's distribution gross. This was expected to push the sale price to six million dollars.

The snag in this deal, a clause in the contract that would wind up costing Fox additional millions, was that the movie version could not be released until June 1971 or when the show closed on Broadway, whichever came first.

Show business trades reported the "early release" escape payment at a rumored one to two million, paid by Fox to Broadway *Dolly!* producer David Merrick. *The Hollywood Reporter* stated on October 21, 1969, that "[Twentieth Century-Fox president Richard] Zanuck had to agree that if Merrick's box office receipts should suffer from the concurrent run of the stage and screen attractions, then 20th-Fox will have to reimburse any losses sustained thereof." This amount reportedly guaranteed to pay the difference on any weekly Broadway gross that fell under sixty thousand dollars.

The film finally saw its premiere on December 16, 1969, at New York's Rivoli Theater, with the West Coast premiere at the Chinese Theater on Hollywood Boulevard on December 19. The film had wrapped shooting more than a year before it premiered.

These elaborate rights payments are another reason that *Hello, Dolly!* and its elephantine cost have become the stuff of legend. The legend, by the way, would have it that *Hello, Dolly!* bankrupted Fox. The picture had cost twenty million dollars, and by the end of its first year in release, its domestic gross was more than thirteen million. In the long run, *Hello, Dolly!* probably broke even or showed a small profit. Fox simply had bankrolled three gargantuan pictures in a row: *Hello, Dolly!*, *Star!*, and *Doctor Dolittle*, none of which were able to duplicate the bonanza of *The Sound of Music*, which is obviously what they were after (as was every studio). *Hello, Dolly!* appears to have simply pulled a *Dick Tracy*—it cost a lot, taxed studio resources, and

made back its cost by a squeak.

Film critic and historian Tony Thomas summed up *Hello, Dolly!* this way: "It is a genial, handsome, old-fashioned musical dogged by bad luck in its timing and in the decision to spend so much money making it."

■

Q: Twentieth Century-Fox, Broadway *Dolly!* producer David Merrick, and *Hello, Dolly!* were at the center of a lawsuit in 1970. Who was the plaintiff?

A: Paramount Pictures Corporation filed suit in New York State Supreme Court on Friday, February 13, 1970, applying for a judgment directing Twentieth Century-Fox and David Merrick to pay Paramount one-third of all moneys due from Fox to Merrick for the Broadway producer's permission to release *Hello, Dolly!* in December 1969.

Let's step back a few years to September 1963, when Paramount Pictures granted The Dolly Venture Company (a joint venture of which Merrick was a principal) the right to produce a stage musical based upon *The Matchmaker*. Paramount held the rights to the original property, and as part of their agreement with Merrick not only held first right of refusal on the film rights to the resulting stage musical, *Hello, Dolly!*, but also "one third of all sums to be received from sale of the motion picture rights" should Paramount pass on them. Pass they did, and when Fox acquired *Hello, Dolly!*, Paramount apparently received one-third of the coin Fox paid for the film rights.

As mentioned above, a clause in the film rights contract stipulated that the movie version could not be released until June 1971 or when the show closed on Broadway, whichever came first. Fox paid Broadway *Dolly!* producer David Merrick a rumored one to two million dollar "early release" escape payment so that the film of *Hello, Dolly!* could be released before the stage musical closed on Broadway.

But Paramount apparently considered this escape payment a part of the "all sums to be received from the sale of the motion picture rights."

The complaint stated that Merrick, without informing Paramount, and despite Merrick's knowledge of the "one-third" agreement with Paramount, entered negotiations with Fox as to restrictions on release of the film, allowing for the December 1969 opening.

■

Q: The *Hello, Dolly!* set made news again in 1977. How?

A: On June 21, 1977, fire broke out on the still-standing Manhattan exterior set, wrapped around the studio buildings of the Twentieth Century-Fox lot. Reported to the Los Angeles County Fire Department at 4:51 P.M., the blaze consumed a three-building section of the set in about eighteen minutes. Nine Los Angeles County fire units and one Beverly Hills Fire Department unit quickly contained the flames, which were visible from the streets outside the studio gate at Pico Boulevard and Motor Avenue. There were no injuries.

"It looked worse than it was," said the Fox Vice President of Operations, Bernie Barron, to *The Hollywood Reporter*. "The bulk of the 'Dolly' street, a city landmark, remains intact." There were no companies shooting on the sets, or scheduled to do so, at the time of the fire.

After filming was completed on *Hello, Dolly!*, the Manhattan set was left more or less intact for a number of years, and can be seen in dozens of Twentieth Century-Fox films and television shows from 1969 to 1992, memorably the "Dreams" episode of "M*A*S*H," where the secondary street set represents Corporal Max Klinger's hometown of Toledo, Ohio. This "Bowery" section of the *Dolly!* set is frequently seen in the TV series "NYPD Blue."

A new master plan for the remaining acreage of the Fox lot, announced in 1993, dictated the final dismantling of entire set over a period of years, revealing the actual facades (some of them quite beautiful) of the Fox studio buildings for the first time in twenty-five years.

■

Q: As they arrive at the hat shop, a quick accounting reveals that Cornelius and Barnaby's funds amount to "Forty cents for the train back, thirty cents for dinner and twenty cents..." to see something. What New York attraction does Barnaby have his heart set on seeing?

hard

Film historian Tony Thomas called *Hello, Dolly!* "a genial, handsome, old-fashioned musical."

A: Barnaby has set aside "twenty cents to see the whale." In Yonkers, Cornelius had listed the attractions of New York to his young associate: "Adventure, Barnaby. Living, Barnaby! Will you come, Barnaby? The lights of Broadway...elevated trains...the stuffed whale in Barnum's Museum!" While the two clerks wait for their dates to change clothes for the evening, Barnaby claims his tourist victory: "We've seen everything—the parade, the Statue of Liberty, the stuffed whale at Barnum's Museum...I could die a happy man right now!"

If the screenplay had been historically accurate, Barnaby would have suffered a terrific disappointment—Barnum's American Museum had burned down 1865. Barnum reopened, but Barnum's New American Museum also burned to the ground in 1868.

Even if visiting the museum had been possible, Barnaby would not have found a stuffed whale there. Barnum's showmanship was above such a pedantic taxidermy display. What Barnum had exhibited, in 1861, were *living* whales!

Melville's *Moby Dick* had provided Barnum's inspiration, and he constructed an eighteen-by-fifty foot concrete and brick holding tank in the basement of his museum on lower Broadway at Ann Street in Manhattan. He put twenty-four French-Canadian fishermen on a daily retainer, and promised a bonus for the capture of a pair—male and female—of living great white whales. The whales were trapped and transported by rail freight cars to New York, a five day journey. The animals were lowered into the basement tank, which contained salted fresh water, as real ocean water was not readily available. Thousands clamored to see the whales, but the unfortunate beasts died only a few days after their arrival.

Barnum was unfazed, and, learning from his initial experience, constructed a new, four thousand dollar, twenty-four-foot-square tank on the second floor of the museum building, with a slate floor and inch-thick glass imported from France. Real salt water was piped from the bay into the tank, and he soon had another pair of white whales...which died nearly as quickly as the first had. Barnum spent another ten thousand dollars on a third pair of whales, but first one and then the other succumbed to captivity. A hippopotamus occupied the tank next, followed by sharks, angel fish, and, finally, porpoises, before the fiery close of the American Museum in 1868—twenty-two years before Cornelius and Barnaby visited New York City.

■

Q: *Hello, Dolly!* has something in common with *Oklahoma!* (1955), *Around the World in 80 Days* (1956), *South Pacific* (1958), *Porgy and Bess* (1959), *Can-Can* (1960), and *The Sound of Music* (1965). What could all of these films have in common? (Well, beyond the obvious things like color, sound, music, actors, etc.)

A: All of the films mentioned above were filmed in the widescreen, stereophonic sound process know as Todd-AO®.

The process employed a wide-gauge 65mm negative, which ran through the camera at 30 frames per second (standard 35mm runs at 24 fps). The wider frame (three and a half times the frame area of 35mm film) and increased frames per second resulted in a sharp, vivid, rock-steady image of superlative quality. (In some cases the image is so realistic it is truly like looking out a window.) When the multi-track magnetic sound track was added, the result was a 70mm positive print, the archetype of the modern 70mm system still in use. The first public showing of Todd-AO was in 1955, with the premiere of *Oklahoma!*

Todd stands for Michael Todd, the flamboyant producer-showman who spearheaded the rebirth of the wide gauge film process. Early attempts to introduce the 70mm process in the 1930s had failed to gain unified support and exhibitor acceptance. (Good God, the exhibitors had barely gotten converted to talkies, and now Hollywood people were pushing a whole new projection system?) AO stands for the American Optical Company, the engineering and technical end of the project.

The initial Todd-AO process faced a drawback: there was no way to show the films in theaters not equipped with special projection systems for wide-gauge film. The initial solution was a laborious one: both *Oklahoma!* and the next Todd-AO picture, *Around the World in 80 Days*, were actually shot twice—once in Todd-AO, and once in CinemaScope™. After these films, the Todd-AO process was refined, its frame speed reduced to the standard 24 fps, and a method of optically printing from the 65mm negative to a 35mm anamorphic print was developed.

The brand name Todd-AO carried a certain prestige until the late 1960s; much like Cinerama, the Todd-AO name had public appeal all by itself. Also, because of the expense of filming in Todd-AO (the cost of the raw stock of the film was, naturally, double) and because using Todd-AO equipment was specialized, time consuming, and cumbersome, producers were very careful about the properties they chose to film in the process. It was a big investment, and the philosophy at Todd-AO was to go after a prestige market. The breathtaking visual result that could be achieved with the Todd-AO process cried out for spectacular subjects and scenery as well.

The Todd-AO credit card does not appear on the titles of the home video versions of *Hello, Dolly!*, since the video was mastered from a 35mm anamorphic print element. In a Todd-AO print, the Todd-AO credit goes with the Color by DeLuxe title, over the shot of the railroad engineer.

■

Q: How many Academy Awards did *Hello Dolly!* win?

A: Three. One of the most-deserved awards in Academy history was given for the **Art Direction** of *Hello, Dolly!* (John De Cuir, Jack Martin

Smith, and Herman Blumenthal; Walter M. Scott, George Hopkins, and Raphael Bretton; set decoration). Other nominees that year were *Anne of the Thousand Days* (Maurice Carter, Lionel Couch, art direction; Patrick McLoughlin, set decoration); *Gaily, Gaily* (Robert Boyle, George B. Chan, art direction; Edward G. Boyle, Carl Biddiscombe, set decoration); *Sweet Charity* (Alexander Golitzen, George C. Webb, art direction; Jack D. Moore, set decoration); and *They Shoot Horses, Don't They?* (Harry Horner, art direction; Frank McKelvy, set decoration).

Lennie Hayton and Lionel Newman won the Oscar for **Best Score of a Musical Picture** (Original or Adaptation). Other nominations in

hard

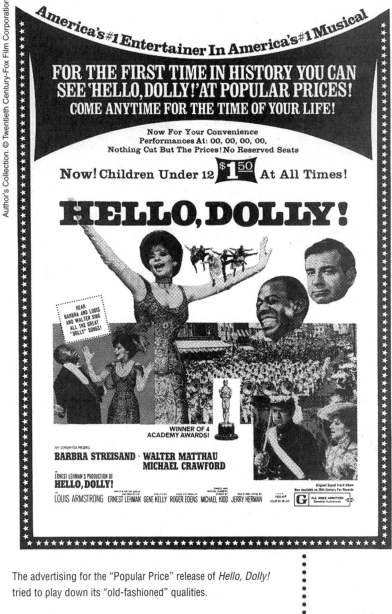

The advertising for the "Popular Price" release of *Hello, Dolly!* tried to play down its "old-fashioned" qualities.

the category were *Goodbye, Mr. Chips* (John Williams; Leslie Bricusse, music and lyrics); *Paint Your Wagon* (Nelson Riddle); *Sweet Charity* (Cy Coleman); and *They Shoot Horses, Don't They?* (Johnny Green, Albert Woodbury).

Dolly's final Oscar went for **Best Sound**, to Jack Solomon and Murray Spivack. The other nominees were *Anne of the Thousand Days* (John Alfred); *Butch Cassidy and the Sundance Kid* (William Edmundson, David Dockendorf); *Gaily, Gaily* (Robert Martin, Clem Portman); and *Marooned* (Les Fresholtz, Arthur Piantadosi).

Hello, Dolly! was nominated in four other Academy Award categories:

Best Picture (no kidding!), along with *Midnight Cowboy* (the winner), *Anne of the Thousand Days*, *Butch Cassidy and the Sundance Kid*, and *Z*.

Cinematography, which was won by *Butch Cassidy and the Sundance Kid* (Conrad L. Hall). Also nominated were *Anne of the Thousand Days* (Arthur Ibbetson), *Bob & Carol & Ted & Alice* (Charles B. Lang), and *Marooned* (Daniel L. Fapp).

Costume Design was won by *Anne of the Thousand Days* (Margaret Furse). Other nominees were *Gaily, Gaily* (Ray Aghayan); *Sweet Charity* (Edith Head); and *They Shoot Horses, Don't They?* (Donfeld).

Finally, *Hello Dolly!* was nominated for the **Film Editing** Oscar, won by *Z* (Francoise Bonnot). Also nominated were *Midnight Cowboy* (Hugh A. Robertson); *The Secret of Santa Vittoria* (William Lyon, Earle Herdan); and *They Shoot Horses, Don't They?* (Fredric Steinkamp).

■

Q: Several changes to the score of the stage musical were made in the film version of *Hello, Dolly!* What songs were cut from the stage musical in the move to film?

A: If you're familiar with both the stage and screen *Dollys*, your first guess might be "I Put My Hand In," but, technically, that song is still in the film score. Its introduction is retained for a new song, "Just Leave Everything to Me," and an instrumental version of it is played during the polka contest at the Harmonia Gardens.

"Motherhood," a patriotic pastiche paean (alliteration!) to motherhood, apple pie, and hot lunch for orphans was excised from the film version.

"Love is Only Love" was a Jerry Herman trunk song, originally written for the Broadway version of *Mame*. It was retrieved for use in this film, and is actually quite appropriate to the segment of the plot that it carries, giving depth and insight to Dolly Levi's pursuit of Horace Vandergelder. It portrays her clear-eyed yet romantic view of her desired relationship with Horace.

The the music that accompanies the choreographed movement at the opening of the film, leading up to "Just Leave Everything to Me," is referred to in production notes as "Clip Clop, Clip Clop" and "Bus Music."

■

Q: Apart from those already mentioned, *Hello, Dolly!* contains some interesting and hard-to-see anachronisms. Can you spot them?

A: During the opening titles, to the far right of frame, when Walter Matthau's credit is on screen, you can see a derelict automobile beside the railroad tracks. In the time context of the film, 1890, Henry Ford was hard at work in the Detroit Edison factory, building the first gas-powered automobile. This is not one of them.

Again in the title sequence, under the credit for Jack Martin Smith and Herman Blumenthal, along the ridge of the hill in the background at top of frame, highway signs for the New York Thruway are clearly visible.

TWENTIETH CENTURY-FOX PRESENTS ERNEST LEHMAN'S PRODUCTION OF

HELLO, DOLLY!

Written for the screen and produced by Ernest Lehman

Directed by Gene Kelly

Associate Producer Roger Edens

Dances and musical numbers staged by Michael Kidd

Music and lyrics by Jerry Herman

Music scored and conducted by Lenny Hayton, Lionel Newman

Director of Photography Harry Stradling ASC

Production designed by John De Cuir (Sr.)

Art Direction Jack Martin Smith, Herman Blumenthal

Costumes designed by Irene Sharaff

Set decorations by Walter M. Scott, George Hopkins, Ralph Bretton

Film Editor William Reynolds, ACE

Unit Production Manager Francisco Day

Assistant Director Paul Helmick

Sound Supervision James Corcoran

Sound Murray Spivak, Vinton Vernon, Jack Solomon, Douglas Williams

Assistant Choreographer Shelah Hackett

Orchestrations Philip J. Lang, Lennie Hayton, Joseph Lipman, Don Costa, Alexander Courage, Warren Baker

Orchestrations Frank Comstock, Herbert Spencer

Dance Arrangements Marvin Laird

Choral Arrangements Jack Latimer

Music Editors Robert Mayer, Kenneth Wannberg

Special Photographic Effects L. B. Abbott, ASC; Art Cruickshank

Make-up Supervision Dan Striepeke

Make-up Artists Ed Butterworth, Richard Hamilton

Hairstyling by Edith Lindon

Wardrobe Ed Wynigear, Barbara Westerland

Antique Jewelry from Laurence W. Ford & Company

Public Relations Patricia Newcomb

Script Supervisor Mollie Kent

Dialogue Coach George Eckert

Based on the Stage Play "Hello, Dolly!" produced on the New York Stage by David Merrick

Book of Stage Play by Michael Stewart

Based on "The Matchmaker" by Thornton Wilder

Music and Lyrics of the Stage Play by Jerry Herman

Directed and Choreographed by Gower Champion

Produced in Todd-AO®, developed by the American Optical Company and MAGNA

Color by DeLuxe

Produced by Chenault Productions, Inc.

Released by Twentieth Century-Fox Film Corporation

MPAA Rated "G" Running time 148 minutes

(World Premiere, New York, December 16, 1969. West Coast Premiere, Los Angeles, December 19, 1969)

Hello, Dolly!

Barbra Streisand . . . . Dolly Levi

Walter Matthau . . . . Horace Vandergelder

Michael Crawford . . . . Cornelius Hackl

Louis Armstrong . . . . Orchestra Leader

Marianne McAndrew . . . . Irene Molloy

E. J. Peaker . . . . Minnie Fay

Danny Lockin . . . . Barnaby Tucker

Joyce Ames . . . . Ermingarde

Tommy Tune . . . . Ambrose Kemper

Judy Knaiz . . . . Gussy Granger/Ernestina Simple

David Hurst . . . . Rudolph Reisenweber

Fritz Feld . . . . Fritz, a German Waiter

Richard Collier . . . . Joe, Vandergelder's Barber

J. Pat O'Malley . . . . Policeman in Park

Scatman Crothers . . . . Mr. Jones, a Railroad Porter

**Snow
White
and the
Seven
Dwarfs**

easy

Snow White and the Seven Dwarfs might be considered the first "integrated" film musical—that is, a musical where the songs enhance the characters and propel the plot. Though this technique had been employed on stage in Show Boat in 1927, and would come to maturity on stage with Oklahoma! in 1943, the structure of musical integration in Snow White is often minimized or overlooked. In fact, Snow White and the Seven Dwarfs has become such a part of popular culture that its many groundbreaking traits are frequently forgotten. Snow White represented a significant risk for the young studio that created it, and particularly for the young leader of that studio. Although Walt Disney was a darling of the contemporary arts set as well as the Hollywood cognoscenti, many felt that he was completely overstepping the bounds of his medium with Snow White. The success of Snow White and the Seven Dwarfs vindicated Walt Disney, stabilized the studio he had founded, and has become such a part of pop culture that even nearly sixty years after its release, a 1994 video release shattered all records.

■

Level One: The Easy Stuff
Story & Characters

Q: **What is the literary source of Disney's *Snow White and the Seven Dwarfs*? Who authored this source story?**

A: The Snow White story existed as an orally transmitted tale until its first publication as "Sneewitchen," part of Jacob and Wilhelm Grimm's 1812 fairy-tale anthology *Kinder- und Hausmärchen* (*Children's and Household Tales*). In 1823, it appeared as the story of "Snow-drop" in an English translation of Grimm by Edgar Taylor, *German Popular Stories*.

The fairy tale was dramatized for the stage in 1912, with Marguerite Clark as Snow White. This version ran for seventy-two performances on Broadway.

In 1915, Clark reprised her role in a silent film version, which was influential to an adolescent Walt Disney, who saw the film at a special screening for newsboys in Kansas City (young Walt had peddled both the *Kansas City Star* and the *Kansas City Times*). The film was shown simultaneously on four large screens, and from where he sat, Walt could see two of them at once. The power of both the time-honored story and the spectacular medium in which it was pre-

sented apparently stayed with Disney for years afterward. According to Disney biographer Bob Thomas, "It had been his most vivid early memory of attending the movies."

■

Q: **Let's get this one out of the way. Can you name the seven dwarfs?**

A: They are Doc, Bashful, Grumpy, Happy, Sleepy, Sneezy, and Dopey. An easy way to remember the names is that there are only five dwarfs whose names end with "y." Most people forget the two dwarfs whose names *don't* end with "y." Just remember Doc and Bashful, and it's pretty easy to fill in the other five.

As many times as the story of Snow White had been retold, and as obvious as it might seem, Walt Disney was one of the first to assign individual names and personalities to the "the seven little men," as he (and Snow White) called them. In the Grimm's original, and in most retellings thereafter, there was no attempt at such character development. The seven dwarfs were treated as indistinct supporting characters, seven of a matched set. English artist John Hasall in 1921 had illustrated the dwarfs with breeches embroidered with the names Plate, Stool, Bread, Spoon, Fork, Knife, and Wine. Another popular version had the dwarfs named Flick, Glick, Blick, Snick, Plick, Whick, and Queen.

Most animated cartoons before Disney's relied heavily on archetypes (cat and mouse, mischievous child and parent) and racial or cultural stereotypes to communicate characters and situations quickly to the audience. Walt recognized that this technique would be at odds with the level of sophistication that he desired for *Snow White*, and was beginning to achieve in design, color, and photography. Pinto Colvig (a versatile and influential talent at the studio) suggested that since the Dwarfs were individual identities, each should possess a name that could also signal a strong personality characteristic.

The names and personalities of the dwarfs went through a lengthy period of development over the production of *Snow White*. Among the names suggested were Jumpy, Baldy, Wheezy, Gabby, Shorty, and Burpy. The strongest characters were decided fairly early in production: Grumpy, Dopey, Sleepy, Doc, Happy, Bashful, and Deafy. Deafy would be replaced by Sneezy (Walt didn't want to play on physical handicaps for comedy), but the Disney staff had established the basic characters, which allowed the creative team to concentrate on the subtleties of personality.

■

Q: Who is Snow White? What relation is she to the wicked Queen?

A: Snow White is a Princess. Her mother, then, would be the Queen. But isn't the Queen that evil gal who plots Snow White's demise? Yep, but she's an example of the wicked stepmother syndrome, a time-honored fairy tale device.

An originally-planned prologue for *Snow White and the Seven Dwarfs* follows the literary original pretty much verbatim. Quoth the Brothers Grimm: "the child was called Snow White, and right after she was born, the Queen died. When a year had passed, the King married another woman, who was beautiful but proud and haughty, and she could not tolerate anyone else who might rival her beauty." The Disney version of this section of the Grimm story, along with a drawing of Snow White's mother, appeared in a contemporary illustrated story book of Disney's *Snow White*, and has turned up in other publications since.

Come on, now. When are these fairy tale widowers ever going to learn?

■

Q: The Queen consults a familiar to predict the future. What is it?

A: A familiar, in black magic, is a spirit, often in the form of an animal, believed to act as servant to a witch.

The Queen uses a Magic Mirror. Or, more accurately, the Queen calls for her "slave in the magic mirror." This haunting reference makes the mirror not a simple household object, but a powerful portrayal of the Queen's black magic and cruelty. Who is the slave? How did he get in that mirror? Why

Author's Collection. © The Walt Disney Company

The seven dwarfs. From left: Dopey, Sneezy, Bashful, Sleepy, Happy, Grumpy, and Doc.

does he have clairvoyant powers? The depth and eeriness of this brief but unforgettable character are created by the things about him that are apparent but unexplained. The cultured near-monotone of Moroni Olsen provides the mirror slave with a complex voice personality that is world-weary but forceful—a sort of Marley's Ghost.

■

Q: The Queen initially enlists a servant to do her dirty work. Who? What does she demand as proof of the completion of his task?

A: "Take her far into the forest. Find some secluded glade where she can pick wild flowers. And there, my faithful Huntsman, you will kill her!" A huntsman's role to the royal household of old was to provide fresh game for the palace table. In modern times, the huntsman was the "manager" of the sporting hunt, usually charged with care of the hound pack.

The Huntsman is instructed: "To make doubly sure you do not fail, bring back her heart…in

Author's Collection. The Walt Disney Company

The wicked Queen and the box intended to carry the proof of her grisly bidding.

this," as the Queen hands him an elaborate box, bearing a carving of a heart with a knife through it. The Huntsman cannot bring himself to kill the innocent Snow White and warns her to flee the Queen's malevolent jealousy, after which he puts a pig's heart in the box, hoping to fool the Queen. The mirror makes the Queen aware of the trick: "Snow White still lives, fairest in the land—'tis the heart of a pig you hold in your hand."

What happened to the Huntsman after the Queen learned of his deception? It can only be assumed that the Queen exacted a punishment—it would certainly be in keeping with her character. Perhaps he's just around the corner in one of the dank dungeons through which the Queen later stalks.

A dungeon sequence, in which the Queen captures the young Prince and imprisons and tortures him in an attempt to find Snow White's hiding place was developed but deleted. A similar scene was played out two decades later in Walt Disney's *Sleeping Beauty*, when Maleficent imprisons and torments Prince Phillip.

■

Q: Snow White and her animal friends make housework seem like such fun. How?

A: "Whistle While You Work," Snow White's anthem to making the best of your labors, by Disney staffers Larry Morey and Frank Churchill (accompanied by multiple sight gags), makes the drudgery of housecleaning seem riotously entertaining.

As he developed the animated art form from the first synchronized sound cartoon, *Steamboat Willie* (1928), Disney saw the advantages that music brought to storytelling. Many bemoaned the fact that bringing sound to film robbed the medium of its universality by inflicting speech on it, but music quickly proved itself to be a unique and dialect-free way of communicating story and character.

In the late twenties, Disney's in-house musical director for the Mickey Mouse shorts, Carl

Stalling, approached Disney with the idea of a series of animated shorts with no central character, based around musical themes. Disney welcomed Stalling's innovative notion, and the studio began production on the first of these shorts, which were dubbed "Silly Symphonies."

One of the later Silly Symphonies was *Three Little Pigs*, an important step in the creation of realistic and fully developed animated character personalities. The wildly successful short also confirmed to Disney the importance of music in animated filmmaking. "Who's Afraid of the Big Bad Wolf?," the film's catchy signature tune by Frank Churchill, became a rallying cry for a nation struggling through the Depression.

Animator Ken Anderson recalled that when Walt first outlined the story of *Snow White* for his key creative staff in early 1934, Disney was "even anticipating the songs and the kind of music..."

Oscar Hammerstein and Jerome Kern had stunned the Broadway stage with the seemingly basic technique of having the songs all serve story or character development without stopping the show cold with *Show Boat* in 1927. *Snow White* is arguably the first original film musical to employ this technique of musical integration.

■

Q: The evil Queen adopts a disguise to entrap Snow White. What is this disguise?

A: The Queen transforms herself by black magic into an aged hag, peddling apples to forest cottages for her evil purposes.

The character of the wicked Queen was first developed as a standard "cartoon" comic villain—vain, portly, and nonsensically dotty. Sort of a Marion Lorne (Aunt Clara on "Bewitched") or Hermione Gingold (Mrs. Shinn in *The Music Man*, q.v.) type.

Albert Hurter and Joe Grant eventually refined her into a coldly beautiful and heartlessly vain monarch, with a face like the masks of con-

temporary mask artist Wladyslaw T. Benda, as had been first suggested in an August 1934 story outline. The Queen was referred to in a 1934 Disney Studio character outline as "a mixture of Lady Macbeth and the Big Bad Wolf," although that doesn't even come close to defining the depth of her egotistical and cruel villainy. Joe Grant was also responsible for the visual realization of the Queen's alter ego, the aged crone.

■

Q: In her dungeon, the Queen is observed and attended by what companion?

A: A raven comrade witnesses the Queen's transformation. The minor character was adapted from Wilhelm Busch's 1867 drawings of *Hans Huckebein der Unglucksrabe* (*Jack Crook, Bird of Evil*). The Queen's mutation from beauty to hag frightens even the oily bird.

In the litany of Disney feature animation, it seems that wicked villains forever associate themselves with henchmen (or hench-beasts) of mindless loyalty, questionable intelligence, and usually comic character. J. Worthington Foulfellow is accompanied by an apparently brain-damaged cat, Gideon, in *Pinocchio* (1940). It can be

Author's Collection. © The Walt Disney Company

Wearing a disguise born of black magic, the wicked queen entices Snow White with a poisoned apple.

171

argued that Lady Tremayne, the wicked step-mother of Disney's *Cinderella* (1950) has "hench-daughters" in Anastasia and Drizella, the ugly stepsisters—and a hench-beast in the cat, Lucifer. Captain Hook has Mr. Smee in *Peter Pan* (1953); Maleficent, who owes much of her graceful evil to Snow White's nemesis, also has a pet raven (never named in the film itself, but known as Diablo in other sources) in *Sleeping Beauty* (1959), as well as a company of frightening troll-like "goons." Mr. Snoops serves as aide to Madame Medusa (as, to a lesser degree, do the alligators Nero and Brutus) in *The Rescuers* (1977). Ursula, the sea witch, is assisted by evil eels Flotsam and Jetsam in *The Little Mermaid* (1989). Gaston has comic foil LeFou in *Beauty and the Beast* (1991), Jafar has wise-cracking Iago in *Aladdin* (1992), and Scar has the hyenas, Shenzi, Banzai, and Ed, in *The Lion King* (1994).

■

Q: Who kills the wicked Queen?

A: Actually, no one commits the well-deserved dirty deed. While being chased by the dwarfs up a rugged cliff during a driving storm, lightning strikes her precarious perch as she tries to send a

The dwarfs mourn the "death" of their princess in this promotional illustration.

huge boulder down on her seven pursuers.

In the original Brothers Grimm version, the Queen has a much more grisly fate—and Snow White herself is an accessory to the murder! The Queen is not aware that Snow White has survived, and unsuspectingly attends the wedding of the Prince:

> At first she did not want to go to the wedding celebration. But, she could not calm herself until she saw the young queen. When she entered the hall, she recognized Snow White. The evil Queen was so petrified with fright that she could not budge. Iron slippers had already been heated over a fire, and they were brought over to her with tongs. Finally, she had to put on the red-hot slippers and dance until she fell down dead.

Yow. Retribution is all well and good, but it's better left to a higher power. Think of the karma damage.

■

Q: When the dwarfs discover their Princess (apparently) dead, what do they do?

A: "So beautiful, even in death, that the dwarfs could not find it in their hearts to bury her...they fashioned a coffin of glass and gold, and kept eternal vigil at her side...the Prince, who had searched far and wide, heard of the maiden who slept in the glass coffin." This plot point, with Snow White awakened by love's first kiss, is lifted from Perrault's retelling of *The Sleeping Beauty*, and is simply a more graceful and romantic way to have Snow White revived by the Prince. In the Grimm original, Snow White is, to all observation, quite dead. The Prince claims her inert body, and as the dwarfs lift her bier for the Prince to take her away, the bite of poisoned apple dislodges from her throat (eeew!), thus reviving her.

Q: Who provided the voice for Snow White?

A: Adriana Caselotti was chosen out of hundreds who auditioned for the role of Snow White. Disney wanted a fresh, innocent girl, with a strong, melodious voice, but without obvious affectations or techniques of vocal training. (The little princess is described in a 1934 character outline as being "fourteen years old.") During the audition process, Disney had a speaker wired into his office, so he could hear the voice qualities of the girls without being influenced by their physical appearance. One of the young women Disney dismissed was Deanna Durbin ("too mature"), who went on to become a popular singing film star at Universal Pictures.

Disney casting director Roy Scott called Los Angeles vocal coach Guido Caselotti to ask for leads and advice in this casting dilemma. Caselotti's daughter, nineteen-year-old Adriana, was listening on an extension, and interrupted. In a trilling, childlike voice she asked if she could be considered for the part. As any father might, the elder Caselotti told her to get off the line, but Scott arranged for an audition anyway. When Walt heard her bell-like voice, he was convinced. "That's our girl! That's Snow White!"

The recording sessions for Snow White lasted a cumulative forty-eight days. Caselotti received a total of $970.00 for her performance.

■

Q: Which two dwarfs are voiced by the same individual?

A: Pinto Colvig provided the voices for Grumpy and Sleepy.

Born in Oregon in 1892, Vance DeBar Colvig was a skinny, bucktoothed kid with so many freckles that he earned the nickname "Pinto." A childhood "class clown," Colvig was fascinated with minstrel shows and circuses, and as a child performed a blackface act with his brother. Colvig was also a musician, and played the E-flat clarinet. At the age of twelve he went to work as a clown on the midway of the Lewis and Clark Centennial Exposition in Portland. For the next four years, he hoboed across America, clowning and performing with various carnivals and circuses, as well as appearing in vaudeville. He also developed his talents as a cartoonist and writer.

He became interested in the budding art of film animation, and made silent cartoons before becoming a title writer and comedian for Mack Sennett. When sound came to film, Colvig partnered with Walter Lantz in an animation business for a time.

In 1930, Colvig signed with Walt Disney, doing gags and voices for Silly Symphony and Mickey Mouse cartoons. In *Mickey's Revue* (1932), Colvig provided the obnoxious guffaw for a hayseed spectator named Dippy Dawg, who would later become famous (with Colvig's voice) as Goofy. In 1933, he was the voice of Practical Pig in *Three Little Pigs*, and the Grasshopper in *The Grasshopper and the Ants*. For this short, he wrote and performed a song that would later be

Author's Collection. © The Walt Disney Company

Snow White and the young woman who provided her distinctive voice.

**Snow
White
and the
Seven
Dwarfs**

medium

used as Goofy's signature tune, "The World Owes Me a Living." Colvig left Disney in 1938, but continued to free-lance at Disney and all over Hollywood. He relocated to Miami with the Max Fleischer Studio that same year, and provided the voice of Gabby in *Gulliver's Travels* (1939) and in the Gabby shorts.

Over the years between *Snow White and the Seven Dwarfs* and his death in 1967, Colvig continued to write, perform, and cartoon for nearly every major animation concern, as well as on radio. In addition to the voice of Goofy, his other great claim to fame was the creation of Bozo the Clown for Capitol Records in 1946.

Colvig often said, "My mother covered me with a crazy quilt when I was born, and I've been clowning ever since."

■

Q: How many Oscars were won by *Snow White and the Seven Dwarfs?*

A: None. Oddly, the film was almost completely overlooked at the time of the Academy Awards. The score, by Disney staffers Leigh

Walt Disney is presented with a special Oscar® for *Snow White* by child star Shirley Temple.

Harline, Frank Churchill, and Paul J. Smith, was *nominated* for an Oscar, but not one of *Snow White's* eight wildly popular songs was named for the prize. However, neither were such classics as "Hooray for Hollywood" and "Let's Call the Whole Thing Off." The award for Best Song went to a little-known tune called "Sweet Leilani" from an equally obscure film called *Waikiki Wedding*.

More popular hit songs originated with *Snow White and the Seven Dwarfs* than in any other Disney animated film. *The Hit Parade* of 1938 featured six tunes from the film, "Whistle While You Work," "Someday My Prince Will Come," "Heigh-Ho," "One Song," "With a Smile and a Song," and "I'm Wishing."

The Victor Records release of "Songs From Walt Disney's *Snow White and the Seven Dwarfs*" marked another important first for the film: the first original motion picture sound track recording offered for sale on record to the public. The Victor copywriters were obviously hard-pressed to explain an "original sound track recording," resulting in this on-album description of the record: "with the same characters and sound effects as in the film of that title." When Victor Records released the *Pinocchio* record album in 1940, they coined the term "sound track."

On February 23, 1939, the Academy of Motion Picture Arts and Sciences finally recognized the phenomenal artistic and cultural success of *Snow White* by presenting Walt Disney with a special Oscar, alongside seven miniature Oscars. The inscription reads "To Walt Disney for *Snow White and the Seven Dwarfs* recognized as a significant screen innovation which has charmed millions and pioneered a great new entertainment field for the motion picture cartoon." Child star Shirley Temple unveiled the award for Disney.

■

Q: Who provided the voice of the evil Queen? Who provided the voice of the Peddler Woman?

A: Lucille LaVerne gave voice to both the cold, elegant monarch and her alter ego, the peddler crone. LaVerne was in her mid-sixties at the time of the recording sessions for *Snow White*, and had been a prominent actress on the stage and silent screen.

Born in 1873, LaVerne began acting at age fourteen. According to her 1945 obituary in *The New York Times*, "Miss LaVerne gave command performances before the late King George V of England, Leopold, King of the Belgians, and Kaiser Wilhelm of Germany. She played with such stars as Ethel Barrymore and Frank Bacon, and trod the boards in theaters bearing her name in Los Angeles, Chicago, New York, London and Paris." Her most famous role was that of Widow Cagle in *Sun-Up*, which she played in more than three thousand performances.

Interestingly, her stage-trained melodramatic flair proved to be a definite asset to her vocal characterizations in *Snow White*. Her long theatrical experience gave her an innate understanding of understatement (as Snow White bites the poisoned apple, the peddler nearly *whispers* the words of incantation: "… her breath will still…her blood congeal …") and bravura (after Snow White falls, the peddler grandly proclaims "Now *I'll* be fairest in the land!").

In *The Disney Villain* (1993, Hyperion), veteran animators Frank Thomas and Ollie Johnston tell the story of one of LaVerne's recording sessions for the peddler woman. Her voice was aged and crafty, its timbre was right, but, in the manner of many stage actors, it sounded too refined, the diction too precise. LaVerne overheard their conversation about her reading and excused herself. When she returned a few minutes later, her reading was everything they had wanted. Story man and character designer Joe Grant exclaimed, "What happened here?"

LaVerne replied, "Well, I just took my teeth out."

■

medium

Q: Who was the voice of Dopey?

A: Sort of a trick question, for two reasons. First, Dopey is well-known as the dwarf who doesn't speak ("You mean he can't talk?" "He don't know—he never tried!"). Second, all the other "vocals" he performs in the finished film are uncredited.

Those vocals include a "shhhh!" to a squeaking door as the dwarfs sneak into their cottage, a holler of frightened surprise when he sees Snow White stirring beneath the covers, a snore as he describes what "the monster" upstairs is doing, a gurgling underwater scream as the other dwarfs dunk him in the water trough, and a pronounced series of hiccups after he swallows a bar of soap.

The human origin of these sounds is lost to time, although veteran Disney sound man Jimmy Macdonald told *Funnyworld* in 1977: "The Studio didn't have a lot of money in the early days, so I would do these things and fill in. Rather than call in an actor, they would call me, because I was on staff. I just fell into doing them." This is true not only of Macdonald, but of many of the Disney staffers at the time of *Snow White and the Seven Dwarfs*, and on through the years since.

Author's Collection. © The Walt Disney Company

Dopey, the guileless, childlike mute, proved to be a phenomenally popular character.

Q: What is the name of Snow White's Prince?

A: The Prince. Many mistakenly believe that he is Prince Charming, but he is never referred to by that name. When Snow White tells the dwarfs of her dream Prince, she *does* say, "Anyone could see that the Prince was charming," but she is referring to an attribute, not his moniker.

The 1958 Disney-produced preview trailer for the re-release of *Snow White* incorrectly refers to the Prince as Prince Charming.

Prince Charming is Cinderella's Prince. Prince Phillip is the beau of Sleeping Beauty (a.k.a. Princess Aurora, a.k.a. Briar Rose). More recently, Ariel (*The Little Mermaid*) had her Prince Eric, Princess Jasmine had Prince Ali (Aladdin in disguise), and, in *Beauty and the Beast*, Belle had…the Prince.

■

Q: A major photographic innovation for animation was used extensively on *Snow White*. What was it?

A: The Multiplane Camera was developed by Disney and his staff in order to enable his animated world to have the visual depth of reality. Animation had progressed little in this sense—animation was generally photographed flat on a table-top, with a camera mounted above and the images piled one on top of the other in a single plane. There was never a feeling of depth, of characters traveling *through* space.

Walt supervised dozens of technicians in the development of the Multiplane Camera. The fourteen-foot-tall, seventy thousand dollar technical marvel enabled the camera to "travel" through several glass plates. As the camera, mounted above, "moved" through each layer, or plane (the *planes* actually raised and lowered, not the camera itself), a different image representing a different level of depth could be moved at a different speed, giving the illusion of dimen-sion. Each glass pane was animated and lighted individually, and adjusted to assure consistent exposure.

Walt Disney considered this innovation essential for an audience to accept the credibility of a feature-length animated film. Disney knew that the simple "cartoon" had to be elevated as an art form in order to equal its live-action contemporaries. As part of this greater illusion of live action, Walt felt the animation camera needed to be as fluid as any on a typical movie set.

Disney's contemporary, Max Fleischer, used a system in which cels were photographed vertically in front of miniature three-dimensional model "sets" to achieve a sense of depth, but it was never much more than a gimmick, and nowhere near the sophistication of the Multiplane Camera.

The Multiplane camera was used extensively on the 1937 short *The Old Mill*, the most successful Silly Symphony since *Three Little Pigs*. Disney described the short subject as "just a poetic thing, nothing but music. No dialogue or anything. The setting of an old mill at sunset. The cows going home. And then what happens in an old mill at night. The spider coming out and weaving its web. The birds nesting, and then the storm coming up, and the windmill going on a rampage. And with morning the cows come back, the spider web was all shattered, and all that. It was just a poetic thing." *The Old Mill* won the Academy Award for best cartoon in 1937, but "the important thing to me," Disney said, "was the proof that I had a feeling of third dimension."

■

Q: The visual style of *Snow White and the Seven Dwarfs* owes a debt to yet another film-making technology. What innovative technology helped create *Snow White*'s kingdom?

A: It is difficult to conceive today, but at the time of the making of Snow White, *color* was a relatively recent innovation in filmmaking.

Walt Disney knew that animation could benefit immensely by the use of color. He encouraged his technicians to experiment with methods of bringing color to film. Tinting, where lengthy scenes could be bathed in a wash of color, had been used extensively. Hand-tinting, frame by laborious frame, had proved too impractical.

The Technicolor company had developed a process that provided a muted palette of color, but it proved more cumbersome and expensive than the result warranted. In 1932, Technicolor devised a "three-strip" system where the primary colors (cyan, yellow, and magenta) were dye-transferred onto a base of black and white. The combination provided just the vivid color that Disney had envisioned. The process was not ready for application to live-action photography—but, luckily, it could be used for animated cartoons. Disney landed a two-year exclusive on the refined Technicolor process, which would prohibit any other animation concern from using the technique.

He stopped production on a black and white Silly Symphony, *Flowers and Trees*, and ordered it remade in the new Technicolor. The release of *Flowers and Trees* brought high praise for the inventiveness of its color, as well as increased popularity in the theaters. *Flowers and Trees* was also awarded the first-ever Oscar for Best Cartoon Short in 1932.

But it was not just the use of Technicolor that set the visual style of *Snow White* apart. The color styling accepted as the norm for animation to this point had relied on vivid, primary colors, rendered in an opaque gouache paint, and an uncomplicated level of detail to give focus to the character action.

The difference in visual style between the typical cartoon of 1937 and *Snow White* is as vivid as the comparison of a comic book to a Seurat painting.

With *Snow White and the Seven Dwarfs*, the backgrounds were painted with a great depth of detail in grayed-down transparent watercolors. This muted color palette not only achieved the overall subtlety that Disney wanted, it was most suitable to the then-new Technicolor process, which was only capable of accurately capturing mid-range colors.

■

Q: Casting Snow White involved *three* talents for each character. What were they?

A: Naturally, voice casting is a key concern in an animated feature, and the casting to which the audience will primarily relate.

People often forget that the casting of an "actor with a pencil"—the animator—is of equal, and usually greater, importance. The character on screen is a reflection of the acting skills of the person doing the drawing.

The third, and least known, "casting" is that of live-action reference models.

All the human characters in *Snow White and the Seven Dwarfs* were "rotoscoped," a process where footage of a live actor is filmed performing some of the action of the animated character. The resulting pictures are then traced, frame by frame, onto animation paper.

Contrary to popular belief, these traced scenes are not actually used in the finished production, but are instead used as reference in order for the animator get a sense of weight, balance, costume movement, and force of motion. If an animator used rotoscope tracings as a source for finished animation, "the animation looked stupid as the devil," according to veteran Disney layout man Ken O'Connor. "It's a funny thing in animation. You have to go further than normal to make it *seem* normal. You have to exaggerate."

The unsatisfactory result of direct tracing is evident in the bizarre Max Fleischer version of Gulliver's Travels and Ralph Bakshi's equally odd *The Lord of the Rings* (1978).

A young dancer named Marge Belcher performed the live role of Snow White before the camera. She would later marry another dancer, and together they became the famous terpsichorean team of Marge and Gower Champion.

Three actual dwarfs were filmed for reference—Erny, Tom, and Major George. Louis Hightower was the model for the Prince, and vaudeville veteran Eddie Collins provided inspiration for many of Dopey's characteristics. Several of the dwarfs' voice actors reportedly performed flat-footed dances before the cameras for reference use in "The Silly Song" sequence.

Don Brodie acted out the role of the peddler hag. Brodie had done voices for several shorts at the Disney Studio, including the voice of the Devil in *Mother Pluto* (1936) and a haunt in *Lonesome Ghosts* (1937). Walt Disney personally asked him to perform the role of the peddler woman for the animator's live action reference. Later, Brodie modeled as Gepetto for the live-action reference of the whale chase in *Pinocchio*.

In 1938, Walt Disney made note of the groundbreaking animation of realistic human characters in *Snow White*. "None of us knew how these drawings of human figures on the screen were going to be taken, " Disney said. "We were prepared for any sort of ridicule."

The dwarfs celebrate the rescue of Snow White by her Prince. One of them didn't get a kiss good-bye.

Author's Collection. © The Walt Disney Company

Q: As Snow White prepares to depart with her charming Prince, she kisses all of the dwarfs except one. Which one? Why does she ignore him?

A: As the film reaches its conclusion, the Prince sets Snow White on his horse, and lifts the dwarfs for a good-bye kiss. First Bashful is lifted, then Grumpy. With one arm, the Prince swoops up Doc, Sneezy, and Happy, all together. And finally Dopey is lifted by himself. Where is Sleepy? Napping, perhaps—but even Sleepy wouldn't fade out during this touching farewell.

Why is Sleepy ignored in this fashion? According to Disney archivist Robert Tieman, the answer comes down to simple logistics. "I was curious about that, too," Tieman relates, "so I asked Frank Thomas, who animated much of that scene. Frank says that when the finale was being completed, they had run out of time. The premiere date had been set, and they were working furiously to meet a deadline. The sequence had already been through layout, everything had been timed, and then Frank realized that there was only space enough for Snow White to reach six of the dwarfs. Restaging was out of the question, and the deadline was looming. Giving the Prince a six-foot arm so he could lift a fourth dwarf was not an option, so leaving one of the dwarfs out made the most sense.

"Most people are so caught up in the emotion of the scene, they don't even notice," Tieman concludes. "Well, until the film came out on video, anyway!"

Level Three: No Easy Stuff
Minutia & Obscuria

Q: The seven dwarfs appeared in four subsequent Disney animated shorts. Can you name them?

A: The seven dwarfs were so popular that Disney was besieged with requests for a sequel to *Snow White*. He resisted, falling back on an oft-quoted phrase, "you can't top pigs with pigs." This quote related to the resounding success of *Three Little Pigs* in 1933, after which Disney's distributor pressured him into making several sequels—*The Big Bad Wolf* (1934), *Three Little Wolves* (1936), and *The Practical Pig* (1939)—none of which lived up to the success of the original *Three Little Pigs*.

There was little to develop in terms of a story, either—always one of Disney's key issues—and by the time of *Snow White's* success, production was well underway on *Pinocchio* and *Bambi*.

The dwarfs were used again, though. Their first appearance was in *The Standard Parade* (1939), a commercial film for the Standard Oil Company. *The Seven Wise Dwarfs* (1941), created to help sell Canadian War Bonds, used existing footage from *Snow White*, along with reshoots of the dwarfs' march home on new backgrounds (the dwarfs now marched to the bank to buy bonds). *The Winged Scourge* (1943) was an educational film created for the U.S. Office of the Coordinator of Inter-American Affairs, about protection against malaria-carrying mosquitoes. This short featured all-new animation of the dwarfs. *All Together* (1942) was another commercial film for the Canadian War Bond Campaign, which also recycled old animation on new backgrounds—one of them the Canadian Parliament Building!

During the Second World War, the Disney Studio received hundreds of requests from different military units of the United States (and many allied units overseas) for specially designed insignia. The Disney team was pleased to respond, and during the course of the war created more than eight hundred different insignia for the Armed Forces. Naturally, the still-popular characters from *Snow White and the Seven Dwarfs* were a favorite design.

There is also a rumor that Walt Disney was lobbied by many of his staff to use Dopey in "The Sorcerer's Apprentice" instead of Mickey Mouse. Obviously, if such lobbying really occurred, it was not successful.

■

Q: What are the six ingredients that the Queen uses to mix the potion that disguises her as an old peddler woman?

A: Mummy Dust ("to make me old"), Black of Night ("to shroud my clothes"), an Old Hag's Cackle ("to age my voice"), a Scream of Fright ("to whiten my hair"), a Blast of Wind ("to fan

Author's Collection. © The Walt Disney Company

The wicked Queen brews a cauldron of evil in this promotional illustration.

my hate"), and a Thunderbolt ("to mix it well"). In the original Grimm's tale, the Queen is "disguised" as an old peddler; she paints her face, hangs the rags on herself, and pretends. In the Disney version, her altered form results not just from disguise, but through powerful black magic, taking her another notch up the wickedness scale.

The Grimm's Queen, while not a practitioner of the black arts, is a persistent one. She tries to do away with Snow White *three* times. First, she tries to suffocate her with a tightened staylace, then she tries to kill her with a poisoned comb. Finally, she hits on the poisoned apple bit. The curious thing is that Snow White is so…uh… innocent that she lets the old bat into the house all three times!

∎

Q: The Slave in the Magic Mirror made a return to Disney a dozen years after the release of *Snow White*. In what project? Who played the Slave?

A: The character of the slave in the mirror was recreated by the Disney team in the studio's first television venture, *One Hour in Wonderland*, in 1950. Veteran character and voice actor Hans Conried (the voice of Captain Hook in Disney's *Peter Pan*) actually portrayed the slave in the mirror in live-action, with a make-up "face mask" duplicating the look of the film character and the rest of his body obscured by black masking, all in an elaborate recreation of the mirror frame from the film.

Conried repeated the role in 1956 for a retrospective of Disney villains, "Our Unsung Villains," on the weekly Disney television show. This program was updated in 1977 under the title "Disney's Greatest Villains."

∎

Q: Graciously (except for Grumpy, naturally), the dwarfs give over their room to Snow White. Where do the dwarfs sleep?

A: Grumpy sleeps—grumpily—in the soup kettle. Doc sleeps in the water trough. Dopey sleeps on a bench, with Sneezy on his butt. Bashful snoozes in a dresser drawer, Sleepy in the woodpile, and Happy snores in the cupboard. These "gags," as they are known in animation, are significant not just for the laugh they contain, but because they are a shorthand way both to develop character and to propel story. Walt Disney was ever on the lookout for good gags to help "plus" a story. It is legend that during the production of *Snow White and the Seven Dwarfs*, Walt Disney offered his staffers five dollars for any single gag that made its way into the finished film. In 1935, five cents could buy a loaf of bread, thirty-five cents could buy lunch, and five thousand dollars could buy a fine new house. Starting pay for an animator at the Disney Studio was fifteen dollars a week.

An individual gag might result in scenes like the dwarfs' sleeping locations, or Doc testing the purity of a gem by its sound, or Sneezy and Dopey "stacking up" to make a full-size dancing partner for Snow White. The "Whistle While You Work" sequence is a masterpiece of well-paced gags that propel story and character and entertain masterfully.

There's even a gag in *Snow White* that shows up again nearly fifty years later in *The Little Mermaid* (1989). In *Snow White*, as the squirrels sweep a mantle, the dust sends a baby squirrel sneezing backwards into a lidded tankard that shuts on him. In *The Little Mermaid*, Sebastian the crab is startled by a distorted reflection, with the same result.

∎

Q: "The Silly Song," where the dwarfs entertain their new house guest with music and dance, actually replaced two earlier songs. What were they?

A: Initial story plans called for an elaborate musical "story" to be told by the dwarfs to the visiting Princess. "The Lady in the Moon" was originally planned as a character developing song for the dwarfs, with each taking a part in the telling of the story. The tale revolved around the creatures of the wood having a falling out, fighting over their desire to serenade the lady in the moon. The dwarfs would each imitate a woodland creature (a bird, a frog, a cricket, an owl, etc.). The animals eventually forget their differences when they discover they've been mistakenly serenading the *man* in the moon.

This song was replaced by "You're Never to Old to Be Young." This song appears on the magnificent 1993 soundtrack compact disc of *Snow White and the Seven Dwarfs*. It contains much of the feel of "The Silly Song," including that song's distinctive yodeling, but it is more structured and lyric-based, lacking the spontaneous feeling of an impromptu party that the final scene in the film joyously portrays.

The yodeling for this scene was performed by professional yodelers (honest), the Fraunfelder Family, along with Jimmy Macdonald, a Disney sound man. In 1977, Macdonald told *Funnyworld* magazine:

> [Walt Disney] looked at me. "Have you ever yodeled?" I said, "No, Walt." He said "Go on down to the stage and try it." So I did a lot of test yodeling. Now they had the Fraunfelders come in, and they did a great job. But as you know [the production of] that picture went on for years and years, and as the picture keeps progressing, they keep changing scenes and so forth. Some of the yodeling would be out, and some they wanted a little more of. They got into the habit of saying "Call Jim down, and let him do it."
>
> I played in the band; I played jugs and ocarina and different things. We had a little five- or six-piece group, and I remember that Art Smith played clarinet without a mouthpiece, and all of these oddball things, and we made the sound of that organ.

■

Q: One of Walt Disney's great concerns with *Snow White* was its distribution, and he went to special lengths to make sure the picture was a hit. Name one of these special efforts.

A: *Snow White* was a worldwide sensation. Disney was so concerned with the international audiences for *Snow White* that he had specially-prepared backgrounds created and certain scenes reshot for selected international versions. The storybook seen at the opening, the writing in the Queen's spell book, and even the carved names on the dwarfs' beds were translated for foreign filmgoers.

The film was initially dubbed into ten languages, with the dwarfs getting some interesting new names: Doc became Prof in French; Grumpy, Sleepy, and Dopey were renamed Butter, Trotter, and Toker in Swedish; Happy became Gongolo in Italian, Bashful was Romantico in Spanish, and Sneezy was Apsik in Polish.

■

Q: Attached to most beloved films are tales (some true) of great scenes that were left on the cutting room floor. Were any scenes cut out of *Snow White and the Seven Dwarfs*?

A: One of Walt Disney's great talents was that of story editor. *Snow White and the Seven Dwarfs* was a remarkably taut story, and little time was wasted by the Disney animation staff in the devel-

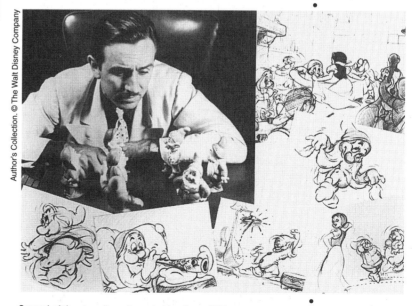

Several of the story "gags" created for *Snow White and the Seven Dwarfs*.

Author's Collection. © The Walt Disney Company

opment of scenes not vital to the overall story. So, unlike live-action films, there are no "outtakes," or finished film scenes cut after production.

Snow White contained a "soup-eating scene" that was to take place (naturally) after the dwarfs finished washing up for supper. The accompanying song, "Music in Your Soup," revealed the dwarfs' joy at their terrible table manners—and just how much fun it is to loudly slurp soup. This song also appears on the 1993 soundtrack compact disc.

The entire sequence was filmed in pencil-test animation before it was decided that it was too reminiscent of the hand-washing scene, slowed down the central action, and offered no further character development. This pencil test of the soup scene was also eventually showcased on several Disney television shows.

A scene where the dwarfs and Snow White's forest animal friends work together to build an elaborate bed for the little princess was also developed at length. Several complicated gags were to be incorporated into the scene, which was intended to strengthen the audience perception of the affection that the seven little men feel for their house guest. It was also ultimately abandoned prior to finished animation.

Both of these scenes can be found in the supplemental material on the deluxe laser disc edition of *Snow White and the Seven Dwarfs* (Walt Disney Home Video, 1994).

■

Q: *Snow White* was the first animated feature, and from it came the first original soundtrack album. In 1993, *Snow White* boasted another "first." What was it?

A: *Snow White and the Seven Dwarfs* became the first film in history to be completely restored by digital technology. This elaborate restoration process exceeded even the complex photomechanical restoration that had been performed

on *Snow White* for its fiftieth anniversary re-release in 1987.

For the 1993 digital restoration, Eastman Kodak's Cinesite digital film center in Burbank provided the technology to scan, record, manipulate, and "write back" to motion picture film at full motion picture resolution.

The 1987 restoration had returned to the original negative for the first time in forty-three years (the negative was "retired" by Technicolor in 1944, which judged the original too brittle for further production printing). At that time, a new nitrate negative and master duplicate negative were created. This work provided the basis for the digital Cinesite restoration.

Not only did the digital restoration repair the visual wear and tear of the years, it actually corrected innate flaws in the original negative (cel dust and fibers), and brought out color and detail visible in the animation art that earlier film processes had been unable to reveal. *Snow White* animator Ollie Johnston remarked, "We never did get on-screen, in our 1937 answer prints, the exact color that was on the cels or backgrounds. It never quite matched what you were shooting for. The problems of photography with the three-color process through the years! We never got exactly what we should have off the cels. What you've got now is closer to the original cel. Snow White's bodice is blue now, rather than black as in the old prints, and that's a great step forward."

Sometimes, the computer algorithms established to remove "artifacts" (photography or processing-related debris) did the job too well. During an initial pass, the automated program removed the red eyes of the doves at Snow White's wishing well, pointing up the need for strict human supervision of the digital process.

The final result was screened for five artists who had worked on the picture (Frank Thomas, Ollie Johnston, Ward Kimball, Marc Davis, and Joe Grant) and Disney Vice Chairman Roy E. Disney. It received their unanimous approval.

The 1993 reissue restoration also returned the

film to its full 1:33 to 1 aspect ratio. The film had been cropped to the modern standard aspect ratio of 1:85 to 1 on its prior several reissues.

■

Q: The currently available 1993 restored version of *Snow White* actually lacks one element that 1937 audiences saw. What is it?

A: The beginning and end title cards of *Snow White and the Seven Dwarfs* were reshot by the Disney Studio in 1958. The original opening title card (actually the third card, after "A Walt Disney FEATURE Production" and "Snow White and the Seven Dwarfs") contained the phrase "Distributed by R.K.O. Radio Pictures Inc." The end title ("A WALT DISNEY FEATURE Production") is superimposed over the RKO Radio Pictures logo. Prior to the founding of Buena Vista Pictures Distribution (Disney's own film distribution company) in 1953, Disney productions had been released by Columbia Pictures, United Artists, and RKO Radio Pictures. When Disney's distribution contracts with these concerns expired, many of his pictures had title elements re-shot to remove the distributor names. This is what happened with *Snow White* on its fourth release in 1958. The titles were re-photographed with new art that eliminated the reference to RKO Radio. Although removed, the original (RKO) titles for *Snow White and the Seven Dwarfs* have been preserved for posterity by the Walt Disney Studios, and appear in the supplemental material of the deluxe laser disc edition of *Snow White and the Seven Dwarfs.*

Q: Which dwarf became a hero of the circus?

A: Here's an obscure one for you, located in John Culhane's *The American Circus: An Illustrated History* (1990, Henry Holt and Company, New York).

In 1938, the Ringling Bros. and Barnum & Bailey Circus built its show around Frank "Bring 'em Back Alive" Buck, but one of the special acts was a parade of "Walt Disney's Seven Dwarfs," seven of the circus's midgets and dwarfs parading to "Heigh-Ho" in character costumes.

Just before show time at Madison Square Garden, a tiger escaped backstage and streaked past the menagerie keepers toward the lobby, which was crowded with children. Standing between the helpless children and the raging tiger was a midget clown named Paul Horompo, dressed in his Dopey costume for the special act. Horompo stepped between the children and the tiger, and struck the tiger on the nose with the prop papier-mâché pick ax that was part of his Dopey wardrobe. Momentarily stunned, the tiger spun about and ran in the opposite direction—into the net that the menagerie men dropped over her.

Thus, Dopey, in the person of Paul Horompo, became the hero of the circus. The story hit the newspapers and the radio, and by the time the circus reached Boston, Horompo was called back to New York, to be honored on a radio show called "We, the People."

hard

WALT DISNEY'S

SNOW WHITE AND THE SEVEN DWARFS

Adapted from Grimm's Fairy Tales

Supervising Director: David Hand

Sequence Directors: Perce Pearce, Larry Morey, William Cottrell, Wilfred Jackson, Ben Sharpsteen

Supervising Animators: Hamilton Luske, Vladimir Tytla, Fred Moore, Norman Ferguson

Story Adaptation: Ted Sears, Otto Englander, Earl Hurd, Dorothy Ann Blank,
Richard Creedon, Dick Rickard, Merril De Maris, Webb Smith

Character Designers: Albert Hurter, Joe Grant

Music: Frank Churchill, Leigh Harline, Paul Smith

Art Directors: Charles Philippi, Hugh Hennesy, Terrell Stapp, McLaren Stewart, Harold Miles,
Tom Codrick, Gustaf Tenggren, Kenneth Anderson, Kendall O'Connor, Hazel Sewell

Backgrounds: Samuel Armstrong, Mique Nelson, Merle Cox,
Claude Coats, Phil Dike, Ray Lockrem, Maurice Noble

Animators: Frank Thomas, Dick Lundy, Arthur Babbitt, Eric Larson, Milton Kahl, Robert Stokes,
James Algar, Al Eugster, Cy Young, Joshua Meador, Ugo D'Orsi, George Rowley, Les Clark,
Fred Spencer, Bill Roberts, Bernard Garbutt, Grim Natwick, Jack Campbell, Marvin Woodward,
James Culhane, Stan Quakenbush, Ward Kimball, Woolie Reitherman, Robert Martsch

Originally released by RKO Radio Pictures

Premiered December 21, 1937
(Subsequent domestic re-releases in 1944, 1951, 1958, 1967, 1975, 1983, 1987, 1993, 1994: Home Video)

Multiplane Technicolor®. Running time: 83 minutes

Voice Talents

Adriana Caselotti	Snow White
Harry Stockwell	Prince
Lucille LaVerne	The Queen/Peddler Woman
Moroni Olsen	Magic Mirror
Billy Gilbert	Sneezy
Pinto Colvig	Grumpy and Sleepy
Otis Harlan	Happy
Scotty Mattraw	Bashful
Roy Atwell	Doc

Chapter Ten
Beauty and the Beast

After the death of Walt Disney in 1966, the Feature Animation department of the Disney Studios began a decline that would last until 1984. That year, The Walt Disney Company underwent a corporate upheaval that resulted in (among other things) a commitment from Disney's new administration to retrieve Disney's eminence in animation. The Great Mouse Detective (1986) marked a recovery for Disney, and, to many, Oliver & Company (1988) marked the "return" of Disney animation. The Little Mermaid (1989) was a thundering success, and animation truly entered a "new golden age." Despite a disappointing response, The Rescuers Down Under (1990) broke enormous technical ground. The next feature, Beauty and the Beast, truly brought feature animation to pinnacles of success, both artistic and fiscal, not seen since the day of Snow White and the Seven Dwarfs.

Much of the success of Beauty and the Beast derives from the fact that, at the heart of it, the film is a solidly structured and skillfully executed piece of musical theatre. Although Beauty and the Beast began a renaissance in feature animation of increasing fiscal success, neither Disney, nor any other organization, has yet produced an animated feature of the artistic merit of Beauty and the Beast.

■

Level One: The Easy Stuff
Story & Characters

Q: Disney fairy tale films have typically begun with the opening of a live-action storybook. How does *Beauty and the Beast* establish its fairy tale?

A: The prologue of *Beauty and the Beast* is revealed through spoken narration and a series of beautifully rendered stained glass windows. Vance Gerry's story sketches were the inspiration for the unique and beautiful framing device. Mac George designed the final windows.

In traditional fashion, the story begins with "Once Upon a Time."

■

Q: The icon of *Beauty and the Beast* is established in the prologue. What is this icon?

The Beast and the cursed reminder of his enchanted fate.

A: An enchanted rose. "The rose she had offered was truly an enchanted rose, which would bloom until his twenty-first year. If he could learn to love another, and earn their love in return, by the time the last petal fell, then the spell would be broken. If not he would be doomed to remain a beast for all time." In dramatic terms, the enchanted rose has become a "ticking clock," creating a point of reference to heighten audience suspense.

In the most famous modern telling of the tale, the father of the young beauty is initially imprisoned by the enraged beast for picking one of the beast's roses as a gift for the beauty. Producer Don Hahn recalled that the rose initially presented a problem: "Why would it tick off Beast so much? What is this guy, a gardener or something? So we changed the function of the rose to be a ticking clock, the hourglass, as it were."

The visual contradiction of the hideous beast and the fragile rose is an eloquent icon of the basic story of *Beauty and the Beast*.

■

Q: What is the occupation of Belle's father?

A: Maurice, Belle's father, joins the cinematic ranks of "crackpot inventors." Real inventors have been the subject of a surprising number of films, including *The Story of Alexander Graham Bell*, *Young Tom Edison* (1939), *The Great Moment* (1944), *Carbine Williams*, *The Sound Barrier* (1952), *The Dam Busters* (1954), and *I Aim at the Stars* (1960).

Disney films have often returned to the archetype of the crackpot inventor. Benjamin Franklin is portrayed as something of a befuddled kook in *Ben and Me* (1953), Ed Wynn is a crackpot toymaker in *Babes in Toyland* (1961), and Rick Moranis plays inventor Wayne Szalinski in *Honey, I Shrunk the Kids* (1989) and *Honey, I Blew Up the Kid* (1992). And let's not forget one of the first, and certainly one of the best—Fred MacMurray as

Ned Brainard in *The Absent-Minded Professor* (1961) and *Son of Flubber* (1963).

Although Disney may seem to have cornered the crackpot market, there was also Jerry Lewis as *The Nutty Professor* (1963) and Dick Van Dyke as tinkerer Caractacus Potts (get it?) in *Chitty Chitty Bang Bang* (1968).

■

Q: The selfish young prince is transformed by a spell. What is he transformed into?

A: If you answered "a beast," well, duh! What kind of beast? According to animator Glen Keane, who refined the final character design of Beast, "the beard and muzzle stem from the buffalo, as well as the feeling in the eyes. The gorilla...has a great, expressive brow, and we used this for Beast. We went for a very lionlike mane...then borrowed the tusks from [a] boar...also the hair on the nose. The horns on the head are something we gave him ourselves. He's got a big tail like a wolf's, and his body is generally like a bear, but with a wolf's legs."

■

Q: The palace household is run by a devoted and motherly character. Who is she?

A: Mrs. Potts is the portly cook and de facto household manager at Beast's palace. She is voiced to perfection by Angela Lansbury. Lansbury says that "Mrs. Potts was just exactly the fat, comfortable little lady I had envisioned in my mind."

Several of the creative team, including Lansbury, point out a common inspiration for Mrs. Potts in the character of Mrs. Bridges, from the TV series "Upstairs, Downstairs." Interestingly, Mrs. Bridges was played by Angela Baddeley, whose sister was Hermione Baddeley, who had played fat, comfortable domestics in several

Disney films, including *Mary Poppins* (q.v.).

So perfect is her vocal quality for the role that it's hard to imagine anyone but Angela Lansbury as Mrs. Potts. Lansbury was born in London, the daughter of a lumber merchant and a famous actress named Moyna Macgill, who was the toast of the London stage in the 1920s and '30s. She began training as an actress at the Webber-Douglas School for Dramatic Arts, but her schooling was interrupted when World War II forced her family to move to the United States. There she enrolled at the Feagin School of Dramatic Arts in New York City, and eventually rejoined her family in California. In 1944, Lansbury was cast by George Cukor as Nancy in *Gaslight*. This first film role earned Lansbury a contract at MGM and a Best Supporting Actress Academy Award nomination. She was nineteen years old. The next year she was again nominated for the Supporting Actress Oscar, this time for the role of Sybil Vane in *The Picture of Dorian Gray*. A variety of films and roles followed, with Lansbury generally playing characters much older than herself. The most memorable are *National Velvet*

(1944); *The Harvey Girls* (1946); *State of the Union* (1948); *Samson and Delilah* (1949); *The Court Jester* (1956); *The Long, Hot Summer*(1958); *The Manchurian Candidate* (1962, her third Oscar nomination); *The World of Henry Orient*; *Dear Heart* (1964); *Mister Buddwing* (1966); *Something for Everyone* (1970); *Death on the Nile* (1978); *The Lady Vanishes* (1979); *The Mirror Crack'd* (1980, as Miss Marple); *The Pirates of Penzance* (1983); and *The Company of Wolves* (1984).

Her first Disney film was the musical *Bedknobs and Broomsticks* (1971). Lansbury has introduced two Academy Award-nominated songs in her Disney film appearances, "The Age of Not Believing" in *Bedknobs and Broomsticks* as well as "Beauty and the Beast." In all, she has appeared in more than forty feature films, and although she has yet to win an Oscar, she has received a British Academy Award for Lifetime Achievement in Motion Pictures.

In 1957, she made her Broadway debut in *Hotel Paradiso* co-starring Bert Lahr, and three years later starred in the drama *A Taste of*

Author's Collection. © The Walt Disney Company

Tony Award-winner and TV favorite Angela Lansbury brings vocal warmth to kitchen crockery.

Honey. She followed this with the starring role in the 1964 Arthur Laurents/Stephen Sondheim musical flop *Anyone Can Whistle*. She attained Broadway stardom in her tour de force performance in the smash musical *Mame* in 1966, for which she won the first of her four Tony awards. She went on to win the others for *Dear World*, the revival of *Gypsy*, and *Sweeney Todd*.

As if all this weren't enough, Lansbury conquered television, too, with her weekly series "Murder, She Wrote," which has run on CBS for more than a decade, and inspired imitators such as "Diagnosis: Murder," "The Cosby Mysteries," and the spin-off "The Law and Harry McGraw," which starred Lansbury's *Beauty and the Beast* co-household object, Jerry Orbach.

■

Q: What is the big French candlestick's name?

A: Lumiere is the valet-turned-candlestick's name. The name is actually a French noun, lumiére, which means "light." Broadway and movie character vet Jerry Orbach provides the voice, inspired in part by Maurice Chevalier. Lumiere is also a caricature of Orbach's distinctive features.

Orbach made his first New York stage appearance in *The Threepenny Opera* as Mack the Knife, after which he originated the role of El Gallo in the legendary off-Broadway musical *The Fantasticks*. He made his Broadway debut in *Carnival*, and won his first Tony award for his portrayal of Sky Masterson in the City Center revival of *Guys and Dolls*. He starred in *Chicago* and *42nd Street*, *The Cradle Will Rock*, *Scuba Duba*, *6 Rms Riv Vu*, and the national tour of Neil Simon's *Chapter Two*. He won another Tony for *Promises, Promises*, the stage musical adaptation of Billy Wilder's *The Apartment*.

Orbach has appeared in the films *The Gang That Couldn't Shoot Straight* (1971), *Prince of the City* (1981), *F/X* (1986), *Someone to Watch Over Me*, *Dirty Dancing* (1987), *Crimes and Misdemeanors* (1989), and *Postcards from the Edge* (1990). He is also a regular lead in the popular and acclaimed television drama series "Law and Order."

Author's Collection. © The Walt Disney Company

Jerry Orbach lent both his engaging voice and distinctive features to his character.

Author's Collection. © The Walt Disney Company

Because Belle is an avid reader, she has a strong point of view. The Beast's heartfelt gift to her shows that he understands and appreciates her unique intelligence.

Orbach began his career behind the scenes, as Tom Bosley's dresser during the Broadway run of *Fiorello!* Bosley originated the role of Maurice, Belle's father, in the stage version of *Beauty and the Beast*.

■

Q: Beast gives Belle a heartfelt gift. What?

A: A library. Belle is a different kind of "Disney Princess." Unlike Snow White, Cinderella, or even the "modern" Ariel in *The Little Mermaid*, Belle couldn't care less about a simple domestic life and isn't about to settle for a man (Gaston) who is all brawn and no brain. She is unabashedly a book-worm, intelligent, curious, brave, and strong— quite a departure for a Disney heroine.

The character was developed by screenwriter Linda Woolverton with such strengths in mind. Belle is "a very strong, smart, courageous woman. Because she is an avid reader, she has a point of view of her life, and that doesn't neces-sarily involve a man getting her there."

Animators James Baxter and Mark Henn set out to create a different physical appearance as well. "Physically, we tried to make her a little more European-looking, with fuller lips, a little bit darker eyebrows, and slightly smaller eyes than Ariel. She's also a few years older than Ariel, and a lot more worldly because she's always reading."

Paige O'Hara provided the voice for Belle. An actress and singer, O'Hara made her Broadway debut as the ingenue in *Gift of the Magi*. She also guested on the daytime dramas "Search for Tomorrow" and "One Life to Live." In 1980, she was cast as Ado Annie in the National Touring Company of *Oklahoma!*, then starred as Ellie in the Broadway revival of *Show Boat*. She appeared as the title character in *The Mystery of Edwin Drood* on Broadway and on tour.

"We were looking for someone who could cre-ate a character completely with her voice," recalls co-director Kirk Wise. "When Gary [Trousdale, co-director] and I heard Paige's voice for the first time, everything just clicked. The more we listened to her, the more we found that she was a really, really strong actress who was equally adept with the sort of light, comic scenes as she was with the very dramatic and heartfelt ones. She was definitely a real find."

Q: The true villain of *Beauty and the Beast* is not Beast at all. Who is?

A: Gaston. At first, Gaston appears to be boorish but comic. He is revealed as a true threat during the course of the film. His mounting frustration reveals an uglier and uglier soul, while Beast's increasing love reveals a more and more beautiful soul.

This tandem character development enabled supervising animator Andreas Deja to create a character design that avoided the blandness that has often afflicted human animated characters. "I tried to retain the whole range of expression—the sarcasm, the broadness, and the expressiveness—that the handsome leading man seldom gets to show," Deja said. He researched much of the look and gesture of Gaston right in Los Angeles. "Los Angeles is full of good-looking guys who just adore themselves," he says. "You see them all over, always admiring themselves in the mirror, making sure their hair and everything else is in place."

Stage veteran Richard White was the voice of Gaston. A Tennessee native, White studied music and acting at The Oberlin Conservatory in Ohio. He made his Broadway debut as Joey in *The Most Happy Fella* with Giorgio Tozzi. He toured the country with Yul Brynner in *The King and I* and has appeared across the country in productions of *1776*, *Carnival*, *A Little Night Music*, *Oklahoma!*, and *The Merry Widow*. He is a favorite leading man at the New York City Opera, where he has appeared in *Brigadoon*, *The Desert Song*, *South Pacific*, and *Naughty Marietta*.

Of his role in *Beauty and the Beast*, White feels that "the best part about the role was getting to sing those great Ashman and Menken songs. It is dramatic music without any artifice and in the best Broadway tradition."

■

Q: Which wing of the castle is forbidden? Why?

A: The west wing holds the remnants of Beast's human past, the enchanted rose, and the magic mirror, Beast's sole contact with the outside world.

The production designers painted the chamber with gloom—the fixtures and furnishings diffuse, the colors subdued. That the rooms were once beautiful and elegant can be seen in the dim light, with only the moonlight and the rose as illumination. It is in this chamber that we see, in the opening montage, Beast destroy a portrait of his human self with his monstrous claws.

The room embodies the conflicting identities of Beast, which are further characterized by the unlikely voice casting of Robby Benson. "The Beast was the most difficult voice to cast," co-director Kirk Wise asserted. "We needed someone who could sound like an eight-foot-tall hairy monster and at the same time express the warmth, sincerity, and intelligence of a human prince. Robby was the first person we heard who actually managed to combine both in a believable way. Robby is also a very creative actor who thinks on his feet and found ways to play scenes that really made the character come alive."

Benson was born in Dallas, Texas, and grew up in New York City. He began acting at age five, in summer stock productions with his mother. By age ten, he had appeared in commercials, recorded voice-overs and jingles, and dubbed children's voices in English for such foreign films as *War and Peace* (1968) and *The Garden of the Finzi-Continis* (1971).

He made his Broadway debut in *Zelda* (at age twelve, 1968) and performed in *The Rothschilds* (1970), *Dude* (1972), and *The Pirates of Penzance* (1981).

Benson made his film debut in *Jory* (1972), and made a career of playing earnest, naïve young men in such films as *Jeremy* (1973), *Lucky Lady* (1975), *Ode to Billy Joe* (1976), *One on One* (1977), *The Chosen*, *The End* (1978), *Walk Proud*, *Ice Castles* (1979), *Tribute* (1980), *Running Brave* (1983), and *Harry and Son* (1984), among others.

Benson held a two-year artist in residence sta-

Author's Collection. © The Walt Disney Company

The unorthodox voice casting of Robby Benson brought both ferocity and sincerity to the Beast.

tus at the University of South Carolina, where he taught courses in screen acting and filmmaking. He has also taught graduate-level film and television acting at UCLA. He is a sought-after director of episodic television, and has directed such shows as the Shelley Long/Treat Williams sitcom "Good Advice," the Edward Asner sitcom "Thunder Alley," "Friends," and "Ellen."

Benson called *Beauty and the Beast* "the most exciting thing that's ever happened in my career. I have always been an incredible fan of Disney animation, and just knowing that my children are going to grow up watching this film makes it so much more special than any other movie I've ever been in."

■

Q: In her palace room, Belle is comforted by whom?

A: A wardrobe. Initially, the wardrobe served as a mentor/advisor to Belle and her role was much larger, something like Grandmother Willow in *Pocahontas*. Anthony DeRosa was scheduled to act as lead animator on the wardrobe, but

bowed out when the role was reduced (he instead assisted Glen Keane in animating Beast). The character of the wardrobe was assigned to veteran Disney animator Tony Anselmo—who is also the official voice of Donald Duck.

The wardrobe was voiced by versatile actress and comedian JoAnne Worley, probably best known for her four years on the revolutionary TV comedy series "Rowan and Martin's Laugh-In."

An Indiana native, Worley studied at Midwestern University, Los Angeles City College, and the Pasadena Playhouse. She was Carol Channing's standby in the original Broadway production of *Hello, Dolly!*, after which she launched her own nightclub act in Greenwich Village. She was seen in this act by Merv Griffin, and appeared on his show more than 150 times. This led to her stint on "Laugh-In." Worley has toured the country in companies of *Mame*, *Gypsy*, and *Into the Woods*, among many others.

In the Broadway musical version of *Beauty and the Beast*, the wardrobe is back in a role of equal significance to that of Lumiere, Cogsworth, and Mrs. Potts. She even has a name, Madame de la Grande Bouche.

Level Two: Not So Easy
The Actors, Artists, & Others

Q: What is the source of the screen story of *Beauty and the Beast*?

A: Here is a question that lacks a definitive answer. It really is a "tale as old as time, song as old as rhyme." Nearly every culture has what *Brewer's Dictionary of Phrase and Fable* defines as

> **Beauty and the Beast**. A handsome woman with an uncouth or uncomely male companion.

According to Betsy Hearne in *Beauty and the Beast: Visions and Revisions of an Old Tale*, "Animal groom and [human] bride stories have varied as widely across time and culture as have versions of the Cinderella theme." There is an Eskimo tale of a girl and a seagull. In Greek myth, the goddess of Love and Beauty, Venus, marries the lame and ugly god of the Forge, Vulcan. In Africa, a girl licks the face of a crocodile, transforming him into a handsome man. In Shakespeare's *A Midsummer Night's Dream*, Titania, Queen of the Fairies, falls in love with the weaver, Bottom, whose head has been changed to that of an ass.

Probably the closest version to the Disney one is the best-known modern literary retelling of the tale, Mme. Marie Leprince de Beaumont's popular 1757 version, *La Belle et la Bête*. Mme. de Beaumont was a governess in England for the offspring of the Prince of Wales, as well as an author of children's books.

Beauty and the Beast was performed in stage versions throughout the nineteenth century, and the first film version was made in 1908. Other films were made in 1912, 1916, and 1936. French director Jean Cocteau made a renowned film version in 1946.

Other stories certainly have their roots in the Beauty and the Beast legend, *Notre Dame de Paris* (*The Hunchback of Notre Dame*) and *Le Fantôme de l'Opera* (*The Phantom of the Opera*)

among them. Even the film *King Kong* compares itself—none too subtly—to the ancient fable.

From 1987 to 1990, CBS-TV broadcast a popular television drama titled "Beauty and the Beast," which transplanted the tale to modern Manhattan. The beast was a deformed crusader dwelling in the city's underground. Ron Perlman played this golden-voiced, leonine beast, known as Vincent. His beauty, Katharine, was played by Linda Hamilton.

Beauty and the Beast had been suggested to Walt Disney as a potential animated feature as early as the 1930s, but the filmmaker and his creative team were frustrated in their attempts to translate the tale to animation. One of the problems that faced them had to do with the clear delineation of hero and villain, victor and victim—the Beast is all of these. Another was that the predominant setting in the legend is the dining room of the Beast's castle, and attempts to "open up" the story created unnecessary narrative tangents that diluted the power of the focal love story. The last development of *Beauty and the Beast* at Disney before 1988 had been in the early 1950s. A 1953 proposal for the "Disneyland" television series suggests "A 'Look In' at Future Product," including *The Sleeping Beauty* [sic], Victor Herbert's *Babes in Toyland*, Kingsley's *Westward Ho*, Cervantes' *Don Quixote*, Humperdinck's *Hansel and Gretel* and Perrault's [sic] *Beauty and the Beast*.

There is a also a distaff version of the Beauty and the Beast legend, defined by *Brewer's* as

> **Loathly Lady**. A stock character of old romance who is so hideous that everyone is deterred from marrying her. When, however, she at last finds a husband her ugliness, the effect of enchantment, disappears, and she becomes a model of beauty.

■

Q: Who is the storyteller who narrates the prologue montage of *Beauty and the Beast*?

A: David Ogden Stiers, the voice of Cogsworth, performs double duty as the resonant, resolute storyteller who provides the prologue for *Beauty and the Beast*.

Stiers, of course, is famous for his portrayal of the pompous surgeon and comic foil Charles Emerson Winchester III on six seasons of the acclaimed television series "M*A*S*H," for which he was twice nominated for the Emmy award. He received a third nomination for the NBC mini-series *The First Modern Olympics*.

Stiers was born in Peoria, Illinois, and began acting with the California Shakespeare Festival and the Actor's Workshop in San Francisco. He studied in New York with John Houseman at The Juilliard School, and with the graduating class became a charter member of Houseman's Acting Company. He toured with that company in *The Beggar's Opera*, *The Three Sisters*, *Measure for Measure*, and *The Lower Depths*. On Broadway, Stiers appeared with Zero Mostel in the revival of

Ulysses in Nighttown (1974) and created the role of "Feldman the Magnificent" in the hit musical *The Magic Show* the same year. Stiers' movie appearances have included *Oh, God!* (1977), *Magic* (1978), and *The Accidental Tourist* (1988). Other television work has included the stuttering WJM station manager in the final season of "The Mary Tyler Moore Show" (1977), *North and South* (1985), *Mrs. Delafield Wants to Marry* (1986), *The Final Days* (1989), and the "Star Trek: The Next Generation" episode "Half-a-Life."

Stiers' passion is music, his avocation is conducting symphony orchestras. Those he has guest conducted include Portland, Maine; San Francisco; San Diego; Honolulu; Los Angeles; and Chicago.

Of the stuffy Cogsworth, Stiers recognized in him the characteristics that are manifest in many of the roles he has played: "Cogsworth strikes me as the sort of person who tries to maintain control but has no real resources at his command."

More recently, Stiers gave voice to a character of unsurprising similarity to both Cogsworth and Winchester, that of Governor Ratcliffe in the Dis-

Author's Collection. © The Walt Disney Company

David Ogden Stiers has made pomposity an art form. His Cogsworth is tightly-wound—but with superb timing.

ney animated feature *Pocahontas* (1995). He has become something of a talisman to the new generation of Disney animators—he also gives voice to the Deacon of Notre Dame Cathedral in Disney's *The Hunchback of Notre Dame* (1996).

■

Q: Who was the creative composing team who brought new life to Disney's *Beauty and the Beast* project?

A: Howard Ashman and Alan Menken. The team had first met in 1978, when Ashman was looking for a composer to collaborate with on a musical adaptation of Kurt Vonnegut's *God Bless You, Mr. Rosewater*. Conductor Lehman Engel, then teaching a musical theatre workshop at BMI, introduced Ashman to Alan Menken. The team clicked, and the play was created and staged in the Spring of 1979 at the WPA Theater.

Ashman and Menken next collaborated on the now-famous musical version of Roger Corman's cult comic horror film, *Little Shop of Horrors*, which received the New York Drama Critics Circle Award for Best Musical of 1982–83. The musical had lyrics and libretto by Ashman and music by Menken, and was directed by Ashman. It became the third longest-running musical in off-Broadway history, and the highest-grossing musical ever to play off-Broadway. The subsequent London production won the Evening Standard Award for Best Musical, and productions were mounted worldwide. The play is now tied with *Our Town* as the most-produced play in American high schools. A film version, directed by Frank Oz, was released by Warner Bros. in 1986. A new Ashman and Menken song written for the film score, "Mean Green Mother from Outer Space," was nominated for the Best Song Oscar.

Jeffrey Katzenberg, then-president of The Walt Disney Studios, was a fan of *Little Shop of Horrors*, and had bid on the film rights. Failing to win that, he asked Ashman to come to Disney, where he com-

The late and much-mourned Howard Ashman (seated left) and his songwriting partner Alan Menken.

posed a song for *Oliver & Company* (1988). Soon, Ashman re-teamed with Menken and created the song score to *The Little Mermaid* (1989), which Ashman also co-produced with John Musker.

Beauty and the Beast began development under the direction of Richard and Jill Purdum, with a screenplay by Linda Woolverton, and produced by Don Hahn. After several months of development, the Purdum's perspective on the work was deemed too dramatic and too dark. It was at this juncture that Katzenberg asked Ashman and Menken to lend their talents to the project. The team brought the structure and archetype of the Broadway musical to *Beauty and the Beast*, further defining the approach that had succeeded so well for them in *The Little Mermaid*.

■

Q: Belle's father is also a Founding Father. How?

A: Rex Everhart, who gave voice to Maurice, played the role of Benjamin Franklin in the original Broadway cast and national tour of the musical *1776*.

medium

195

Rex Everhart, a veteran stage actor, brought a half-century of acting experience to his role in *Beauty and the Beast*.

Although Howard Da Silva originated the role of Franklin, he was hospitalized after the first performance of *1776* on March 16, 1969. His stand-by, Rex Everhart, stepped in. Not only that, but Da Silva was still hospitalized when the Broadway cast recording was made on March 23, 1969, and so it is Rex Everhart who is immortalized on the *1776* "original" cast album!

Everhart actually received a master's degree in speech pathology before deciding on an acting career. While visiting California in the late 1930s, he met some students from the renowned Pasadena Playhouse and soon found himself studying there with the likes of William Holden and Robert Preston.

Everhart has been principally a stage actor over the fifty years of his career, with roles in twenty-seven Broadway shows as well as numerous national and regional touring companies. He starred as Eli Whitney opposite Patti Lupone in the hit revival of *Anything Goes* (1987), and appeared in *Chicago* (1976), *Woman of the Year* (1981), *Rags* (1986), and *Working* (1978), for which he received a Tony Award nomination. He

spent several seasons at American Shakespeare Theatre, and was in the London company of Neil Simon's *The Odd Couple* (1965).

He has appeared in few films, among them *Friday the 13th* (1980), *Power* (1985), *The Rosary Murders* (1987), and *Family Business* (1989), as well as hundreds of TV shows.

His approach to Maurice paid homage to another great character actor: "His whole demeanor is a bit tentative and I tried to play him with a little Frank Morgan thrown in."

■

Q: **Maurice's horse, Philippe, has a voice credited. (Honest.) Name the famous character actor who gave Philippe his neigh.**

A: Hal Smith. Smith began his show business career as a band singer in the 1930s, which led him to radio work. He was a staff announcer on Los Angeles radio station KFI in the 1940s, then launched his acting career. For most of the rest of his life, Smith appeared both on-camera in character roles in dozens of films and television shows, and off-camera as a voice artist. He briefly voiced Winnie the Pooh, on The Disney Channel series "Welcome to Pooh Corner," and was the voice of Owl in several Pooh projects for Disney.

The role for which Smith is best and most fondly remembered is that of Otis Campbell, the town drunk of Mayberry, North Carolina, in the 1960s television landmark "The Andy Griffith Show," and its successor, "Mayberry R.F.D."

Smith died at the age of seventy-seven in 1994.

■

Q: **As the Beast prepares for his big dinner with Belle, homage is paid to another favorite movie musical. How?**

A: As the Beast is being bathed, groomed, and dressed, he appears with his mane combed, curled, and beribboned—bearing a striking resemblance to Bert Lahr in *The Wizard of Oz* (q.v., 1939).

Beauty and the Beast is actually teeming, from beginning to end, with references to other motion pictures, most of which are absolutely intentional. Sometimes the references are meant with a nudge and a wink, as in the unabashed allusion to the extravagant musical numbers of Busby Berkeley movies, Esther Williams swimfests, and even Disney's own *Fantasia* (1940) in "Be Our Guest."

Other referential uses are meant to evoke subconscious memories and emotional reactions in the audience. As Belle proclaims her heart's desire—"I want adventure in the great wide somewhere"—she sweeps onto a hilly meadow, all very reminiscent of the opening shots of *The Sound of Music* (1965), and intentionally so. *Beauty and the Beast* editor John Carnochan admitted to "shamelessly" fine-tuning the *Beauty and the Beast* scene into a Julie Andrews "*Sound of Music* shot" after watching the film at a Los Angeles theater. He felt that the Julie Andrews scene gave the feeling that he was trying to capture with Belle.

Frankenstein (1931) is evoked as the torch-bearing mob of villagers ascend to the castle on the hill. *The King and I* (1956) is likewise called to mind in the title ballad, a sort of slow restatement of "Shall We Dance?"

Production designers also readily admit to studying such varied films as *Bambi* (1942) and *Doctor Zhivago* (1965) for the feel and mood of certain scenes in *Beauty and the Beast*.

The most direct "lifted" scene in *Beauty and the Beast* is in the finale dance of Belle and the transformed Beast. This animation was actually redrawn from animation created for the finale waltz of Prince Phillip and Princess Aurora in Disney's *Sleeping Beauty* (1959).

■

Q: **Early in the story development of *Beauty and the Beast*, "Be Our Guest" served a different story purpose. At what point in the story was this musical number originally planned?**

A: The number was initially scripted, storyboarded, and animated to be a welcome number for Maurice, Belle's father, upon his accidental

The "*Sound of Music* shot" in *Beauty and the Beast*.

medium

arrival at the Beast's palace. During production, the song was moved. The number would now be used to cheer the bereft Belle and better define her relationship with the household objects. The character of Maurice is pretty much a technical contrivance, and such a lavish number directed to him might also have shifted the audience focus away from the central character of Belle.

Oddly, very little work was required to change the number's location in the picture. The shots of Maurice were simply edited out and re-animated with Belle. The real difficulty was with the music track. On the initial finished recording, all the gender references were masculine. Jerry Orbach, Angela Lansbury, and the chorus were summoned to re-record the song, changing "he" to "she" and "monsieur" to "cherie."

■

Q: How many Academy Awards were won by *Beauty and the Beast*?

A: Two. *Beauty and the Beast* was nominated for six Oscars (although in only four categories), including

Best Picture of the Year: *Beauty and the Beast, Bugsy, JFK, The Prince of Tides*, and *The Silence of the Lambs* (the winner).

Best Achievement in Music (Original Score): *Beauty and the Beast* (the winner, Alan Menken), *Bugsy* (Ennio Morricone), *The Fisher King* (George Fenton), *JFK* (John Williams), and *The Prince of Tides* (James Newton Howard).

Best Achievement in Music (Original Song): Three of the songs from the *Beauty and the Beast* score were nominated, "Belle," "Be Our Guest," and "Beauty and the Beast" (the winner, all three with music by Alan Menken, lyrics by Howard Ashman). Also nominated were "(Everything I Do) I Do It For You" from *Robin Hood: Prince of Thieves* (music by Michael Kamen, lyrics by Bryan Adams, Robert John Lange), and

"When You're Alone" from *Hook* (music by John Williams, lyrics by Leslie Bricusse).

Best Achievement in Sound: *Beauty and the Beast* (Terry Porter, Mel Metcalfe, David J. Hudson, Doc Kane), *Backdraft* (Gary Summers, Randy Thom, Gary Rydstrom, Glenn Williams), *JFK* (Michael Minkler, Gregg Landaker, Todd A. Maitland), *The Silence of the Lambs* (Tom Fleishman, Christopher Newman), and *Terminator 2: Judgment Day* (the winner, Tom Johnson, Gary Rydstrom, Gary Summers, Lee Orloff).

Finally, a special technical Academy Award Plaque was given to Randy Cartwright, David B. Coons, Lem Davis, Thomas Hahn, James Houston, Mark Kimball, Peter Nye, Michael Shantzis, and David F. Wolf of the Walt Disney Feature Animation Department, for the design and development of the "CAPS" production system for feature film animation.

■

Q: *Beauty and the Beast* carries a poignant dedication. To whom?

A: The final title card at the end of Beauty and the Beast carries this message:

TO OUR FRIEND, HOWARD,
WHO GAVE A MERMAID HER VOICE
AND A BEAST HIS SOUL,
WE WILL BE FOREVER GRATEFUL.
HOWARD ASHMAN
1950–1991

Howard Ashman died in March 1991, of complications from AIDS. His contribution to the renaissance of the animated feature, and (one hopes) the film musical, is immeasurable. His loss was devastating, and the loss of the works that he might have contributed to the world is even more frightening to imagine.

Level Three: No Easy Stuff
Minutia & Obscuria

Q: How many Disney animated features have been based on fairy tales?

A: As of this writing, only five. *Snow White and the Seven Dwarfs* (q.v., 1937), *Cinderella* (1950), *Sleeping Beauty* (1959), *The Little Mermaid* (1989), and *Beauty and the Beast*.

It may seem that Disney and his creative heirs are actually choosing an "easy out" when choosing a fairy tale as the basis for a new film project. They actually walk a very fine line between the ease of accessing a culture of the familiar and failing to capture the essential elements of the story that are the important part of the collective memory of the tale.

For example, Bruno Bettleheim, in his landmark work *The Uses of Enchantment*, objects to the names and personalities Disney assigned to the seven dwarfs, feeling that such a retelling "interferes with the unconscious understanding that [the dwarfs] symbolize an immature pre-individual form of existence which Snow White must transcend."

It is this delicate balance between retelling and bowdlerization that may account for the few times that Disney has relied on the works of Grimm, Perrault, and Andersen in the making of animated features.

■

Q: On his way to the fair, Maurice consults a faded road sign. What towns does the road sign point to?

A: Those signs that are decipherable (just barely) read "Newhall," "Valencia," and "Anaheim."

Newhall is located in the Santa Clarita Valley, about thirty miles north of the Disney Studios. It is the small town adjacent to:

Valencia, the site of California Institute of the Arts, the multi-disciplinary arts college founded by Walt Disney. Many of the artists and animators associated with *Beauty and the Beast* attended CalArts.

Anaheim is, of course, the former orange grove about thirty miles south of the Disney Studios, where Disneyland was built in 1954–55.

This type of "in-joke" is not unheard of in all manner of films, animated features among them. It has become somewhat more common recently, and certainly easier to spot with the advent of home video technology.

■

Q: The Disney Studio did something with *Beauty and the Beast* that had never been done with an animated feature before. What?

A: *Beauty and the Beast* actually had its public premiere *before* it was finished, at the New York Film Festival on September 29, 1991, six weeks before its November 13, 1991, World Premiere in New York.

The showing of an animated film in its unfinished form was unprecedented, and was a big worry to the creative team behind *Beauty and the Beast*. "We were scared green," co-director Gary Trousdale recalled.

The presentation, only 70 percent complete, showed *Beauty and the Beast* in all stages of the animation process: story sketch, rough animation, pencil tests, clean-up animation, and finished animation in color. Festival director Richard Pena called the work-in-progress "educational in the best sense of the word."

Janet Maslin of *The New York Times* felt that the festival screening

offered a rare analytical look at the animation process which will never again be taken for granted by anyone who sees [the film] this way. This will be a revelation, particularly for viewers who grew up watching animated films and have come to feel blasé about them. And when the radiant sight of Beauty and the Beast waltzing together, to the sound of the lilting theme by Alan Menken and Howard Ashman, stirs emotion even in this sketchy form, then both the power and the artifice of animation make themselves felt.

Co-director Kirk Wise recalled, "It was wonderful to see people relating to these animated characters, and losing themselves in characters that are just lines on paper...and relating to them as though they were flesh and blood. That was really overwhelming."

Luckily for the Disney fan, the animation buff, and posterity, this work-in-progress edition of *Beauty and the Beast* was released on laser disc in 1992.

■

Q: Another "first" for *Beauty and the Beast* was a pretty impressive one. Can you name it?

A: *Beauty and the Beast* was the first animated feature ever nominated for the Academy Award for Best Picture of the Year.

Amazing as it may seem today, films such as *Snow White and the Seven Dwarfs* (q.v., 1937), *Pinocchio*, and *Fantasia* (1940)—considered "classics" of the stature of *The Wizard of Oz* (q.v., 1939), *Citizen Kane* (1941), and *Casablanca* (1942), all nominees—were never given the Oscar nomination in the Best Picture category.

It can be surmised that Academy members might have felt that to honor a "cartoon" in this fashion might be a slight to "real" films with "live" actors. It might also be theorized that the New York Film Festival screening of the unfinished *Beauty and the Beast* opened a great many eyes to the complex and laborious process involved in creating a believable animated world.

■

Q: On April 19, 1994, *Beauty and the Beast* became one more important Disney "first." What was it?

A: *Beauty and the Beast* became the first Disney film to be adapted into a full-fledged Broadway musical.

In their reviews of the film *Beauty and the Beast*, critic after critic saw the connection of the film's structure and sophisticated score to that of a Broadway musical. Janet Maslin of *The New York Times* felt that "Broadway is as vital to this film's staging and characterizations as it is to the songs themselves." Gene Siskel of *The Chicago Tribune* called *Beauty and the Beast* "an instant classic, with songs worthy of a Broadway musical." *The Kansas City Sun Newspaper* said, "The Broadway musical is alive and well...at least in the movies." Frank Rich in *The New York Times* said, "What is the best Broadway musical com-

Terrence Mann brought the Beast to actual life in the Broadway musical *Disney's Beauty and the Beast*.

Author's Collection. Photo: Joan Marcus/Marc Bryan-Brown/Walt Disney Theatrical Productions. © The Walt Disney Company

edy score of the year? Make no mistake about it, it is *Beauty and the Beast*. I must say I was knocked out by this one—even though, as a theatergoer, I had to regret that Broadway's loss has been Hollywood's gain."

Naturally, these kudos were not lost on the powers-that-be at The Walt Disney Company. They had actually been looking for an entree into the world of musical theatre for some time, and when stage director Robert Jess Roth presented Disney management with a creative stratagem for bringing *Beauty and the Beast* to the musical stage, they enthusiastically approved.

Produced in association with Theatre Under the Stars, the show previewed at the Music Hall Theater in Houston, Texas, on November 27, and its official opening was on December 2, 1993. Broadway previews began on March 9, 1994, with the public opening on April 19, 1994 at the legendary Palace Theatre.

Portraying the Beast was Broadway veteran Terrence Mann, who appeared in *Jerome Robbins' Broadway* and the original casts of *Les Miserables* (1987, for which he received a Tony nomination), as well as *Barnum* (1980), *Cats* (1982), and *Rags* (1986). Off-Broadway he appeared in Stephen Sondheim's *Assassins* (1991), and in the feature films *A Chorus Line* (1985), *Solarbabies* (1986), and *Big Top Pee Wee* (1988).

Belle was played by Susan Egan, who starred with Tommy Tune in the national tour of *Bye Bye Birdie*. Her regional theatre credits include Lizzie in *Baby*, Nellie in *South Pacific*, Margy in *State Fair*, Edythe in *My One and Only*, Peggy in *42nd Street* and Kathy in *Singin' in the Rain*.

Tom Bosley returned to the Broadway stage in the role of Maurice. Bosley won the Tony in the title role of *Fiorello!* before going on to star in the long-running television series "Happy Days" and "Father Dowling Mysteries."

Disney's Beauty and the Beast: A New Musical was directed by Robert Jess Roth, with costumes created by Ann Hould-Ward, who designed for Stephen Sondheim's Pulitzer Prize- and Tony Award-winning *Sun-*

day in the Park with George (1984) and Tony Award-winning *Into the Woods* (1987).

The original film score was supplemented by an additional Howard Ashman and Alan Menken composition (composed for the film but not used), as well as new songs by Menken and Academy Award-winner Tim Rice.

David Ogden Stiers is the only member of the film cast to repeat a role. Stiers recorded the prologue narration that is heard in the stage show.

On May 17, 1994, the American Theatre Wing nominated *Disney's Beauty and the Beast: A New Musical* for nine Tony Awards:

Best Musical (Walt Disney Productions, Producer), Best Performance by a Leading Actor in a Musical (Terrence Mann), Best Performance by a Leading Actress in a Musical (Susan Egan), Best Performance by a Supporting Actor in a Musical (Gary Beach), Best Book of a Musical (Linda Woolverton, book), Best Original Score (Music & Lyrics) Written for the Theatre (Alan Menken, music; Howard Ashman & Tim Rice, lyrics), Best Direction of a Musical (Robert Jess Roth), Best Costume Design (the winner, Ann Hould-Ward), and Best Lighting Design (Natasha Katz).

■

Q: One song was cut from the film score of *Beauty and the Beast*. Can you name it?

A: The song "Human Again" was originally to be sung by the enchanted objects as the relationship between Belle and Beast develops and strengthens. It was written by Ashman and Menken for the film, but discarded. In the film, it was to be staged over the passage of the seasons, and in this sense it more visually and clearly portrayed the length of Belle's stay with Beast. It also underlined the threat to the household servants, since a similar fate awaits them if the curse on Beast is allowed to run its course. The creative team, however, felt that the growing love of Belle and Beast would be more clearly expressed by the principles involved (Belle and Beast), rather than by bystanders (the enchanted objects). "Human Again" was replaced by "Something There" in the final film.

Luckily, the lovely "Human Again" was rescued from the trunk and used (albeit in truncated form) in the stage musical version of *Beauty and the Beast*. The demo version of the complete song, performed by Howard Ashman and Alan Menken, appears on Walt Disney Records' collection *The Music Behind the Magic: The Musical Artistry of Alan Menken, Howard Ashman and Tim Rice*.

■

Q: The animator of the Beast has a famous father. Who?

A: Glen Keane's father is cartoonist Bil Keane, who has been writing and drawing the popular single-panel cartoon "The Family Circus" since March 1, 1960.

Glen Keane, the Beast animator, graduated from California Institute of the Arts in 1974 and became an animation assistant at Disney that same year.

Beauty and the Beast Supervising Animator Glen Keane, carrying on a family tradition in the field of art.

He worked under the tutelage of the great animators Ollie Johnston, Milt Kahl, Eric Larson, and Frank Thomas. He worked on scenes in *The Rescuers* and *Pete's Dragon* (1977), and became supervising animator on *The Fox and the Hound* (1981). Keane animated the Ghost of Christmas Present (Willie the Giant from *Mickey and the Beanstalk*) in *Mickey's Christmas Carol* (1983), and the villainous Ratigan in *The Great Mouse Detective* (1986). Keane was supervising animator for Ariel in *The Little Mermaid* (1989) and created the magnificent golden eagle Marahute in *The Rescuers Down Under* (1990). After *Beauty and the Beast*, Keane supervised animation of Aladdin in *Aladdin* (1992) and Pocahontas in *Pocahontas* (1995).

Keane's fine animation acting skill brings to the screen all of Beast's contradictions, physical and emotional. He moves with weight and mass, but also with grace. He exhibits fearsome anger, and is capable of sweet gentility. He is ugly and repellent, but expressive and captivating. Quite a feat for lines on paper.

■

Q: One favorite character was an afterthought. Which one?

A: Chip, the precocious teacup-son of Mrs. Potts, was originally a bystander in many scenes and had only one line. When the vocal talent for Chip was being auditioned, the creative team was so taken with the voice of Bradley Pierce that it was agreed his role should be expanded.

Ultimately, Chip had a supporting role in the film, and replaced a Music Box as the stowaway who follows Belle when she rushes from Beast's palace to be with her father.

Chip was also given the film's final line. Originally, Belle looked quizzically at her newly-handsome prince, squinted and wrinkled her nose, and asked, "Do you think you could grow a beard?"

This was replaced by Chip's query of Mrs. Potts, "Do I still have to sleep in the cupboard?"

Q: In particularly uncharacteristic fashion, Gaston quotes Shakespeare! Where?

A: In the lyric to "The Mob Song," Gaston sings, "Screw your courage to the sticking place." This is a direct quote from *Macbeth*, Act One, Scene Seven, where Macbeth and Lady Macbeth are plotting the demise of King Duncan:

> MACBETH: If we fail?
> LADY MACBETH: We fail! Screw your courage to the sticking place, and we'll not fail.

Hearing the boorish, brutal, book-hating Gaston quoting the immortal Bard as he incites a mob of villagers to "kill the Beast!" is about as disconcerting and iconoclastic as Mr. Spock quoting the Bible in the "Star Trek" episode "The Trouble with Tribbles."

■

Q: The inking and painting of the animation art in *Beauty and the Beast* employed an impressive new animation technique. What was it?

A: The inking and painting of *Beauty and the Beast* didn't use ink or paint. A new system of bringing color to animation was employed, using artists at monitors coloring drawings scanned into a computer.

This is part of CAPS (Computer Animation and Production System). Engineers at Disney and Pixar began creating CAPS in 1987, and following the use of the system on a brief scene in *The Little Mermaid* moved into full production using CAPS on *The Rescuers Down Under*.

Disney animated features are still created much as they have been since the beginning, with artist and pencil, painter and brush. The characters are still hand-drawn by animators, frame by frame; the backgrounds are painted by artists with traditional brush and airbrush techniques. But once the pencil test and layout are approved, the tools used are no longer the same. The exposure sheet, once a laborious, lengthy, hand-written document, is now digital. Backgrounds, foregrounds, and other painted layers are scanned into the computer where they are digitally composited. Final digital files are sent to a film recorder to create a film positive.

CAPS was intended to give Disney animation the look of the laborious hand processes of the Golden Age such as hand-applied paints, colored inking lines, and airbrushing, which had all but disappeared after the advent of the Xerox™ animation process in 1961. CAPS has not only allowed the replication of these techniques in a fiscally feasible system, it has now surpassed the original technical processes.

hard

Author's Collection. © The Walt Disney Company

The boorish, book-hating Gaston is hardly the type to quote Shakespeare. But he does...

Walt Disney Pictures presents in association with Silver Screen Partners IV

BEAUTY AND THE BEAST

Directed by Gary Trousdale and Kirk Wise

Produced by Don Hahn. Executive Producer Howard Ashman

Animation Screenplay by Linda Woolverton

Songs by Howard Ashman and Alan Menken. Original Score by Alan Menken

Associate Producer Sarah MacArthur. Art Director Brian McEntee

Edited by John Carnochan

Artistic Supervisors: Story Roger Allers, Layout Ed Ghertner, Background Lisa Keene, Cleanup Vera Lanpher, Visual Effects Randy Fullmer, Computer Graphics Images Jim Hillin

Story: Brenda Chapman, Burny Mattinson, Brian Pimental, Joe Ranft, Kelly Asbury, Christopher Sanders, Kevin Harkey, Bruce Woodside, Tom Ellery, Robert Lence

Character Animation

Belle: Supervising Animator James Baxter. Animators Michael Cedeno, Randy Cartwright, Lorna Cook, Ken Duncan, Doug Krohn, Mike Nguyen. Florida Supervising Animator Mark Henn

Beast: Supervising Animator Glen Keane. Animators Anthony DeRosa, Aaron Blaise, Geefwee Boedoe, Broose Johnson, Tom Sito, Brad Kuha

Gaston: Supervising Animator Andreas Deja. Animators Joe Haidar, Ron Husband, David Burgess, Alexander S. Kuperschmidt, Tim Allen

Lumiere: Supervising Animator Nik Ranieri. Animators David P. Stephan, Rejean Bourdages, Barry Temple

Cogsworth: Supervising Animator Will Finn. Animators Michael Show, Tony Bancroft

Mrs. Potts and Chip: Supervising Animator Dave Pruiksma. Animators Phil Young, Dan Boulos

Maurice: Supervising Animator Ruben A. Aquino. Animators Mark Kausler, Ellen Woodbury, Cynthia Overman

Le Fou: Supervising Animator Chris Wahl. Animators Rick Farmiloe, Lennie Graves

Philippe: Supervising Animator Russ Edmonds

Wolves: Animator Larry White

Wardrobe: Animator Tony Anselmo. Animating Assistants Tom Bancroft, Arland Barron, Bob Bryan, Brian Ferguson, Michael Gerard, Mark Kennedy, Michael Surrey. Rough Inbetweeners Ken Culotta, Henry Sato, Jr., Eric Walls, David Zaboski

Clean-Up Animation

Belle: Supervising Character Lead Renee Holt. Key Assistants Dorothea Baker, Merry Kanawyer Clingen, Margie Daniels, Daniel A. Gracey, Lureline Kohler, Christine Lawrence, Kaaren Lundeen, Teresa Martin, Brett Newton, Jennifer Gwynne Oliver, Ginny Parmele. Assistant Animators Kent Culotta, Juliet Stroud Duncan, Teresa Eidenbock, Denise Meara Hahn, Karen Hardenbergh, Leticia Lichtwardt, Steve Lubin, Laura Nichols, Natasha Selfridge. Breakdown Wendie Fischer, Tamara Lusher, Anthony Wayne Michaels, Bryan M. Sommers. Inbetweeners Elliot M. Bour, Ken Kinoshita

Beast: Supervising Character Lead Bill Berg. Key Assistant Tracy M. Lee. Assistant Animators Scott Anderson, Johan Klingler, Rick Kohlschmidt, Susan Lantz, Terry Naughton, Priscillano A. Romanillos, Marshall Toomey. Breakdown Kris Heller, James Y. Jackson, Wendy Werner. Inbetweeners Travis Blaise, Vincent DeFrances, Paul McDonald, Charles R. Vollmer

Gaston: Supervising Character Lead Marty Korth. Key Assistants Kathleen M. Bailey, Sam Ewing, Randy Sanchez, Bruce Strock. Assistant Animators James Davis, Dana Reemes, Maria Rosetti. Breakdown Robert O. Corley, James Fuji. Inbetweeners Lillian Chapman, Anthony Cipriano, Laurey Foulkes, Dylan Kohler, Mary-Jean Repchuk

Lumiere: Character Lead Debra Armstrong. Key Assistants Matt Novak, Gilda Palinginis. Assistant Animators Arland Barron, Trey Finney, Richard Green, Brian McKim. Breakdown Hee Rhan Bae, Edward Gutierrez. Inbetweener Maurilio Morales

Cogsworth: Supervising Character Lead Nancy Kneip. Key Assistant Marianne Tucker. Assistant Animator Karen Rosenfield. Breakdown Beverly Adams, Bill Thinnes. Inbetweener Marsha Park

Mrs. Potts: Character Lead Stephen Zupkas. Key Assistant Dan Tanaka. Assistant Animators Mike McKinney, Susan Sugita

Maurice: Supervising Character Lead Richard Hoppe. Assistant Animators Marcia Dougherty, Peggy Tonkonogy. Breakdown Norma Rivera, Elizabeth Watasin

Le Fou: Character Lead Emily Jiuliano. Key Assistant Gail Frank. Assistant Animators Sue Adnopoz, Michael Hazy

Phillipe: Supervising Character Lead Brian Clift. Breakdown Allison Hollen. Inbetweener Jaquelin M. Sanchez

Wolves: Character Lead Alex Topete. Key Assistant Terry Wozniak Assistant Animator Eric Pigors. Inbetweener Grant Hiestand

Objects, Townspeople and Others: Supervising Character Lead Vera Lanpher. Character Lead Dave Suding. Key Assistants Philip S. Boyd, Ken Coupe, Lou Dellarosa, Ray Harris, Bette Holmquist, William Recinos, Maureen Trueblood. Assistant Animators Carl Bell, Jesus Cortes. Breakdown Noreen Beasley, Inna Chon, Kellie Deron Lewis, Cheryl Polakow, Martin Schwartz, Ron Westlund, Dave Woodman. Inbetweeners Ken Hettig, Tom LaBaff, Jane Misek, Kevin Smith, Michael Swofford, Daniel A. Wawrzaszek. Corrections Diana Falk, Miriam McDonnell, John Ramirez

Special Effects

Supervising Effects Animators Dave Bossert, Ted Kierscey, Dorse Lanpher, Mark Myer

Effects Animators Ed Coffey, Christine Harding, Chris Jenkins, Eusebio Torres, Kelvin Yasuda. Key Effects Assistants Allen Blyth, Dan Chaika, Mabel Gesner, John Tucker. Assistant Effects Animators Mark Barrows, Jeff Dutton, James Mansfield, Cynthia Neill-Knizek, Steve Starr, Allen Stovall. Effects Breakdown/Inbetweeners Kennard Betts, Kristine Brown, Peter DeMund, Sandra Groenveld, Paul Lewis, Dan Lund, Masa Oshiro, Lisa Ann Reinert, Tony West. Key Layout/Workbook Dan St. Pierre, Larry Leker, Fred Craig, Lorenzo Martinez, Tom Shannon, Tnya Wilson, Thom Enriquez, Rasoul Azadani, Bill Perkins. Layout Assistants Mac George, Jeff Dickson, David Gardner, Mitchell Bernal, Daniel Hu, Allen Tam, Davy Liu, Mark Wallace. Blue Sketch Madlyn O'Neill. Background Doug Ball, Jim Coleman, Donald Towns, Cristy Maltese, Phil Phillipson, Dean Gordon, Robert E. Stanton, Tom Woodington, Tia Kratter, Diana Wakeman, John Emerson, Gregory Alexander Drolette

Assistant Backgrounds Debbie DuBois, Natalie Franscioni-Karp, Serge Michaels, William Dely, Bill Kaufmann, Kevin Turcotte. Visual Development Kelly Asbury, Michael Cedeno, Joe Grant, Jean Gillmore, Kevin Lima, Dave Molina, Sue C. Nichols, Christopher Sanders, Terry Shakespeare. Production Consultants Hans Bacher, Mel Shaw

Pre-Production Script Development Jim Cox, Dennis Edwards, Tim Hauser, Rob Minkoff, Rebecca Rees, Darrell Rooney. Associate Editor Gregory Perler

Assistant Editors Deirdre Hepburn, Pamela G. Kimber, Jim Melton

Florida Editorial Staff Chuck Williams, Beth Ann Collins. Casting by Albert Tavares. Production Manager Baker Bloodworth. Scene Planning Supervisor Ann Tucker. Animation Check Supervisor Janet Bruce. Color Models Supervisor Karen Comella. Ink and Paint Manager Gretchen Maschmeyer Albrecht. Final Check/Paint Supervisor Hortensia M. Casagran. Digitizing Camera Supervisor Robyn Roberts. Scene Planning Dave Thomson, Annamarie Costa. Scene Planning Assistant Donna Weir. Animation Checking Karen Hepburn, Karen S. Paat, Gary Shafer, Mavis Shafer, Barbara Wiles. Color Model Assistants Penny Coulter, Ann Sorenson

Artistic Supervisors Florida Unit: Layout Robert Walker. Background Richard John Sluiter. Cleanup Ruben Procopio. Visual Effects Barry Cook. Production Manager Florida Unit Tim O'Donnell. Pre-Production Manager Ron Rocha. Production Administrator Dorothy McKim. Assistant Production Managers: Editorial Deborah Tobias. Layout Patricia Hicks. Animation Leslie Hough. Effects/Computer Graphics Brett Hayden. Background/Color Model/CheckingBruce Grant Williams. Compositing & Retakes Suzi Vissotzky. Florida Unit Paul Steele. Ink & Paint Assistant Manager Chris Hecox. Computer Animation Linda Bel, Greg Griffith, James R. Tooley. Computer Animation Software Engineers Mary Jane "M.J." Turner, Scott F. Johnston, Edward Kummer. Digital painting Thomas Cardone. Sr. Production Coordinator Rozanne Cazian. CGI Manager Dan Philips. Engineering Managers Dave Inglish, David F. Wolf

Engineering Development David Coons, Scot Greenidge, James D. Houston, Mark R. Kimball, Marty Prager. Engineering Support Raul E. Anaya, Michael Bolds, Randy Fukada, Bruce Hatakeyama, Pradeep Hiremath, Kiran B. Joshi, Brad Lowman, Michael K. Purvis, Carlos Quinonez, Grace Shirado, Michael Sullivan, Mark M. Tokunaga, Paul Yanover. PIXAR Thomas Hahn, Peter Nye, Michael A. Shantzis. Assistant to the Producer Patricia Conklin. Production Coordinators Charlie Desrochers, Kevin Wade. Production Assistants Kirk Bodyfelt, Holly E. Bratton, Kevin L. Briggs, Greg Chalekian, Matthew Garbera, Sean Hawkins, Eric Lee, Tod Marsden, Karenna Mazur, Janet McLaurin, Laura Perrotta, Laurie Sacks, Dale A. Smith, Christopher Tapia, Kevin Traxler, Anthony Faust Rocco. Production Secretary Stephen Bove. Florida Production Secretary Barbara J. Poirier. Production Accountants Kyle Patterson, Carole Constantineau, Darrell L. Brown, Robin J. Flynn. Character Sculpture Ruben Procopio, Kenny Thompkins. Title Design by Saxon/Ross Film Design. Stained Glass Designed by Mac George. Digitizing Mark-Up Gina Wooten. Line Repair Angelika Katz. Digitizing Camera Operators Tina Baldwin, Jo Ann Breuer, Karen China, Bob Cohen, Lynette Cullen, Gary Fishbaugh, Cindy Garcia, Kent Gordon. Assitant Paint Supervisors Barbara Lynne Hamane, Rhonda L. Hicks. Color Model Mark-Up Leslie Ellery, Rhonda L. Hicks, Beth Ann McCoy. Paint Mark-Up Irma Velez, Micki Zurcher. Painting Carmen Sanderson, Phyllis Bird, Russel Blandino, Sherrie Cuzzort, Phyllis Fields, Paulino Garcia DeMingo, Anne Hazard, David Karp, Harlene Cooper-Mears, Deborah Jane Mooneyham, Karen Nugent, Leyla C. de Pelaez, Bruce Phillipson, Heidi Shellhorn, Fumiko Roche Sommer, Britt Vandernagel, Susan Wileman. Final Check Teri McDonald, Saskia Raevouri. Compositing James "JR" Russell, David J. Rowe, Shannon Fallis-Kane. Camera Manager Joe Jiuliano. Film Recording Supervisor Ariel Shaw. Film Recording Operator Christopher Gee, Chuck Warren, Christine Beck. Animation Camera Supervisor John Cunningham. Animation Camera John Aardal, Mary Lescher, Gary W. Smith

New York Casting Associate Matt Messinger. Songs Produced by Howard Ashman and Alan Menken. Songs Arranged by Alan Menken and Danny Troob. Songs and Score Orchestrations Danny Troob. Additional Score Orchestrations Michael Starobin. Vocal Arrangements and Music Conducted by David Friedman. Supervising Music Editor Kathleen Bennett. Music Editing Segue Music. Songs Recorded and Mixed by Michael Farrow at BMG Recording Studio, New York. Score Recorded and Mixed by John Richards at Evergreen and Sony Studios. Orchestra Contractors/New York Emile Charlap, Los Angeles Ken Watson. End Title Duet "Beauty and the Beast" performed by Celine Dion and Peabo Bryson, Produced by Walter Afanasieff, Arranged by Walter Afanasieff and Robbie Buchanan. Sound Effects by Mark Mangini and Dave Stone, M.P.S.E., Weddinton Productions. Special Sound Effects John P. Sound Editors Julia Evershade, Michael Benavente, Jessica Gallavan, J.H. Arrufat, Ron Bartlett. Assistant Sound Editors Sonya "Sonny" Pettijohn, Oscar Mitt. Additional Sound effects by Drew Newman. Foley by TAJ Soundworks, Buena Vista Sound East. Foley Artists John Roesch, Catherine Rowe, Vanessa Theme Ament. Rerecorded at Buena Vista Sound Studios. Rerecording Mixers Terry Porter C.A.S., Mel Metcalfe, David J. Hudson. Dubbing Recordist Denis Blackerby. PDL Judy Nord. ADR Mixers Doc Kane, Vince Caro. Optical Supervisor Mark Dornfeld. Optical Consultant Peter Montgomery. Optical Camera Allen Gonzales, S.O.C. Black and White Processing Joe Parra, John White. Effects Graphics Bernie Gagliano. Color Timer Dale Grahn. Live-Action Reference Sherri Stoner, Dan McCoy, Peter Hastings. Dance Sequence Models Mary Anderson, Duane May. Live-Action Video Crew Al Vasquez, David Weiss. Projection Don Henry. Rendering on Silicon Graphics Computer Systems. Modeling Software by Alias Research, Inc. Digital Film recorders by Celco. Titles and Opticals by Buena Vista Visual Effects. Special Thanks to the Los Angeles Zoo and Vance Gerry. Prints by Technicolor®. Produced and Distributed on Eastman Film. Dolby Stereo in Selected Theaters. Soundtrack Available on Cassette and Compact Disc from Walt Disney Records

MPAA Rated G. Running time 84 minutes

Voice Talents

Robby Benson	Beast
Jesse Corti	LeFou
Rex Everhart	Maurice
Angela Lansbury	Mrs. Potts
Paige O'Hara	Belle
Jerry Orbach	Lumiere
Bradley Michael Pierce	Chip
David Ogden Stiers	Cogsworth
Richard White	Gaston
Jo Anne Worley	Wardrobe
Mary Kay Bergman	Bimbette
Brian Cummins	Stove
Alvin Epstein	Bookseller
Tony Jay	Monsieur D'Arque
Alec Murphy	Baker
Kimmy Robertson	Featherduster
Hal Smith	Phillipe
Kath Soucie	Bimbette
David Ogden Stiers	Narrator
Frank Welker	Footstool/Special Vocal Effects

Additional Voices

Jack Angel, Bruce Adler, Scott Barnes, Vanna Bonta, Maureen Brennan, Liz Callaway, Philip Clarke, Margery Daley, Jennifer Darling, Albert de Ruiter, George Dvorsky, Bill Farmer, Bruce Fifer, Johnson Flucker, Larry Hansen, Randy Hansen, Mary Ann Hart, Alix Korey, Phyllis Kubey, Hearndon Lackey, Sherry Lynn, Mickie McGowan, Larry Moss, Panchali Null, Wilbur Pauley, Jennifer Perito, Caroline Peyton, Patrick Pinney, Cynthia Richards-Hewes, Phil Proctor, Stephani Ryan, Gordon Stanley, Stephen Sturk

Acknowledgments

My agent, David Andrew, told me "the Acknowledgment isn't where you thank everyone you've ever known, it's where you quickly thank your agent and get on with it." But David, what if this is my only chance? (I know that kind of pessimism is unacceptable, but I need an excuse to "thank everyone I've ever known.") So to David Andrew and Sasha Goodman, thanks for taking a chance on me. To my publisher, Glenn Young, thank you for your patience, understanding, and kindness.

So if you believe David Andrew, stop here. Acknowledgments are over. Keep reading if you want to see how many people it took to get this wee book into your paw.

My parents and grandmother always indulged my predilection for movies and Disney, and never made me feel as if I was wasting my time, or should pursue something else. I've since discovered that such guidance is rare. None of them ever wanted to live vicariously through me, so, thanks Mom, Dad, and Grandma Mick.

There came a time some years ago when my brothers and I stopped picking on each other for our differences and started respecting each other for them. That's when we stopped being kids and became real brothers. Ron and Jerry have been, and continue to be, my friends and protectors, and I'd rather hang with them than just about anyone. Thanks, Chuck; thanks, Bill.

Dan Long is one of those friends you'd pray for if you knew they were out there. He gave me my first job back in 1978, and—even when I was sixteen years old—made me feel that my ideas and opinions were of value. He helped me get through adolescence, the hardest part of growing up, and remains my dear friend to this day. Always encouraging, always supportive, Dan was my first mentor.

When I started working for Betsy Richman at Walt Disney Imagineering in September 1989, it still hadn't occurred to me that I was a writer. So thanks go to Betsy, for pushing me onto the path and showing me what a good editor does, so I can recognize one. Betsy, my Auntie Mame, showed me that life's a banquet, and taught me how to spot the Mr. Babcocks of the world and laugh out loud at them. Betsy was my second mentor.

The idea for this book came about in December 1992, and is in your hands because of Stephanie F. Ogle, owner of Cinema Books in Seattle. She suggested it, and without her I probably wouldn't have thought of it. She also has a terrific film and theatre book store. Stop in and say hello when you're in Seattle.

When the notion of this book began to take shape, I found loving hearts and sharp minds at my beck and call.

Robert Tieman and I found common ground early in our friendship, and I think we both wonder now what we did for laughs before we met each other. Robert is a tough, fair, concerned, and funny editor, proofreader, fact-checker, nitpicker, and commentator. I am both lucky and grateful for the benefit of his friendship, his regard, his perspective, and his ruthless purple pen. You'd be holding a very different (and not better) book right now without the insights of Robert Tieman.

I fell in love with Paul Wolski the minute I met him, and I haven't really felt much different about him since then. My blood brother, my shadow, my bestest friend. I have very few words to describe my feelings for Paul. But he knows.

Joe Morris has been a one-man fan club and cheering section for me since I met this blooming bougainvillea on a sternwheeler riverboat in 1986. Caring, tough, and fiercely loyal, Joe made research trips to the Los Angeles Central Library a joy instead of a chore.

Jean Cress belies one of my favorite pseudo-platitudes, "Never trust a redhead." Jean made me see things in myself that I knew were there, but needed someone to coax out of me. She gave me professional breaks that created the opportunity for my independence. Jean is generous and supportive, and I always know that she is a safe haven in a weary world.

Tim O'Day is another surprising redhead—a big lovable galoot, and even though he never told me, I know what a sensitive and loving guy he is, because I always felt it. He even made me really groove on Sinatra (who I liked) and respect John Wayne (who I didn't).

Sean Markland and I met on line at a movie theater in Seattle in 1981. Since then, we've been friends, family, roommates, and comic conspirators. Sean has been a consistent and comforting presence through my adult life. Without knowing it, he was even a twentysomething Zen Master.

Garrett Hicks has unselfishly offered his support and friendship to me in the best way he could—he stayed out of the way and let me work, all the while letting me know he was there, concerned, and watching out for me.

The last of this group is Ric Edinger. Steadfast and guileless, Ric has often reminded me of the joy there is to be found in simplicity, and craft, and earnest hard work for something or someone you love. He set me up in my writer's den and let me be, offering encouragement and support when I needed it, and making me sit down and get to work when I really didn't want to, and leaving me alone to do what needed to be done.

These people helped me through the hard part of ceasing to be one thing and becoming something else. I'm an author today due to the extra effort they all put forth on my behalf. Each of them read my drafts, played devil's advocate, cajoled, and complimented, and the love I have to give them is feeble payment for what I've received.

My research was made possible by the indispensable collections and staff of the Margaret Herrick Library of The Academy of Motion Picture Arts and Sciences.

Another indispensable resource was the USC Library of Cinema and Television under the guidance of Ned Comstock; and the Warner Bros. Archives at the USC Library of Cinema and Television, under Bill Whittington and Stuart Ng. And thanks to Leith Adams of the Warner Bros. Archives for connecting me with all of them.

The Disney content in this book would simply not have been possible without the infallible Walt Disney Archives: David R. Smith, Robert Tieman, Rebecca Cline, Colette Espino, Adina Lerner Steve Rogers, and Ed Squair.

The Los Angeles Central Library provided a wealth of information, and the author is grateful that Los Angeles has such a rich resource. It is also the only library that is open on Sunday.

Special thanks to Shirley Jones and Marty Ingels. They took a chance that I wasn't a bozo, and graciously committed their time, effort, and enthusiasm to my project.

Thanks go as well to Terry Anderson, Tony Baxter, Frawley Becker, Richard Bontems, Gordon and Jane Connell, Mary Alice Drumm, Robert J. Fitzpatrick, Ken Gehrig, Stephanie Goode, Milton W. Hamlin, Richard Jordan, Paul Lanner, Dotty Lew of The Wells Fargo Company, Hisato Masuyama, Armistead Maupin, Tom Miller, Scott Murcheson, David J. Negrón, Rex Poindexter, Cessido Priore, Kay Radtke, Rachel Reiss, Lorraine Santoli, Dea Shandera, Richard M. and Ursula Sherman, Robert B. and Joyce Sherman, Martin A. Sklar, Edward Sotto, and Gilles C. Wheeler.

Bibliography

Books

Ashman, Charles and Robert J. Wagman. *The Nazi Hunters*. New York: Pharos Books, 1988.

Atkinson, Brooks. *Broadway*. New York: The Macmillan Company, 1970.

Bacon, James. *How Sweet It Is: The Jackie Gleason Story*. New York: St. Martin's Press, 1985.

Bartlett, John. *A Collection of Familiar Quotations*. Facsimile Edition. Secaucus, NJ: Poplar Books, 1965.

Behlmer, Rudy and Tony Thomas. *Hollywood's Hollywood: The Movies About the Movies*. Secaucus, NJ: Citadel Press, 1975.

Belton, John. *Widescreen Cinema*. Cambridge, MA: Harvard University Press, 1992.

Berg, A. Scott. *Goldwyn: A Biography*. New York: Alfred A. Knopf, 1989.

Bettleheim, Bruno. *The Uses of Enchantment: The Meaning and Importance of Fairy Tales*. New York: Alfred A. Knopf, 1977.

Bricusse, Leslie and Anthony Newley. *Willy Wonka and the Chocolate Factory*. Vocal Selections/Sheet Music. Beverly Hills, CA: Taradam Music, Inc., 1971.

Brown, Dee. *Hear the Lonesome Whistle Blow: Railroads in the West*. New York: Holt, Rinehart and Winston, 1977.

Burrows, Abe. *Honest, Abe*. Boston: An Atlantic Monthly Press Book/Little, Brown and Company, 1980.

Cabarga, Leslie. *The Fleischer Story*. New York: Nostalgia Press, 1976.

Comden, Betty and Adolph Green. *Singin' in the Rain*. Published Screenplay. London: Lorrimer Publishing Limited, 1986.

Culhane, John. *The American Circus: An Illustrated History*. New York: Henry Holt, 1990.

Dahl, Roald. *Charlie and the Chocolate Factory*. New York: Alfred A. Knopf, 1964.

———. *Charlie and the Great Glass Elevator*. New York: Alfred A. Knopf, 1972.

Davis, Kenneth C. *Don't Know Much About History*. New York: Avon Books, 1990.

Dunne, John Gregory. *The Studio*. New York: Farrar, Straus & Giroux, 1969.

Finch, Christopher. *The Art of Walt Disney*. New York: Abrams, 1973.

Fjellman, Stephen M. *Vinyl Leaves: Walt Disney World and America*. Boulder, CO: Westview Press, 1992.

Fordin, Hugh. *The World of Entertainment*. New York: Doubleday and Company, Inc., 1975.

Fricke, John. *The Wizard of Oz: The Official 50th Anniversary Pictorial History*/John Fricke, Jay Scarfone, William Stillman. New York: Warner Books, 1989.

George, Richard. *Roald Dahl's Charlie and the Chocolate Factory: A Play*. New York: Alfred A. Knopf, 1976.

Goodman, Randolph G. *From Script to Stage: Eight Modern Plays*. San Francisco: Rinehart Press, 1971.

Goodwin, Betty. *Hollywood du Jour: Lost Recipies of Legendary Hollywood Haunts*. Santa Monica, CA: Angel City Press, 1993.

Grant, John. *The Encyclopedia of Walt Disney's Animated Characters*. New York: Hyperion, 1993.

Halliwell, Leslie. *The Filmgoer's Companion, Sixth Edition*. New York: Avon, 1978.

———. *Halliwell's Film Guide, Seventh Edition*. New York: Harper & Row Perennial Library, 1989.

Hansen, Bruce K. *The Peter Pan Chronicles*. New York: Birch Lane Press, 1993.

Harmetz, Aljean. *The Making of the Wizard of Oz*. New York: Alfred A. Knopf, 1977.

———. *Round Up the Usual Suspects*. New York: Hyperion, 1992.

Haver, Ronald. *A Star is Born: The Making of the 1954 Movie and its 1983 Restoration*. New York: Alfred A. Knopf, 1988.

Hearn, Michael Patrick. *The Annotated Wizard of Oz*. New York: Clarkson N. Potter, 1973.

Hirsch, Julia Antopol. *The Sound of Music: The Making of America's Favorite Movie*. Chicago: Contemporary Books, 1993.

Hirschorn, Clive. *The Hollywood Musical*. New York: Crown Publishing, 1981.

———. *Gene Kelly*. New York: St. Martin's Press, 1984.

Hirshberg, Jack. *Hello, Dolly! Journal*. Los Angeles: Twentieth Century-Fox Film Corporation, 1969.

Hollis, Richard and Brian Sibley. *The Disney Studio Story*. New York: Crown Publishers, Inc., 1988.

———. *Walt Disney's Snow White and the Seven Dwarfs & the Making of the Classic Film*. New York: Hyperion, 1994.

Holloway, Stanley, as told to Dick Richards. *Wiv a Little Bit O' Luck*. New York: Stein & Day, 1967.

Johnston, Ollie and Frank Thomas. *The Disney Villain*. New York: Hyperion, 1993.

Jones, Chuck. *Chuck Amuck*. New York: Farrar Strauss Giroux, 1989.

Kalter, Suzy. *The Complete Book of M*A*S*H*. New York: Abrams, 1984.

Katz, Ephraim. *The Film Encyclopedia*. New York: Harper & Row Perennial Library, 1990.

Krause, Martin and Linda Witkowski. *Walt Disney's Snow White and the Seven Dwarfs: An Art in Its Making*. New York: Hyperion/Indianapolis Museum of Art, 1994.

Lamparski, Richard. *Whatever Became Of?* Tenth Series. New York: Crown Publishers, 1986.

Laufe, Abe. *Broadway's Greatest Musicals*. New York: Funk & Wagnalls, 1977.

Liebling, Howard. *The Sound of Music Souvenir Book*. New York: National Publishers, 1965.

Logan, Joshua. *Movie Stars, Real People, and Me*. New York: Delacorte Press, 1978.

Lupoff, Dick and Don Thompson. *All In Color for a Dime*. New York: Ace Books, 1970.

Macaulay, David. *Underground*. Boston: Houghton Mifflin Company, 1976.

Maltin, Leonard. *Leonard Maltin's TV Movies and Video Guide 1991 Edition*. New York: Signet Books, 1990.

———. *Leonard Maltin's TV Movies and Video Guide 1995*. New York: Penguin Group/Plume, 1994.

———. *Leonard Maltin's Movie Encyclopedia*. New York: Penguin Group/Dutton, 1994.

———. *The Disney Films*. New York: Crown Publishers Inc., 1984.

Mandelbaum, Ken. *Not Since Carrie: 40 Years of Broadway Musical Flops*. New York: St. Martin's Press, 1991.

Manso, Peter. *Brando: The Biography*. New York: Hyperion, 1994.

McCabe, James D., Jr. *New York by Sunlight and Gaslight: Facsimile of 1882 Edition*. New York: Greenwich House, 1984.

McClelland, Doug. *Hollywood Talks Turkey: The Screen's Greatest Flops*. Boston: Faber and Faber, 1989.

McGovern, Dennis and Deborah Grace Winter. *Sing Out, Louise!: 150 Stars of the Musical Theatre Remember 50 Years on Broadway*. New York: Macmillan/Schirmer Books, 1993.

Mitz, Rick. *The Great TV Sitcom Book*. New York: Richard Marek Publishers, 1980.

Mordden, Ethan. *The Hollywood Musical*. New York: St. Martin's Press, 1981.

———. *Rodgers & Hammerstein*. New York: Harry N. Abrams, Inc., 1992.

Morris, Lloyd. *Incredible New York*. New York: Random House, 1951.

National Theatre, London. *The Guys and Dolls Book*. London: Methuen, 1982.

Norton, Mary. *Bed-Knob and Broomstick*. New York: Scholastic Book Sevices, 1972.

Peary, Danny. *Cult Movies 2*. New York: Dell, 1983.

Perry, George. *The Complete Phantom of the Opera*. New York: Henry Holt and Company, 1987.

Plotkin, Fred. *Opera 101: A Complete Guide to Learning and Loving Opera*. New York: Hyperion, 1994.

Runyon, Damon. *The Best of Damon Runyon*, selected by E.C. Bentley. New York: Triangle Books, 1940.

——. *Guys and Dolls: The Stories of Damon Runyon*. New York: Viking, 1992.

Sackson, Sid. *Charlie and the Chocolate Factory: A Game*. New York: Alfred A. Knopf, 1978.

Santoli, Lorraine. *The Official Mickey Mouse Club Book*. New York: Hyperion, 1995.

Shakespeare, William. *The Complete Works of William Shakespeare*. New York: Avenel Books, 1975.

Shale, Richard. *Academy Awards: An Ungar Reference Index*. New York: Frederick Ungar Publishing Co., 1978.

Shipman, David. *Judy Garland: The Secret Life of an American Legend*. New York: Hyperion, 1993.

Spada, James. *Barbra: The First Decade*. Secaucus, NJ: Citadel Press, 1974.

Spears, Richard A. *Slang and Euphemism*. New York: Penguin Group/Signet, 1982.

Stallings, Penny. *Flesh and Fantasy*. New York: St. Martin's Press, 1978.

Steinberg, Cobbett. *TV Facts*. New York: Facts on File Publications, 1985.

Stone, Peter and Sherman Edwards. *1776: A Musical Play*. New York: The Viking Press, 1970.

Taylor, Telford. *The Anatomy of the Nuremberg Trials*. New York: Alfred A. Knopf, 1992.

Thomas, Bob. *Walt Disney:An American Original*. New York: Hyperion, 1994.

——. *Walt Disney: The Art of Animation*. New York: Golden Press, 1958.

——. *Disney's Art of Animation: from Mickey Mouse to Beauty and the Beast*. New York: Hyperion, 1992.

Thomas, Tony. *The Films of Gene Kelly, Song and Dance Man*. Secaucus, NJ: Citadel Press, 1974.

Travers, P.L. *Mary Poppins*. New York: Hartcourt Brace Jovanovich, 1971.

——. *Mary Poppins*. Revised Edition. New York: Dell Yearling, 1981.

Warner Bros. Presents My Fair Lady. Souvenir Book. Burbank: Warner Bros. Pictures, 1964.

Waldron, Vince. *The Official Dick Van Dyke Show Book*. New York: Hyperion, 1994.

Wallace, Irving. *The Fabulous Showman*. New York: Signet Paperback, c.1980.

Walt Disney Studios, The. *Facilities, Production and Post Production Services (Facility Brochure)*. Burbank: The Walt Disney Studios/CIA Creative Group, L.A., 1992.

Willson, Meredith. *But He Doesn't Know the Territory*. New York: Van Rees Press, 1959.

——. *The Music Man* (Play). New York: G.P. Putnam's Sons, 1958.

——. *The Music Man* (Novel). New York: Pyramid Books, 1962.

Wollen, Peter. *Singin' in the Rain* (BFI Film Classics Series). London: British Film Institute, 1992.

Wurman, Richard Saul. *New York City Access*. Fifth Edition. New York: Access® Press, 1993.

Wystotsky, Michael Z. *Wide-Screen Cinema and Stereophonic Sound*. New York: Communication Arts Books, 1971.

Zadan, Craig. *Sondheim & Co.* (Second Edition). New York: Harper & Row, 1986.

——. *Sondheim & Co.* (Second Edition, updated). New York: Da Capo Press, 1994.

Video Laser Discs

CBS/Fox Video. *My Fair Lady* (Special Widescreen Edition). New York: CBS/Fox Video, 1990.

Criterion Collection (A Joint Venture of Janus Films and Voyager Press). *Singin' in the Rain* (CAV). Santa Monica, CA: The Voyager Company, 1988.

Fox Video. *Hello, Dolly!* (Special Widescreen Edition). Beverly Hills: Fox Video, 1992.

——. *My Fair Lady* (Restored Version). Beverly Hills: Fox Video, 1994.

MGM/UA Home Video. *Good News* (New Technicolor Restoration). Culver City, CA: MGM/UA Home Video, 1991.

——. *Singin' in the Rain* (New Technicolor Restoration). Culver City, CA: MGM/UA Home Video, 1991.

Pioneer Artists Video. *Barbra Streisand: One Voice*. New Jersey: Laserdisc Corporation of America, 1986.

Pioneer Special Edition. *Ross Hunter's Lost Horizon*. New Jersey: Laserdisc Corporation of America, 1992.

Walt Disney Home Video. *Beauty and the Beast*. Burbank: Walt Disney Home Video, 1993.

——. *Beauty and the Beast: Work in Progress*. Burbank: Walt Disney Home Video, 1992.

——. *Mary Poppins* (Disney's Exclusive Archive Collection). Burbank: Walt Disney Home Video, 1993.

——. *Snow White and the Seven Dwarfs* (Deluxe CAV Laser Disc Edition). Burbank: Walt Disney Home Video, 1994.

Warner Home Video. *Robin and the 7 Hoods* (Widescreen Edition). Burbank: Warner Home Video, 1991.

Audio Records and Compact Discs

Capitol Records. *The Music Man* (Original Broadway Cast). Hollywood: Capitol Records, 1958.

Columbia Records. *My Fair Lady* (London Cast Album). New York: Columbia Records, 1959.

Columbia Special Products. *Greenwillow* (Original Broadway Cast). New York: CBS Records, 1974.

GNP/Crescendo Records. *Victor/Victoria* (Soundtrack). Hollywood: GNP/Crescendo, 1994.

MCA Classics Broadway Gold. *Mack & Mabel* (Original Broadway Cast). Universal City, CA: MCA Records, 1992.

PolyGram Records. *Hello, Dolly!* (Soundtrack). New York: PolyGram Records, 1994.

RCA Victor/BMG Classics. *Hello, Dolly!* (Original Broadway Cast). New York: BMG Music, 1989.

——. *Guys and Dolls* (1992 Revival Cast Recording). New York: BMG Music, 1992.

Sony Masterworks. *My Fair Lady* (Remastered Soundtrack). New York: Sony Music Entertainment, Inc., 1994.

Sony Broadway. *Here's Love* (Original Broadway Cast). New York: Sony Music Entertainment, Inc., 1994.

TER Limited. *Anthony Newley in Scrooge* (Original Cast Recording). London: TER Ltd., 1992.

——. *John Mills in Goodbye Mr. Chips* (Original Cast Recording). London: TER Ltd., 1992.

Walt Disney Records. *Beauty and the Beast* (Soundtrack). Burbank: Walt Disney Records, 1991.

——. *Disney's Beauty and the Beast* (Original Broadway Cast). Burbank: Walt Disney Records, 1994.

——. *Mary Poppins* (Soundtrack). Burbank: Walt Disney Records, 1989.

——. *The Music Behind the Magic: The Musical Artistry of Alan Menken, Howard Ashman & Tim Rice*. (Burbank: Walt Disney Records, 1994.

——. *The Music of Disneyland, Walt Disney World and EPCOT Center*. Burbank: Walt Disney Records, 1988.

——. *Snow White and the Seven Dwarfs* (Soundtrack). Burbank: Walt Disney Records, 1993.

Warner Bros. Records. *The Music Man* (Soundtrack). (Burbank: Warner Bros. Records, 199?)

Broadcasts

Sibley, Brian. *P. L. Travers Talking to Brian Sibley*. London: BBC World Service Meridien, 3 January 1989.

——. *Roald Dahl Talking to Brian Sibley*. London: BBC World Service Meridien, 1988.

Index

THE MUSICAL
A LOOK AT THE AMERICAN MUSICAL THEATER
by Richard Kislan
New, Revised, Expanded Edition

Richard Kislan examines the history, the creators, and the vital components that make up a musical and demonstrates as never before how musicals are made.

From its beginnings in colonial America, the musical theater has matured into an impressive art and business, one that has brought millions the experience that director-choreographer Bob Fosse describes as when "everybody has a good time even in the crying scenes."

Kislan traces the musical's evolution through the colorful eras of minstrels, vaudeville, burlesque, revue, and comic opera up to the present day. You'll learn about the lives, techniques, and contributions of such great 20th-century composers and lyricists as Jerome Kern, Rodgers an d Hammerstein, Stephen Sondheim and others. Kislan explains all the basic principles, materials and techniques that go into the major elements of a musical production—the book, lyrics, score, dance and set design.

Richard Kislan's acclaimed study of America's musical theatre has been updated to bring it up to the cutting edge of today's musicals. A new section entitled: Recent Musical Theater: Issues and Problems includes chapters on **The British Invasion • Competition from the Electronic Media • Escalating Costs • The Power of the Critics • The Depletion of Creative Forces • Multiculturalism • The Decline of the Broadway Neighborhood* Stephen Sondheim** and his influence on the present day musical theater.

Paper $16.95 ISBN: 1-55783-217-X

❦ **APPLAUSE** ❦

A LITTLE NIGHT MUSIC

Music and Lyrics by Stephen Sondheim, Book by Hugh Wheeler

"Heady, civilized, sophisticated and enchanting. Good God! An adult musical."
—Clive Barnes, The New York Times

Cloth $19.95 ISBN: 1-55783-070-3 • Paper $9.95 ISBN: 1-55783-069-X

A FUNNY THING HAPPENED ON THE WAY TO THE FORUM

Music & Lyrics by Stephen Sondheim, Book by Burt Shevelove & Larry Gelbart

"A good, clean, dirty show! Bring back the belly laughs" —Time
"It's funny, true nonsense! A merry good time!" —Walter Kerr, Herald Tribune

Cloth $19.95 ISBN: 1-55783-064-9 • Paper $9.95 ISBN: 1-55783-063-0

SUNDAY IN THE PARK WITH GEORGE

Music and Lyrics by Stephen Sondheim, Book by James Lapine

"*Sunday* is itself a modernist creation, perhaps the first truly modernist work of musical theatre that Broadway has produced."
—Frank Rich, The New York Times

Cloth $19.95 ISBN: 1-55783-068-1 • Paper $9.95 ISBN: 1-55783-067-3

SWEENEY TODD

Music and Lyrics by Stephen Sondheim, Book by Hugh Wheeler

"There is more artistic energy, creative personality, and plain excitement than in a dozen average musicals." —Richard Eder, The New York Times

Cloth $19.95 ISBN: 1-55783-066-5 • Paper $9.95 ISBN: 1-55783-065-7

John Willis
SCREEN WORLD

THE ENDURING FILM CLASSIC!

•Complete filmographies: cast and characters, credits, production company, month released, rating, and running time.

•Biographical entries; a priceless reference for over 2,250 living stars, including real name, school, place and date of birth.

"Essential for any film library...Quite frankly, the handiest, most useful chronicle of a year spent in the dark...**A BOOK EVERY FILM LOVER SHOULD HAVE!"** —Jeffrey Lyons, THE LYONS DEN

"THE DEFINITIVE RECORD OF THE PAST MOVIE SEASON."
—Theatre Crafts

"For fan, film student or scholar, SCREEN WORLD is **THE DEFINITIVE REFERENCE** ...handsomely produced." —Digby Diehl, Playboy

"ONE OF THE BEST MOVIE INVESTMENTS YOU CAN MAKE. YES WE SAID INVESTMENTS! You see it in selected short subjects; dozens of members selling their back issues for premium prices. Naturally they're hard to find. **MOST PEOPLE WOULD RATHER PART WITH THEIR VCRS!"**
—Movie/Entertainment Book Club

SCREEN WORLD 1995 FILM ANNUAL VOLUME 46
Cloth $49.95 ISBN: 1-55783-233-1 • Paper $27.95 ISBN: 1-55783-234-X

SCREEN WORLD 1994 FILM ANNUAL VOLUME 45
Cloth $49.95 ISBN: 1-55783-201-3 • Paper $27.95 ISBN: 1-55783-202-1

SCREEN WORLD 1993 FILM ANNUAL VOLUME 44
Cloth $45.00 ISBN: 1-55783-175-0

SCREEN WORLD 1992 FILM ANNUAL VOLUME 43
Cloth $45.00 ISBN: 1-55783-135-1

❦ **APPLAUSE** ❦

MICHAEL CAINE
ACTING IN FILM
An Actor's Take on Movie Making

Academy Award winning actor Michael Caine, internationally acclaimed for his talented performances in movies for over 25 years, reveals secrets for success on screen. *Acting in Film* is also available on video (the BBC Master Class).

"Michael Caine knows the territory...*Acting in Film* is wonderful reading, even for those who would not dream of playing 'Lets Pretend' in front of a camera. Caine's guidance, aimed at novices still dreaming of the big break, can also give hardened critics fresh insights to what it is they're seeing up there on the screen..."
   –Charles Champlin, LOS ANGELES TIMES

BOOK/PAPER: $9.95• ISBN: 1-55783-124-6
BOOK/CLOTH: $14.95 • ISBN: 0-936839-86-4
VIDEO: $29.95 • ISBN: 1-55783-034-7

WILLIAM GOLDMAN FOUR SCREENPLAYS

William Goldman, master craftsman and two-time Oscar winner continues his irreverent analysis with merciless essays written expressly for this landmark edition of his screen work. Nobody covers the psychic and political terrain behind the Hollywood lot with more cynical wisdom and practical savvy than the much celebrated author of ADVENTURES IN THE SCREEN TRADE.

William Goldman won Academy Awards for BUTCH CASSIDY AND THE SUNDANCE KID and ALL THE PRESIDENT'S MEN

Includes the screenplays:

BUTCH CASSIDY AND THE SUNDANCE KID

THE PRINCESS BRIDE

MARATHON MAN

MISERY

$25.95 • CLOTH
ISBN 1-55783-198-X

❦ APPLAUSE ❦